THE PURSUIT OF LEARNING IN THE
ISLAMIC WORLD, 610–2003

ALSO BY HUNT JANIN
AND FROM MCFARLAND

*Medieval Justice: Cases and Laws in
France, England and Germany, 500–1500* (2004)

*Four Paths to Jerusalem: Jewish, Christian, Muslim,
and Secular Pilgrimages, 1000 BCE to 2001 CE* (2002)

*Fort Bridger, Wyoming: Trading Post for
Indians, Mountain Men and Westward Migrants* (2001)

The India-China Opium Trade in the Nineteenth Century (1999)

The Pursuit of Learning in the Islamic World, 610–2003

Hunt Janin

McFarland & Company, Inc., Publishers
Jefferson, North Carolina, and London

The present work is a reprint of the illustrated bound edition of The Pursuit of Learning in the Islamic World, 610–2003, first published in 2005 by McFarland

LIBRARY OF CONGRESS CATALOGUING-IN-PUBLICATION DATA

Janin, Hunt, 1940–
The pursuit of learning in the Islamic world, 610–2003 / Hunt Janin.
p. cm.
Includes bibliographical references and index.

ISBN-13: 978-0-7864-2904-2
ISBN-10: 0-7864-2904-6 (softcover : 50# alkaline paper) ∞

1. Learning and scholarship — Middle East. 2. Islamic learning and scholarship.
3. Civilization, Islamic. 4. Middle East — Civilization. I. Title.
AZ771.J36   2006   001.2'0917'67 — dc22   2004020950

British Library cataloguing data are available

©2005 Hunt Janin. All rights reserved

No part of this book may be reproduced or transmitted in any form or by any means, electronic or mechanical, including photocopying or recording, or by any information storage and retrieval system, without permission in writing from the publisher.

Cover photograph ©2005 Photodisc

Manufactured in the United States of America

*McFarland & Company, Inc., Publishers
Box 611, Jefferson, North Carolina 28640
www.mcfarlandpub.com*

Contents

Preface	1
Introduction: Why This Book?	3

PART ONE : FUNDAMENTALS OF ISLAMIC LEARNING

I	The World of Islam: Doctrines and Structure	11
II	The Prophet Muhammad and His Times (c. 500–632)	25
III	The Quran	31

PART TWO : THE GROWTH OF ISLAMIC LEARNING

IV	Islam Becomes the Dominant Faith of an Empire (632–873)	39
V	The Flowering of Islam (873–1041)	61
VI	Population Movements and Islamic Cities (1041–1453)	77
VII	The Age of Great Empires (1453–1699)	111
VIII	The Impact of the West (1699–2003)	128

PART THREE : ISLAMIC FUNDAMENTALISM AND THE FUTURE

IX	The Challenge of Fundamentalism	157
X	Conclusions: Future Prospects for Islamic Learning	176

Appendix 1 : The Decorative and Other Arts of Islam	181
Appendix 2 : Expertise in Islamic Thought	193
Appendix 3 : Ethical Traditions in Islam	195
Appendix 4 : Noteworthy Islamic Personalities and Cultural Achievements	199
Glossary of Selected Islamic Terms	201
Notes	205
Selected Bibliography	219
Index	227

Preface

The Pursuit of Learning in the Islamic World, 610–2003 is a primer on Islamic learning, a phrase which is used here in a very broad sense to mean *the realms of thought, architecture and arts of the Islamic world*. It focuses on noteworthy Islamic personalities and cultural achievements over a period of nearly 1,400 years, namely, from 610, when Muslims believe that the angel Gabriel[1] first appeared to the Prophet Muhammad, to the year 2003. Ninety-two of these personalities and achievements are discussed in the text, most of them only briefly due to space limitations. For ease of reference they are all listed in chronological order in Appendix 4.

This book is arranged in chronological order, too. As the table of contents shows, it consists of three main parts. Part One gives some of the fundamentals of Islamic learning. Since Islamic learning is inextricably bound up with Islam itself, it is essential to examine this religion in some detail. This will set the stage for Part Two, which discusses the growth of this learning. Finally, Part Three analyzes fundamentalism as an integral part of Islamic learning and tries to forecast what it may have in store for us in the years ahead. It is important to note here that "Islamic fundamentalism" is a convenient but potentially misleading term which requires careful definition — a task that will be undertaken in Chapter X.

To keep this text as uncluttered as possible, three issues which are important but which cut across chronological lines (and thus do not lend themselves readily to chronological treatment) are discussed in separate appendices. These issues are the decorative and other arts of Islam, expertise in Islamic thought, and the ethical traditions of Islam.

Very few diacritical marks or other phonetic conventions have been used when transliterating words from Arabic or other Islamic languages into English.[2] Such words can legitimately be spelled in numerous ways, e.g., "Koran," "Qur'an" or "Quran." Any variations in spellings in this book come about because of citations from other authors.

A number of Arabic words have been used in this book. This is necessary because some concepts must be described precisely, i.e., by their Arabic names. A few readers may be put off by this use of Arabic, but since the purpose of reading this book is to learn about Islamic intellectual and cultural achievements, it is worthwhile to make the small extra effort needed to become familiar with a few foreign terms. Actually, this should not pose much of an intellectual challenge: in all cases, foreign words which are not familiar to English speakers are defined when they are first used and are defined again thereafter if this seems necessary. They are also listed in the glossary.

To avoid digressions on the frequently changing political geography of the Middle East, the names of countries as they exist today have in most cases been used in this book, e.g., Iran rather than Persia.

There are many English translations of the Quran. Unless otherwise noted, the translation used here is N.J. Dawood's *The Koran*, originally published by Penguin in 1956 and revised frequently thereafter.

The endnotes in this book are worth skimming. They have been used very freely, not only for attribution but also to elaborate on points in the text and to cite some of the astute comments offered by readers of this book while it was in manuscript form. Many of these readers are Muslims themselves; others are non–Muslims who have a professional or a personal interest in studying Islam.

It is also worthwhile mentioning that a clear distinction must be drawn between Islamic *learning*, on the one hand, and an Islamic *education*, on the other. The former is a recognized and more or less fixed body of knowledge; the latter is the process of mastering it or other kinds of knowledge. Islamic learning, not an Islamic education, is the focus of this book.

It should also be clear to the reader that just as the average Christian rarely takes the trouble to master the history or subtleties of Christian learning, so, too, the average Muslim-in-the-street has never been an expert in Islamic learning. What matters more to him or her today is simply getting on with life and practicing Islam just as the neighbors do.

I owe thanks to a far-flung range of friends and scholars who have been very generous with their time and critical comments. Chief among these is Petronella van Gorkom, a Dutch editor who has helped turn my rough drafts into what I hope is a coherent whole.

Sincere thanks are due as well to the following friends and Internet contacts, who are listed here in random order: Ulrika Mårtensson, André Kahlmeyer, Mona Katawi, Arendina F. Tieleman, Martine Kommer, Gillian Webb, Munawar Anees, Muhammed Hassanali, Shahab Mushtaq, Fazl Rahman, Jean-Louis Duvigneau, Knut Vikør, Vika Gardner, Charles Buckner, Munir Zilanawala, Jonathan Berkey, Leor Halevi, Sajjad Rizvi, Leon Sherman, Gudmar Aneer, Nahyan Fancy, and Kamran Bokhari. Whatever errors or misjudgments may remain in this book, however, are my responsibility alone.

St. Urcisse, France
Fall 2004

Introduction: Why This Book?

The rigidity and conservatism of some forms of Islamic fundamentalism are widely assailed today. Much of what has been written about Islam in recent years, especially after the terrorist attacks on the United States of 11 September 2001, reflects this negative point of view. Terrorism invariably reinforces the stereotypical view that Muslims are incorrigibly fanatical, violent, and morally and culturally "different." Such comments are, in fact, only the current version of a much longer running historical feud.

Negative reporting has almost always constituted the West's traditional response to Islam. As Edward W. Said pointed out in his brilliant polemic, *Orientalism* (1978),

> After Muhammad's death in 632, the military and later the cultural and religious hegemony of Islam grew enormously. First Persia, Syria, and Egypt, then Turkey, then North Africa fell to the Muslim armies; in the eighth and ninth centuries Spain, Sicily, and parts of France were conquered. By the thirteenth and fourteenth centuries Islam ruled as far east as India, Indonesia, and China. And to this extraordinary assault Europe could respond with very little except fear and a kind of awe... Not for nothing did Islam come to symbolize terror, devastation, the demonic, hordes of hated barbarians. For Europe, Islam was a lasting trauma. Until the end of the seventeenth century the "Ottoman peril" lurked alongside Europe to represent for the whole of Christian civilization a constant danger.[1]

As a result of this perceived Islamic threat — buttressed later on by scathing contempt for Islam's political, military, economic and social weaknesses — negative reporting on Islamic subjects became the stock-in-trade of most Western writers. This is still largely true today. It is critically important for us to remember, however, that such Western criticism of Islam almost always overlooks the fact that Islamic civilization has been refined, prestigious, and has had a highly developed intellectual component.

History proves that Islam is not intrinsically hostile to the life of the mind: there have been periods of brilliance when Islamic learning has flourished. The tenth, eleventh and twelfth centuries (the Western calendar is used in this book) may have been decentralized politically but, intellectually, they could boast of a roster of world-class thinkers. These include the philosopher and physician Ibn Sina (d. 1037), the mathematician and physicist Ibn al-Haytham (d. 1040), the multifaceted genius al-Biruni (d. 1048), and the great religious thinker al-Ghazali (d. 1111).[2]

The Middle East Institute, a research organization in Washington, D.C., reminds us that

> From the second half of the eighth century to the end of the eleventh century, Islamic scientific developments were the basis of knowledge in the world. At a period of history when the scientific and philosophical heritage of the ancient world was about to be lost, Islamic scholars stepped in to preserve that heritage from destruction. Indeed, without the cultivation of science in these early centuries by Islamic scholars, it is probable that texts which later exercised a formative influence over Western culture would never have survived intact.
>
> It is certain, moreover, that the modern world would look much different than it does today. For the culture and civilization that were founded on Islam not only preserved the heritage of the ancient world but codified, systematized, explained, criticized, modified, and, finally, built on past contributions in the process of making distinctive contributions of their own.[3]

A similar point has been made by Professor David King of Frankfurt University, an expert on the history of science in Islamic civilization. In a lecture entitled "Astronomy in the Baghdad of the Caliphs," which was delivered at several universities in Europe during 2003, he noted that

> From the eighth to perhaps the twelfth century Baghdad was the intellectual capital of the world. The history of at least one part of this intellectual activity — astronomy — is still being written. The Institute for the History of Science at Frankfurt University has conducted intensive research on a series of Arabic manuscripts from libraries between Spain and Uzbekistan which record the scientific achievements in the new Muslim capital of Baghdad, especially in the ninth and tenth centuries. These texts document the mastery of Greek and Indian astronomy by the Muslim scientists, the emergence of Arabic as the new language of science, [and] the application of inherited and newly-conceived techniques to the religious ritual of the emergent Muslim society.[4]

Under Muslim rulers, the philosophic and scientific texts of the ancient Greeks were translated first into Syriac and then into Arabic. The reason for this circuitous method was that the translators (usually Christians) who knew Greek also knew Syriac. Muslim translators found it easier to learn Syriac, which is similar to Arabic, than to learn Greek itself.[5]

In this manner, Greek texts became accessible to Muslim scholars and later on, after they had been translated into Latin, to Western scholars as well. These texts encouraged rapid progress in a wide range of fields — in mathematics, astronomy, medicine, pharmacology, optics, chemistry, philosophy, physics, medicine, and astronomy.[6]

The book you have in your hands tries to blaze a new trail through a tangled subject. This is a survey — indeed, almost an *anthology* — of noteworthy Muslim personalities and cultural achievements, written for the general reader. Its goals are clarity and simplicity, not academic hairsplitting. At the same time, it tries to fill a scholarly gap. Almost all of the information presented here can be found in other published sources, but it tends to be fragmentary and scattered there. As far as is known, no other book now in print focuses on all the intellectual and cultural Islamic achievements discussed here or tries to set them in their general historical context.

The following chapters are organized chronologically along a two-track approach. As suggested by the titles of many of these chapters, the first track consists of the key military, political or economic events in the periods under discussion. Most chapters will begin with a brief but vital historical background overview of these events. These overviews are printed in italics to set them off from the main body of the text, which focuses on the second track — that is, the key intellectual and cultural forces of the times. Individuals are listed in chronological order according to the year of their death. The last chapter offers a personal summary of Islamic learning and a forecast of its prospects for the future.

It must be recognized that a survey such as this cannot offer encyclopedic coverage of what is in fact an extraordinarily complicated subject. Because of space limitations, a survey must necessarily be highly selective. As a result, some of the significant political, economic, military, religious or social events of the nearly 1,400-year span of Islamic history discussed here will be mentioned only in passing or perhaps not at all. For example, it has not been possible to include most of the Islamic scholars who are teaching and writing today.

The reader who wants further information on Islamic history will find some excellent sources in the bibliography. The more broadly based works listed there are useful starting points. Good examples, listed here in order of publication, include the second edition of Ira Lapidus's *A History of Islamic Societies* (2002); Karen Armstrong's *Islam: A Short History* (2002); Jonathan Bloom and Sheila Blair's *Islam: Empire of Faith* (2001); Francis Robinson's *Cambridge Illustrated History of the Islamic World* (1998); Marilyn Waldman's comprehensive *Encyclopædia Britannica* article, "Islamic World,"[7] apparently written in the late 1980s; Edward W. Said's *Orientalism* (1979); and Marshall Hodgson's definitive trilogy entitled *The Venture of Islam* (1974).

Islamic learning is a timely subject today because of the increasing importance of Islam in the modern world. The West can no longer afford to dismiss Muslims in the contemptuous words of Lord Cromer, Britain's consul general in Egypt from 1883 to 1907. What Cromer had to say about the "Oriental mind," i.e., the Muslim mind, in his two volumes of memoirs entitled *Modern Egypt* (1908) is worth citing here. Cromer wrote:

> Sir Alfred Lyall [a minor Victorian poet] once said to me: "Accuracy is abhorrent to the Oriental mind. Every Anglo-Indian should always remember that maxim." Want of accuracy, which easily degenerates into untruthfulness, is in fact the main characteristic of the Oriental mind.
>
> The European is a close reasoner; his statements of fact are devoid of any ambiguity;... his trained intelligence works like a piece of mechanism. The

mind of the Oriental, on the other hand, like his picturesque streets, is eminently wanting in symmetry. His reasoning is of the most slipshod description. Although the ancient Arabs acquired in a somewhat higher degree the science of dialectics, their descendants are singularly deficient in the logical faculty. They are often incapable of drawing the most obvious conclusions from any simple premises of which they may admit the truth. Endeavor to elicit a plain statement from any ordinary Egyptian. His explanation will generally be lengthy, and wanting in lucidity. He will probably contradict himself half-a-dozen times before he has finished his story. He will often break down under the mildest process of cross-examination.[8]

Many Muslims today are worried about the undercurrent of hostility toward Islam that has been evident in the West even before 1095, when Pope Urban II preached (called for) the first Crusade to "liberate" Jerusalem. Muslim concerns appear to be well-founded. Many Westerners, consciously or not, probably still agree with Lord Cromer. For example, one observer (who must remain nameless) can be cited here. She is a British woman who lived for years in Saudi Arabia and who, only half-jokingly, offered the following advice to the author of this book:

> Do not think for one second that the Muslim world will appreciate your efforts to elucidate their appalling faith in such a clear and rational manner. It's more likely that a little *fatwa* [in this context, a formal opinion of a religious scholar that embodies a death threat] will follow publication, especially as you are an American imperialist.[9]

A solitary example does not, of course, make a case. All it really shows is that bigotry is still alive and well. But, like it or not, in the twenty-first century the West may be forced to improve its understanding, if not its liking, of Islam. The reasons are crystal-clear.

There are more than 190 countries in the world. In about 57 of them, Muslims now form the majority of the population.[10] There are about 23 million Muslims in Europe alone, at least 7 million of whom live in Western Europe. Experts estimate that there are approximately 6 million Muslims in the United States, roughly three-quarters of whom are immigrants. The U.S. State Department reports that

> Islam is one of the fastest-growing religions in the U.S. By the year 2010, America's Muslim population is expected to surpass the Jewish population, making Islam the country's second-largest faith after Christianity.[11]

Twenty percent of the world's population is now Muslim — about 1.5 billion men, women and children — and this number is growing every day.[12] Except for specialists, the Islamic world is not well-known or well-understood in the West today. Learning a bit more about it would therefore seem to be a sensible policy.[13]

"The pursuit of knowledge is incumbent on every Muslim."
—A *hadith* (saying) attributed to the Prophet Muhammad

Part One

Fundamentals of Islamic Learning

Chapter I

The World of Islam: Doctrines and Structure

Much of Islamic learning is based directly on Islamic theology. Our first task must therefore be to come to some understanding of this religion. A fundamental tenet of Islam, and thus of Islamic learning as a whole, is that the faithful must submit themselves totally to God.[1] In many ways, this concept encourages a search for knowledge—that is to say, knowledge of the Quran (the holy scripture of Islam), knowledge of the life of Muhammad, and knowledge of the conclusions reached by generations of Muslim theologians and jurists. The search for such knowledge has traditionally played a central role in Islamic life.

Muslim folklore, for example, affirms that "an hour of learning is worth more than a year of prayer."[2] For Muslims, all forms of learning, whether acquiring the practical information necessary to get on with life, or memorizing passages from the Quran or studying the subtleties of Islamic theology, are themselves "an act of worship."[3] To understand what this act of worship entails, we must begin with a brief introduction to a few key Islamic concepts, recognizing that such an overview cannot hope to do justice to them.

It must be kept in mind here that the finer points of Islamic thought are extremely complex. Any definitive understanding of Islam, for example, would have to include four interdependent disciplines: philosophy (*falsafa*), theology (*kalam*),[4] jurisprudence (*fiqh*), and Sufism (the mysticism of Islam), which will be described below in the section on the great theologian al-Ghazali.[5] Expertise in Islamic thought, moreover, is said to demand mastery of certain highly specialized subjects. Although these subjects lie far outside the reach of almost all foreigners (and most Muslims as well), they are listed in Appendix 2 because of their intrinsic interest.

Islamic Doctrines

Islam, a world religion which has links both to Judaism and to Christianity, was founded by the Prophet Muhammad in the seventh century in what is now Saudi

Arabia. Muhammad is considered to be the last of a series of prophets. His teachings are held to consummate, complement and elucidate those of the earlier prophets, whose messages are thought to have been corrupted over time.

In Arabic, *islam* is a verb which means "to surrender." It refers to this religion's requirement that believers must surrender themselves totally to the will of Allah (God). A Muslim is one who so surrenders himself or herself. This surrender is considered essential because Allah is seen as the sole creator, preserver and restorer of the universe. As the Quran enjoins the faithful:

> Praise be to God, Creator of the heavens and the earth... He multiplies His creatures according to His will. God has power over all things... You people! Bear in mind God's goodness to you. Is there any other creator who provides for you from heaven and earth? There is no god but Him. How can you turn away?[6]
>
> Fight [strive] for the cause of God with the devotion due to Him. *He* has chosen you, and laid on you no burdens in the observance of your faith, the faith of Abraham your father. In this, as in former scriptures, He has given you the name of Muslims, so that the Apostle [Muhammad] may testify [i.e., bear religious witness] against you, and that you yourselves may testify against your fellow-men. Therefore attend to your prayers, render the alms levy [used to support the poor], and hold fast to God; for He is your Guardian. A gracious guardian and a gracious helper![7]

Islam is an all-embracing faith. In theory, at least, in a purely Islamic state there can be no difference between the temporal sphere of life (the state) and the religious sphere of life (the church). Thus such a state cannot, by definition, be a secular state: it must be a religious state. In practice, however, the situation has been quite different: historically, religion has an important but usually not a dominant role. As the modern scholar Ira Lapidus notes,

> [I]n the pre-modern era there were two alternative concepts of Islamic society. One was the "Caliphate," which integrated the state and the community. The second was the "Sultanate," or secular state, which ruled over the quasi-independent religious associations that were the true bearers of Muslim religious life. In one image the state was the all-encompassing expression of an Islamic society; in the other, an Islamic society was divided into separate state and religious institutions... The legacy of pre-modern [Islamic] societies to the modern era, then, was not a defined structure of state and society, but *a spectrum of variation and an inherent ambiguity in the relations between the two*.[8]

Today, only in an Islamic fundamentalist state would religious laws and institutions totally govern private life. This would be in marked contrast with the West, where church and state have often been considered as different entities and have often been separated. Historically, a number of factors contributed to this separation: the struggles between emperors and popes during the European Middle Ages; the Renaissance; the Reformation; the Enlightenment, which stressed the primacy of reason; and the scientific revolution in Europe, which was characterized by empirical research.

It is critically important to remember that, like two other world religions—Christianity and Judaism—Islam (or more precisely, the *Islamic world* or the *Muslim world*) is not a monolithic structure. Today, to borrow a term from Christianity, Islam is a "broad church," that is to say, it has room for a wide variety of practices. There is no central authority—no papacy—that can set standards for all believers.[9] Islamic practices range across a spectrum which includes the

- traditionally tolerant, inclusive Islam usually practiced in Indonesia, the world's most populous Muslim nation (although Indonesia now has several extremist Islamic organizations, most notably Jemaah Islamiya, a Muslim terrorist group that wants to create an Islamic state spanning much of Southeast Asia);
- hard-core, literalist, but not necessarily violence-prone interpretation of Islam known as Wahhabism, which is still the dominant pattern of belief in Saudi Arabia; and
- xenophobic religious nationalism advocated by Al Qaeda, the international organization founded by the Saudi terrorist Osama bin Laden.

We must remember, too, that in Islam, as in other religions, there is often a cyclical movement, back and forth, between the two poles of liberalism and reaction. Both these terms, moreover, have only local, not absolute, meanings: they are always a function of the geographical locations and historical eras being discussed.[10]

GOD, HUMAN BEINGS AND THE DEVIL

According to the Quran, God is all-powerful and unique, having no partner and no equal. As the Quran puts it majestically,

> God: there is no god but Him, the Living, the Eternal One. Neither slumber nor sleep overtakes Him. To Him belongs all that the heavens and the earth contain. Who can intercede with Him except by His permission? He knows what is before and behind men. They can grasp only that part of His knowledge which He wills. His throne is as vast as the heavens and the earth, and the preservation of both does not weary Him. He is the Exalted, the Immense One.[11]

Muslims believe that God brought the cosmos into being with a single word of command: "Be." The creation and maintenance of the universe are seen as proof of His infinite mercy. He responds to human needs and teaches man how to follow "the straight path," i.e., the Muslim way of life. Such divine guidance is necessary because while human beings are believed to be inherently good (very young infants are considered to be *masoom*, that is, innocent or pure, and thus die sinless), adults are subject to the cardinal sin of pride.

Although Islam teaches that human beings have an innate ability to know God (*fitra*), there is always the danger that they will begin to think of themselves as God's *partners* rather than as his *dependants*. In Arabic, this is known as *shirk* (idolatry)—literally "making a partner (of someone)," i.e., elevating another being to the dignity of God. In Islamic jurisprudence, it is legally the equivalent to unbelief (*kufr*) and is the direct opposite of *tawhid*, the oneness of God (see the following section).

When *shirk* occurs, man is guilty of violating the divine unity of God by associating a mere creature (himself) with the Creator. Polytheism is a form of *shirk*.

True faith consists instead of totally submitting oneself to the divine will. Recognizing human frailties, God has sent previous messengers (prophets) to man, but most of their teachings have been corrupted or lost over time. Previous prophets, whose Islamic names are given in parentheses, included Abraham (Ibrahim), Moses (Musa), David (Dawood), Solomon (Suleman) and Jesus (Isa). Muhammad is held to be the last and greatest of the prophets: in him all the messages of former prophets are thought to have been completed, superseded and fulfilled.

Although Satan (known as Shaytan or Iblis) will try his best to tempt man to follow other deviant paths, what might be called "heaven-oriented" behavior consists not only of prayer and religious acts but, equally important, of taking concrete steps to improve the quality of life of fellow human beings, e.g., easing human suffering and helping the needy. For this reason, Islam strongly urges its followers to help create an equitable society by performing community services, e.g., contributing money to charity.[12]

THE DIVINE UNITY: TAWHID

Tawhid (literally "to make one," meaning "to conceive of God as one") is an important theological concept in Islam. It refers to the singularity and uniqueness of God. *Tawhid* means that God is one; that there is no other god but He; and that, unlike the Christian Trinity, He is an uncompounded unity. Muslims try to acknowledge this divine unity by worshipping God and by bringing their behavior and institutions into accordance with the divine will, as expressed in the Quran and the *sunna*.

THE FIVE PILLARS OF ISLAM

Muslims are expected to try to adhere to the five Pillars of Islam.

1. The profession of faith, known as the *shahada* (literally "witness"): "I testify that there is no god but God, and Muhammad is his Messenger [or Prophet]"). All that is required to become a Muslim is that, in the presence of two Muslim men or four Muslim women, a person must recite this formula aloud, correctly, with full understanding, and with genuine assent. In practice, most Sunni Muslims have always given more importance to correct religious behavior than to adherence to correct doctrines. That is, *doing* has traditionally been seen as more important than simply *believing*.

2. Obligatory prayers (*salat*) five times a day. These are said at dawn, noon, mid-afternoon, sunset and nightfall. Worshippers face the Kabah, a sanctuary which is located in Mecca. A cave outside Mecca was the scene of the first revelations, so the city became the spiritual center of the Muslim world.

3. Paying an annual religious levy (*zakat*), which is distributed to the poor. The amount due varies but, traditionally, it has been 2½ percent.

4. Fasting (*sawm*) every year from first light until sundown during the month of Ramadan, the ninth month of the Muslim lunar year. The Quran states:

Trumpeters and horsemen celebrating the Id al–Fitr feast marking the end of Ramadan. (Bibliothèque Nationale, MS. Arabe 5847 folio 19, A74/817.)

Pilgrim caravan leaving Ramla (Palestine) for Mecca. From Hariri's *Sessions* (al-Maqamat), calligraphy and illustrations by Wasiti. Baghdad, 1237. (Bibliothèque Nationale MS. Arabe 5847, folio 94v. A76/365.)

> In the month of Ramadan the Koran was revealed, a book of guidance for mankind with proofs of guidance distinguishing right from wrong. Therefore whoever of you is present in that month let him fast. But he who is ill or on a journey shall fast a similar number of days later on.[13]

5. Making the pilgrimage (*hajj*) to Mecca if one is financially and physically able to do so. For Muslims, the most sacred spot on earth is the Kabah sanctuary in Mecca,

said to have been built by Abraham and one of his sons. It houses the Black Stone (probably a meteorite), which was already an object of worship at the pilgrimages to Mecca before Islamic times.

SOURCES AND MANIFESTATIONS OF RELIGIOUS DOCTRINE

Islamic thought, jurisprudence and traditions draw on a number of revered sources in Arabic. The most important of these can be noted here briefly.

The Quran
Literally the "recitation" or "reading" of God's word, the Quran is believed by Muslims to have been verbally transmitted to the Prophet Muhammad by the Angel Gabriel. In its written form, it is held to be the earthly reproduction of an uncreated, heavenly original. The text itself states, "Surely this is a glorious Quran, inscribed on an imperishable tablet."[14] (There was, however, and still is a debate among Muslims about this heavenly original.[15])

In any case, because it is seen as infallible — its transmissional integrity is thought to have been preserved accurately by recitation from one generation to the next — the Quran is the ultimate authority on all religious and legal matters affecting Islam. This holy scripture will be discussed in more detail in Chapter III.

Traditions: The Sunna
Literally the "well-trodden path" of the Prophet, i.e., the examples which the faithful must follow, the *sunna* is the body of customary social and legal traditions and obligations of the Muslim community based on the life, teachings and practices of Muhammad. Early local variations of the *sunna* were reconciled by the legal scholar al-Shafii (767–820). He explicitly recorded some of the principles he used to sift through, authenticate, and interpret the huge mass of reports (*hadith*: see the following section) that constituted the *sunna*. The *sunna* became even more authoritative later on as scholars devised new ways to test the authenticity of the *hadith* themselves. It was also used to explain the meaning of Quranic texts and to make legal decisions on issues not mentioned or resolved in the Quran.

Reports: Hadith
Literally "report" or "story," *hadith* (in Arabic the plural is *ahadith* but in English *hadith* is often used for both singular and plural) are records of the life, utterances, teachings or actions of Muhammad. These were remembered and recorded by his close companions and his family. Over time, *hadith* proliferated until they numbered in the hundreds of thousands. There are six canonical Sunni collections of *hadith*,[16] dating from the ninth century, and other (Shiite) collections from the tenth and eleventh centuries. (The Sunni/Shiite schism is discussed later in this chapter.) All of these discuss legal and theological issues as well as provide guidance on personal, social and commercial matters.[17]

Hadith and the *sunna* are so intertwined that it may be difficult to separate them conceptually. The essential difference is that *hadith* constitute the biographical basis of Islamic law; the *sunna* is the system of religious, legal and social obligations derived from them. Following is a lightly edited example of a *hadith*. It was sourced to Aisha, Muhammad's favorite wife, in whose arms he died, and was collected by the great scholar al-Bukhari (see below):

> Al-Harith bin Hisham asked Allah's Apostle [Muhammad] "O Allah's Apostle! How is the Divine Inspiration revealed to you?" Allah's Apostle replied, "Sometimes it is revealed like the ringing of a bell; this form of Inspiration is the hardest of all and then this state passes off after I have grasped what is inspired. Sometimes the Angel [Gabriel] comes in the form of a man and talks to me and I grasp whatever he says." Aisha added: "Verily I saw the Prophet being divinely inspired on a very cold day and noticed the sweat dropping from his forehead [as the Inspiration ended]."[18]

One reason for the huge number of *hadith* was that they were invented to confer legitimacy on conflicting points of view on the issues of the day. This is not surprising. As Islam expanded territorially, it very rapidly embraced a wide variety of peoples and had to find (or create) religious and legal standards that would be acceptable to them all. Later, the Islamic scholar al-Bukhari (d. 870) limited his own collection of *hadith* to those he considered the soundest. He ended up with a total of only 2,602 *hadith* (9,082 with repetitions), but the total number of "authentic" *hadith* is now thought to be about 10,000.

These *hadith* were graded into various categories. For example, a *hadith* was considered to be "sound" if the chain of oral transmission from person to person, known as *isnad* (literally "support"), was reliable and unbroken and the text itself did not clash with orthodox beliefs. It was thought to be "good" if the lineage or the content of the *hadith* was in some question. If the *hadith* was vulnerable to serious challenge, it was said to be "weak." To mix a modern metaphor, because of its exclusively oral transmission, *isnad* can be defined as a *verbal* paper trail.[19] This concept of reliable oral transmission is so important in Islam that al-Mubarak, an early Muslim scholar, tells us that "the example of one who studies his religion without an *isnad* is like the one who attempts to ascend a roof without a ladder."[20]

The traditional format used in presenting a *hadith* was to use the first person and to specify carefully the chain of transmission. An example would be: "I was told by A, who received this report from B, on the authority of C, who learned it from D, who was told by E [a companion of Muhammad], that the Prophet said...." The litmus test for the authenticity of a *hadith* was neither its subject matter (*matn*) nor its plausibility, but only the validity of its chain of transmission. (Nevertheless, "weak" *hadith* proliferate in the Sufi world, which will be discussed later.)[21]

Consensus: Ijma

Literally "consensus," that is, the consensus of Muslim scholars on religious issues, *ijma* has played an important role in Islamic thought. One key *hadith* states that "My people [i.e., Muhammad's community] will never agree upon an error." Since the community's views were expressed by its scholars, their agreement on a given issue gave it legitimacy. At the same time, *ijma* also permitted scholarly divergences of opinion, since these were seen as an essential part of the process of reaching a consensus.

Independent Reasoning: "Closing the Door of Ijtihad" (or Idjtihad)
Ijtihad (literally "exerting oneself") is an important technical term in Islamic law. It involves the use of independent reasoning to find new legal or doctrinal solutions to problems, basing such solutions on the Quran and the *sunna*. Because many Westerners have difficulty with this concept, it may be useful here to quote at some length the definition of *ijtihad* given by the current edition of the *Encyclopaedia of Islam*:

> During the first two and a half centuries of Islam [or until about the middle of the ninth century C.E.], there was never any question of denying to any scholoar or specialist of the sacred Law the right to find his own solutions to legal problems. It was only after the formative period of Islamic law had come to an end that the question of who was qualified to exercise *idjtihad* was raised. From about the middle of the 3rd [Muslim calendar]/9th [Western calendar] century the idea began to gain ground that only the great scholars of the past, and not the epigones [followers], had the right to *idjtihad*. By the beginning of the fourth century [about 900 C.E.], the point had been reached when the scholars of all schools felt that all essential questions had been thoroughly discussed and finally settled, and a consensus gradually established itself to the effect that from that time onwards no one might be deemed to have the necessary qualifications for independent reasoning in law, and that all future activity would have to be confined to the explanation, application, and, at the most, interpretation of the doctrine as it had been laid down for once and for all. This "closing of the door of *idjtihad*," as it was called, amounted to the demand for *taqlid*, the unquestioning acceptance of the doctrines of established schools and authorities.[22]

The Islamic Community: Umma
One of Muhammad's most revolutionary ideas was that both personal security and family security were achievable within the Islamic community itself: they did not have to be based on the exclusive "blood" relationship of the tribe. Muhammad's emphasis on the importance of the Muslim community (*umma*), which is open to all comers, whether related or not, became a powerful abstract symbol that won increasing support for his new religion. The community was seen as the instrument through which the commands and ideals of the Quran could be made manifest in daily life. Indeed, two of Muhammad's most important teachings—submission to Allah and membership in the Muslim community—are still the distinguishing hallmarks of Islam.

Holy War or Holy Struggle: Jihad
The great importance attached by Muslims to a closely knit Islamic community also gave rise to the concept of *jihad*, which literally means "endeavor" or "struggle." It is difficult to generalize about this concept because there has been (and still is) so much diversity in the Islamic world that what may have been true in one time and place may not have been true in another.

In the language of Islamic practice, *jihad* technically refers to a believer's struggle to lead an upright, religious life in the face of opposition. Since this opposition may come from within, that is, from lustful or base impulses (combating these is known as "great" or "major" *jihad*), or from without, i.e., from tyranny or violent oppression (these challengers are dealt with by "small" or "minor" *jihad*), the concept *jihad* can apply to a wide range of activities. These include the struggle for spiritual refinement, activism to promote social justice, and armed struggle against oppression.[23] On this latter point, for example, the Quran enjoins the faithful:

> Fight [struggle] for the sake of God those that fight against you, but do not attack them first. God does not love aggressors."[24]

With the later expansion of Islam, *jihad* took on new meanings. It conferred legitimacy on military offensives against nonbelievers, e.g., the Romans, and provided doctrinal justification for Muslim political dominion over them. Thus for many Muslims at that time the world came to be conceptually divided into two parts: *Dar al-Islam*, the "Abode of Peace," i.e., the Islamic world, and *Dar al-Harb*, the "Abode of War," i.e., the non–Muslim or the not-yet-Muslim world.[25]

Islamic Jurisprudence and Its Practitioners: The Sharia

The *sharia* (literally "the path leading to the watering hole," i.e., in a desert climate, the path leading to salvation and, by extension, the path leading to the well of Paradise) is the body of Islamic sacred law, which was first systematized during the eighth and ninth centuries.

In the world today, there is great diversity in the actual use of the *sharia*. Most Muslim countries have replaced it with new legal codes and with secular tribunals based on Western models, though the *sharia* still has an impact on marriage laws, heritage and adoption. In a few states — Saudi Arabia is now perhaps the best-known example — the *sharia* is selectively applied, although secular laws are also used there to address the many issues that the *sharia* does not cover explicitly.

The collective sources of Islamic jurisprudence are referred to as the *usul al-fiqh*. These sources include the Quran, the *sunna*, *ijma*, and *qiyas*. *Qiyas* consist of legal reasoning, i.e., strict analogical deductions from the first three sources. Such analogies helped Muslim lawyers bring past legal decisions to bear on present cases where no clear law applied. A *mujtahid* is a scholar of Islamic law who is permitted to use independent thought (*ijtihad*) on doctrinal issues and can thus interpret the application of Islamic law. A *qadi* (judge) administers the law itself. Muslim jurisprudence, known as *fiqh* ("understanding"), looks for the proper provisions of the *sharia* to apply in a given case.

It is important to recognize that, as the American scholar Barbara Metcalf has pointed out, "Islamic law at its core is not rigid but profoundly contextual."[26] Governing a country requires many more laws than are specified in the Quran: only about 80 of the Quran's 6,000 verses lay down clear rules of public law.[27] As a practical matter, legal guidance is offered by Muslim jurists, who, drawing on the ethical and moral obligations which form the core of the Islamic message, offer informed legal opinions on matters not directly covered by the Quran.

Human actions are traditionally graded on a five-point scale: obligatory acts (for example, paying the religious levy, fasting); recommended acts (charity, kindness); permitted acts (those on which the *sharia* is neutral); reprehensible acts (Muslim opinions differ on what these are); and forbidden acts (murder, adultery, blasphemy, theft, intoxication). These categories are further set by jurists within a dual framework of obligations: those toward God and those toward society itself. In each instance, transgression is perceived in both legal and theological terms, as constituting a crime as well as a sin.[28]

It is important to realize that the *sharia* is unlike Western civil law in two fundamental respects. First, its scope is much broader. The *sharia* deals not only with a person's relations with other people and with government authorities but also with his private beliefs and his relations with God. Ritual practices and moral standards thus fall under the *sharia*'s purview. In essence, then, the *sharia* is not just a collection of laws but, more importantly, it is a fully comprehensive code of behavior, covering ritual, ethics and law, that regulates many private and public undertakings.[29]

The other major difference with Western law is that Muslims see the *sharia* as a clear expression of God's will. This belief has an important consequence. According to Islamic thought, after Muhammad died in 632 there was no further transmission of the divine will. This meant that what *had been revealed* was, as it were, set in stone. Still, there is some flexibility here: the actual application of the *sharia* has been different in different places, and especially among the various schools of Islamic thought.[30]

ETHICAL TRADITIONS IN ISLAM

Ethics can be defined as "the process of determining what is good and what is bad and the moral duties and obligations flowing from such a determination." This is a subject that has not attracted in Islamic thought the same degree of attention it has traditionally received in Western philosophy. As Abdul Haq Ansari, an Indian scholar, explains,

> Islamic ethics as a discipline or subject does not exist at present. We do not have works that define its concept, outline its issues, and discuss its problems. What we have, instead, is a discussion by various writers, philosophers, theologians, Sufis, and political and economic theorists in their particular fields of some issues that are either part of, or relevant to, Islamic ethics.[31]

Islam does not have a separate academic discipline called "ethics," but ethics have always been an integral part of dogmatics—the branch of theology that develops and interprets the dogmas of Islam. Ethical reflection plays an important role in Islamic learning because it addresses a fundamental question of life: namely, what ought or ought not to be done? Ethics thus merits discussion in this book, but because of their diffuse nature, it seems best to outline the issues in an appendix rather than in the text itself. They are therefore discussed in Appendix 3.

The Structure of the Islamic World

Shortly after the death of Muhammad in 632, the Muslim world began to expand rapidly, though it was often torn by internal divisions. The raid (*ghazu*) was an integral component of *bedouin* (nomadic) life; this expansion arguably gave Muslim tribesmen some external enemies to confront so they would no longer have only each other to fight. There was always a considerable ebb and flow in the spread of the Islamic world, but on balance this process was extraordinarily successful.

For example, if we look at the expansion of Islam at its greatest extent (between 900 and 1700), it is clear that this new world was indeed far-flung. A tally of the Islamic world at that time would have to include all the following lands:

most of Spain and Portugal

the northern third of Africa and two-thirds of that continent's eastern coastline, including the northern half of Madagascar

much of the Balkans

part of the Ukraine and southern Russia

the whole of the Middle East

central Eurasia and parts of China

most of India

Indonesia, Malaysia and parts of the Philippines

Islamic power reached its zenith under the rule of Suleyman the Magnificent (1520–1566). Until the eighteenth century, Islam was able to maintain its position as the dominant power in Africa, the Middle East and the Mediterranean region. By the end of that century, however, Western Europe was in the ascendancy. This was largely due to the specialized, efficient, well-armed and increasingly industrialized society which had developed there.[32]

Western Europe's new society was so powerful that it proved to be virtually impossible for traditional cultures, e.g., the Islamic world, to compete with it. The Islamic world was so eclipsed in this new world order that in 1853 Czar Nicholas I of Russia, using a memorable turn of phrase, could say of the Ottoman Empire, which had been in decline for many centuries: "We have on our hands a sick man, a very sick man." Accordingly, until this empire finally came to an enfeebled end after the end of World War I in 1918, it was known as "the sick man of Europe."

Since then, there has been a great demographic if not a political, economic or military resurgence of Islam. As mentioned earlier, there are now approximately 1.5 billion Muslims in the world, who form the majority of the population in about 57 countries.

Sunnis and Shiites: The Major Branches of Islam

The Islamic world is divided into two major branches: Sunnis and Shiites. Sunnis constitute the overwhelming majority—about 90 percent—of all Muslims.

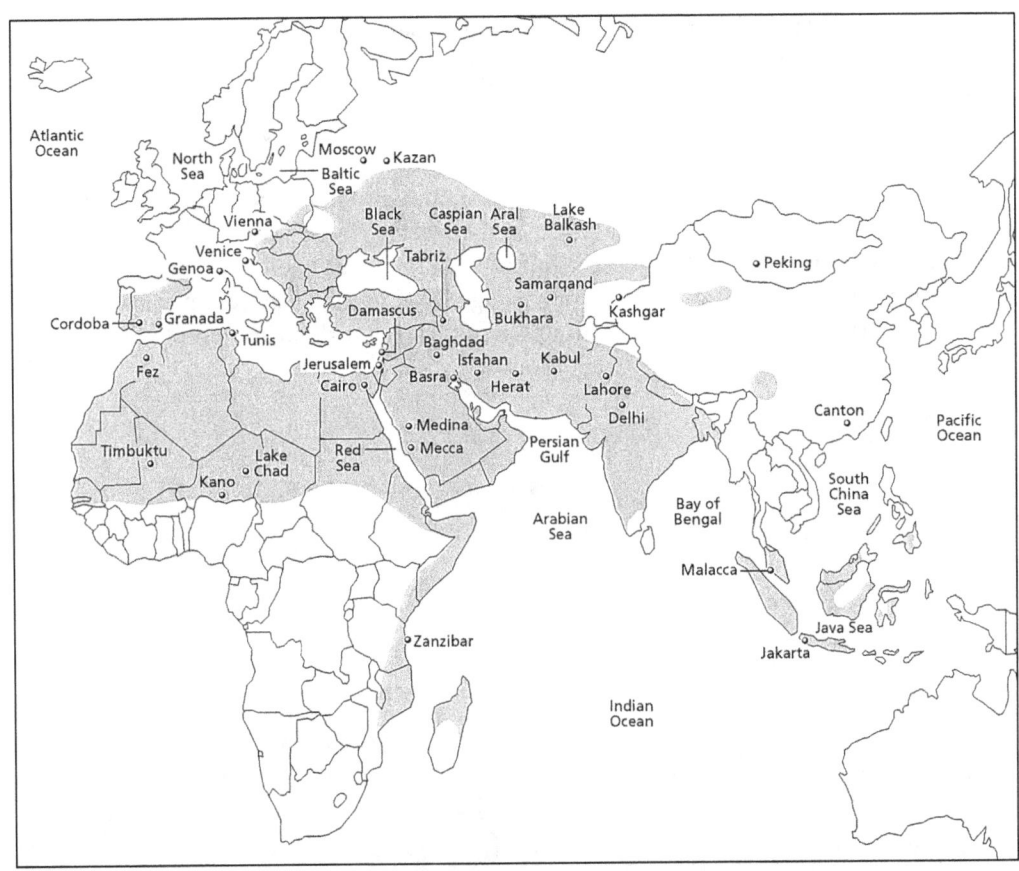

Shaded areas show the expansion of Islam at its greatest extent, i.e., between 900 and 1700. This expansion was not a uniform or an unbroken process but was characterized by marked ebbs and flows. After having been part of the Islamic world, some of the lands shown here were lost to Islam between 1300 and 1700. Muslim power in Spain, for example, arose in 711 and came to an end in 1492. (Map by Graeme Bandeira.)

Their name reflects the importance attached to the *sunna* — the set of traditional social and legal customs of the Muslim community. Sunnis revere the four *Khalifa al-Rashidin*, i.e., the four "rightly guided" caliphs who were the companions and immediate successors of the Prophet. "Rightly guided" refers to the fact that these leaders governed in accordance with the principles laid down by Muhammad; "caliph" comes from the Arabic *khalifa* and means a deputy or a successor. These four caliphs were: Abu Bakr, Umar ibn al-Khattab, Uthman ibn Affan and Ali ibn Abi Talib.

Shiite Muslims share almost all of the fundamental beliefs of the Sunnis. Their name is derived from the Arabic phrase *shi'at Ali*, which means the "party" or "faction" of Ali. They now live chiefly in Iran, Iraq, Bahrain, Yemen, Lebanon, India and Pakistan. They believe that the last of these four caliphs, Ali ibn Abi Talib, should by rights have succeeded the Prophet because Ali was Muhammad's cousin, his ward, his son-in-law, and, most importantly, his only male "blood relative." Shiites say that Muhammad himself wanted his male relative, i.e., Ali, to be his successor.[33]

As a result, Shiites revere Ali as the First Imam (in this context, the absolute ruler) of the Islamic community.³⁴ All later imams are the direct male descendants of Ali and his wife Fatimah, Muhammad's daughter. The Shiite imamate is thus strictly hereditary, and the Shiites have raised it to a metaphysical plane of infallibility.³⁵

This is where Sunni and Shiite ways of thought fundamentally differ. Most importantly, Shiites believe that the only true wellspring of Islamic belief is, ultimately, loyalty to Ali and his descendants.³⁶ There are also some minor Sunni/Shiite differences in the prayer ritual, in heritage laws, in marriage ceremonies, and in the validity of "independent reasoning" to solve legal or doctrinal problems.

Chapter II

The Prophet Muhammad and His Times (c. 500–632)

Historical Background

The Quraysh, a formerly nomadic tribe, in the fifth century had settled in Mecca, on the west coast of what is now Saudi Arabia, and had transformed this desert hamlet into a small but relatively prosperous trading city which lay at the intersection of important trade routes. It seemed extremely unlikely that the Quraysh would ever be able to expand into a powerful, well-organized state. But thanks to a middle-aged Meccan merchant named Muhammad ibn Abdallah ibn Abd al-Muttalib, who was later known as the Prophet Muhammad, this is precisely what happened.

The Physical and Social Environment

To appreciate the remarkable developments brought about in Mecca, we must first note the exceedingly difficult physical and social environment in which they took place. Indeed, this austere environment was arguably responsible for the puritanical nature of "pure," i.e., early, Islam.

Arabia before the rise of Islam (a period known to Muslims as *jahiliyya*—"the time of ignorance") was a ruthless, impoverished, lightly populated land. Because there were not enough worldly goods to go around, raiding and counterraiding by nomadic tribesmen was the de facto social mechanism used to distribute, more or less evenly, what little surplus there was. Population growth had to be kept under control by drastic measures. The Quran deplores the pre-Islamic custom of infanticide: "when the infant girl, buried alive, is asked for what crime she was slain...."[1] This is an allusion to the *bedouin* tradition of burying alive in the desert any unwanted newborn girl.

Mecca itself is located on the dry beds of a river valley (the Wadi Ibrahim) and its tributaries. The city is surrounded by low mountains, including Jabal Hira (2,080 feet in height), which contains the cave in which Muhammad stayed during his spiritual retreats and where he received some of his angelic revelations. Temperatures in Mecca remain high throughout the whole year and in summer can reach 113 degrees F. (45 degrees C.). The single best description of traditional nomadic life in the great heat of the Hijaz (the northern half of the west coast of Saudi Arabia) comes from Charles Montague Doughty, a British explorer with a unique, highly idiosyncratic writing style who was one of the greatest nineteenth-century adventurers. In the 1870s Doughty spent two years wandering through Arabia, living with the *bedouin*. This is what he has to say about "Summer Days in the Wilderness":

> The sun, entering as a tyrant upon the waste landscape, darts upon us a torment of fiery beams, not to be remitted till the far-off evening.... Grave is that giddy heat upon the crown of the head; the ears tingle with a flickering shrillness, a subtle crepitation it seems, in the glassiness of this sun-stricken nature; the hot sand-blink is in the eyes, and there is little refreshment to find in the tents' shelter; the worsted booths [the tents, made of heavy, loosely-woven cloth] leak to this fiery rain of sunny light. Mountains looming like dry bones through the thin air, stand far around about us.... This silent air burning about us, we endure breathless until [evening]: when the dazing Arabs in the tents revive after their heavy hours ... and the morrow will be as this day, days deadly drowned in the sun of the summer wilderness.[2]

Although there is very little rain in Mecca (less than 5 inches a year), in the past the city was subject to seasonal flash floods. Animal and plant life has always been scarce and is limited to desert species which can tolerate great heat and aridity. Mecca did, of course, have water — not enough for extensive agriculture, to be sure, but enough to support large herds of camels. By about the year 500 it had evolved into a regional trading center which staged two great camel caravans each year: one, in the winter, to Yemen; the other, in summer, through northwest Arabia to Palestine and Syria.[3]

The Quraysh decreed that Mecca would become a sanctuary from the constant raiding and counterraiding which was a vital part of *bedouin* life. The town thus became a safe place to hold trade fairs timed to coincide with an annual pilgrimage to a local holy site, the Kabah, where at this time many gods were worshipped — one for each day of the year. Deities included not only Allah, the High God of the Arabs, but also his divine daughters— Al-Lat, Al-Uzza, and Manat. These latter three represented, respectively, the sun, the planet Venus, and fortune.[4] Despite its numerous gods, however, pre-Islamic Arabia, when compared to other ancient civilizations, remained strikingly impoverished in its economy, military prowess, social structure, mythology, ceremonial rituals and festivals.[5]

The Life of Muhammad (c. 570–632)

A thumbnail biographic sketch of Muhammad's life may be useful here.[6] From a secular point of view, two caveats must be borne in mind at the outset. First, we can never know how much of the traditions surrounding Muhammad are actually true: as is the case with many other religions, pious legend has become inextricably intertwined with historical fact. The earliest document bearing on Muhammad's life is the Quran itself.[8] Non–Muslims, however, believe that this is basically a collection of Muhammad's own statements and tells us very little about the Prophet as a person.

The first major biography of Muhammad was not produced until long after his death in 632. This was the edition by Ibn Hisham (d. 833) of a work initially written by Muhammad ibn Ishaq (d. 767). Such a relative paucity of historical detail, coupled with the passage of time and with the extreme devotion Muslims have always attached to Muhammad as the "perfect man" because of his total surrender to the will of God, has given ample scope for pious legends to penetrate deeply and permanently into the historical record. What we do know about Muhammad dates not from his own lifetime but from what his followers said four generations later. The earliest biographies show him as more "human" than the later ones.

In the interest of brevity only a few of the many pious legends will be cited in this book. Muhammad ibn Ishaq, for example, tells us that before the Prophet was born, his mother Amina became aware of a heavenly light within her. This was so intense that when it radiated forth from her one day, she could miraculously see castles in far-off Syria. She also heard a heavenly voice say to her:

> Thou carriest in thy womb the lord of this people; and, when he is born, say: "I place him beneath the protection of the One [God], from the evil of every envier"; then name him Muhammad [this Arabic name means "praised" or "glorified"].[8]

The second caveat to be kept in mind is that Western scholars believe that traditional accounts of the origins of Islam fail to give sufficient weight to historical factors long considered by Muslims to be politically and religiously incorrect. These include the roles of Jews and of Christians in Muhammad's Arabia and the nature of the pagan deities he rejected in favor of his one god, Allah. While these scholarly controversies lie beyond the scope of this book, they deserve mention here to alert the reader to their existence.

Traditional accounts relate that Muhammad was born in Mecca in about 570 into a merchant clan which was part of the prosperous Quraysh tribe but whose own fortunes had been on the decline. Like other babies of this sedentary merchant society, he was given to a *bedouin* nurse so that he could pass his earliest years in the desert, which was considered a healthier environment than a town like Mecca.

His nurse Halimah and her husband were very poor, but little Muhammad turned out to be a great blessing for them. As the biographer Muhammad ibn Ishaq tells the tale, Halimah reported that when she received baby Muhammad from his mother,

> I carried him back to where our mounts [camels] were stationed, and no sooner had I put him in my bosom than my breasts overflowed with milk for him. He drank his fill, and with him his foster-brother likewise drank his fill. Then they both slept; and my husband went to that old she-camel of ours, and lo! her

udders were full. He milked her and drank of her milk and I drank with him until we could drink no more, and our hunger was satisfied....

We reached our tents in the Bani Sa'd country, and I know of no place more barren than that then was. But after we brought him to live with us, my flock would come home to me replete at every eventide and full of milk. We milked them and drank, when others had no drop of milk.[9]

When he grew up, Muhammad eked out a modest existence as a trader in charge of leading camel caravans to Syria and Iraq. In 595, however, he had an unexpected stroke of good luck. Khadija bint Khuwaylid, a widow who was a distant relative and a rich businesswoman, commissioned him, at the age of 25, to lead a camel caravan of her goods to Syria and sell them there. It is said that Muhammad accomplished this assignment so successfully that Khadija doubled her money. Whether it was because of his financial acumen or because of his good looks, Khadija decided to marry him, even though he was 15 years younger than she was. Their marriage was a happy one.

Muhammad had a reputation for honesty, compassion and piety. He often went by himself to a cave in the mountains near Mecca to meditate and pray. According to one tradition, in about 610, when he was asleep or in a trance in this cave, the angel Gabriel appeared to him at night and commanded him: "Recite!" Muhammad replied: "What shall I recite?" (Muhammad's reply can also be translated as "I cannot read," i.e., he could not comply because he was illiterate.) Gabriel gave no explanation but simply repeated the order three times. Since Muhammad still did not know what to say, the angel ordered him:

> Recite in the name of your Lord, who created — created man from clots of blood. Recite! Your Lord is the Most Bountiful One, who by the pen taught man what he did not know.[10]

Another version holds that when Gabriel appeared before him, Muhammad was so terrified he thought about killing himself by leaping out of the cave. The angel steadied him, saying "Muhammad, I am Gabriel and you are the messenger of God. Recite!" When Muhammad could not reply, Gabriel grabbed him and squeezed him so tightly that he was forced to utter the above statement. This would later become the opening verses of *sura* (chapter) 96 of the Quran.

THE NIGHT JOURNEY (ISRA)

After this shattering religious experience, Muhammad began to preach, aided by further messages he continued to receive from Gabriel until the end of his life. His greatest mystical experience came in 620, when he made a miraculous Night Journey (*Isra*) from Mecca and thence to heaven. The Quran states in *sura* 17:1:

> Glory be to Him who made His servant go by night from the Holy Mosque (*al-masjid al-haram*) to the Farther Mosque (*al-masjid al-aqsa*) whose surrounding We have blessed, that We might show him some of Our signs. He is the All-hearing, the All-seeing.[11]

Some Muslims accept this passage at face value as a description of a physical journey; others believe that it refers, symbolically, to a vision or a dream experienced by Muhammad. In any case, it is agreed that the servant of God referred to in this *sura* was Muhammad and that the Holy Mosque was in Mecca.

The Farther Mosque was at one time thought to be heaven. It was therefore at first believed that this *sura* referred to Muhammad's ascension into heaven (an event known as *miraj*), which also originated in Mecca. By the end of the eighth century, however, Jerusalem, not heaven, was considered to be the Farther Mosque. Later on, to resolve any lingering uncertainty, *isra* was defined as the Night Journey itself and Jerusalem as the point from which Muhammad ascended into heaven.

Moving to Medina (Hijra)

Muhammad's monotheistic teachings so annoyed the polytheist Meccans that they wanted to kill him. For this reason, in 622 he decided to lead his followers to the town of Yathrib, about 200 miles north of Mecca, in response to an invitation from the leaders of the city. Yathrib subsequently became known as Medina (literally "city") but was also termed, more poetically, "The Luminous City" (*al-Madinah al-Munawwarah*) or the "city of the messenger of God" (*Madinat Rasul Allah*). Muslims still date the beginning of the Islamic era from this *hijra* ("flight" or "migration") of 622 to Medina.

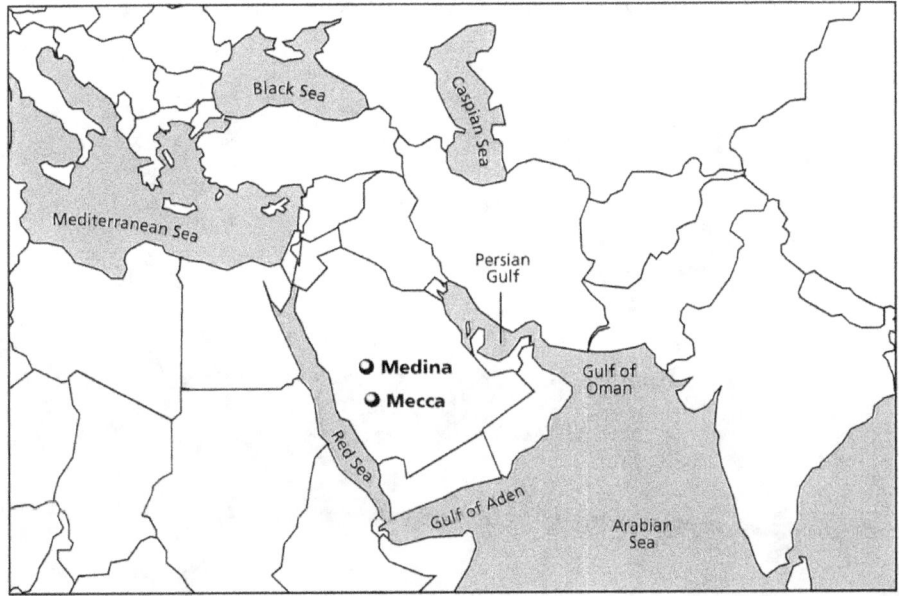

Mecca and Medina, the two holy citites of Saudi Arabia. The Kabah sanctuary in Mecca houses the Black Stone and is the most sacred spot on earth for Muslims. Muhammad's *hijra* ("migration") to Medina in 622 marks the beginning of the Muslim calendar. Medina is also the site of the Prophet's tomb. (Map by Graeme Bandeira.)

The final decade of Muhammad's life, i.e., from the *hijra* until his death in 632, was marked by small-scale but frequent military clashes and by intense diplomatic maneuvering against his opponents. The Prophet's efforts were crowned with ultimate success. Notable events of this last decade include the following[12]:

battle of Badr (624), known as the "Miracle Battle" because there the Muslims, though outnumbered ten to one, defeated the Quraysh (had the Muslims lost this battle, there probably would not be any Muslims today);

battle of Uhud (625), when the Muslims were defeated;

expulsion by the Muslims of the Jewish tribe of al-Nadir (626);

"battle of the ditch," (627), where a mounted Meccan attack against Medina was foiled by a protective ditch dug on Muhammad's orders;

Muslim raid against the Jewish tribe of Qurayzah (627);

truce with the Quraysh (628), who then permitted Muhammad to preach without hindrance;

killing by Muslims of the Jews of Khaybar (629)[13];

peaceful capture by Muhammad of Mecca itself (630), when the Kabah became the center of this new religion; and, finally,

"the year of embassies" (631), during which Islam was accepted by most of the other tribes of Arabia. Because Muslims were not to fight other Muslims, this final event marked the beginning of the end of tribal warfare in Arabia.

Chapter III

The Quran

Historical Background

Muhammad himself was illiterate, but his utterances, revealing what he had heard from Gabriel and delivered over a period of more than twenty years, usually when he was in a state of trance or ecstasy, were memorized by the faithful. Tradition also avers that Muhammad had some of his utterances written down by literate followers on whatever material was readily available, said to have included pieces of paper, stones, palm-leaves, shoulder-blades, ribs, and bits of leather. After his death, an authoritative text, now known as the Uthmanic recension (discussed later in this chapter), was established during the reign of Caliph Uthman (r. 644–656). Believers were encouraged to memorize the whole Quran—a remarkably difficult feat even in their largely oral and aural society, which gave more weight to the spoken than to the written word.[1]

"The Word of God"

Considered by Muslim and Western scholars alike to be the finest work of Classical Arabic rhymed prose, the Quran still forms the bedrock of all Islamic learning because it is usually held to be the Word of God.[2] With the exception of the opening verses and a few passages where Muhammad or Gabriel is the speaker, the speaker is God Himself, who speaks in the *pluralis majestatis* ("We"), the first person singular ("I") or the third person singular ("He").[3] Along with the Torah and the Bible, it can legitimately claim to be one of the most influential books of all time. This chapter discusses the Quran's origins, format, interpretations, translations and enduring importance to Muslims.

SOME DIFFICULTIES

The Quran presents considerable challenges for non–Muslim readers. Roughly comparable in length to the Christian New Testament, it has 114 *suras*, each of which bears a traditional name. These names reflect a creature, object or event mentioned

Decorative covers of a Moroccan Quran.

in the text. Examples include "The Cow" (*sura* 2), "The Table" (*sura* 5), and "He Frowned" (*sura* 80).

The *suras* are not arranged in chronological order but in order of their length, generally with the longest chapters coming first and the shortest at the end of the book. (An exception is the first *sura*, the relatively short *fatihah*, which is quoted in the following section.) To understand the longer and more complicated *suras*, which appear in the early part of the Quran, some knowledge of events during Islam's earliest years, and of what had happened just prior to the revelation of a given verse, is essential.

Perhaps most importantly, the Quran is at its best when it is *recited aloud*, not read silently like a history textbook or a novel. Indeed, many Muslims believe that only when it is so recited can the eloquence, denseness, complexity and allusiveness of its Arabic be fully appreciated. They insist that any translation of the Quran, no matter how conscientiously it is done, will always fall far short of the Arabic original: no human effort can hope to imitate the beauty and perfection of the word of God. For this reason, "Islamic" translations are usually entitled something along the lines of "The Meaning of the Quran" rather than "The Quran."

As if these potential stumbling blocks were not enough, some *suras* also begin with *fawatih*, which are detached, cryptic letters from the Arabic alphabet. "The Cow," for example, begins with the letters *alif lam mim*. Sometimes these letters are pronounced as individual letters. To use an example in English, this is like saying "kay" for the letter *k*. At other times, their enunciation is specially lengthened according to the rules of the discipline of *tajwid*, i.e., the "beautification of Quranic recitation."[4]

Various theories have been put forward to explain these letters but, in fact, their meaning and their function are not known. Islamic commentators traditionally pass over them with a rueful comment: "God alone knows what He means by these letters."[5] Despite such obstacles, however, the attentive non–Muslim reader can still find much literary excellence in a translation of the Quran. Only three of many possible examples will be cited here.

The Fatihah ("Opening") of the Quran

The first example of a translation with literary excellence is that of the *fatihah*, a short prayer which comprises the opening lines of the Quran. It begins with a traditional invocation known as the *bismillah*: "In the Name of God, the Compassionate, the Merciful" and then continues in these stately cadences:

> Praise be to God, Lord of the Universe,
> The Compassionate, the Merciful,
> Sovereign of the Day of Judgment!
> You alone we worship, and to You alone
> we turn for help.
> Guide us to the straight path,
> The path of those whom You have favored,
> Not of those who have incurred Your wrath,
> Nor of those who have gone astray.[6]

This is the first *sura* in the Quran, though not the first one to be revealed to Muhammad. The faithful know it by heart because its primary place in the liturgy of Islam ensures that it will be recited at least seventeen times each day.[7]

The Day of Judgment

The second example of literary excellence is a lovely, evocative *sura* entitled "The Cessation" (*sura* 81), which describes the Day of Judgment. Here is the bulk of its text:

> When the sun ceases to shine; when the stars fall and the mountains are blown away; when camels big with young are left untended, and the wild beasts are brought together; when the seas are set alight and men's souls are reunited; when the infant girl, buried alive, is asked for what crime she was slain; when the records of men's deeds are laid open, and heaven is stripped bare; when Hell burns fiercely and Paradise is brought near: then shall each soul learn what it has done.
>
> I swear by the turning planets, and by the stars that rise and set; by the night, when it descends, and the first breath of morning: this [the Quran] is the word of a gracious and mighty messenger [Gabriel], held in honor by the Lord of the Throne, obeyed in heaven, faithful to his trust.[8]

Verses from "Light"

A third example of literary excellence comes from *sura* 24 ("Light"):

> God is the light of the heavens and the earth. His light may be compared to a niche that enshrines a lamp, the lamp within a crystal of star-like brilliance. It is lit from a blessed olive tree neither eastern nor western. Its very oil would almost shine forth, though no fire has touched it. Light upon light; God guides His light to whom He will.[9]

The Uthmanic Recension (644–656)

Muhammad died in 632. Many of his followers, who had memorized his teachings, fell the next year in the battle of Yamamah. These cumulative losses raised the real possibility that any knowledge of the holy scripture might disappear. Thus a decision was made to assemble whatever written sources remained and to consult "the hearts of the people," i.e., the collective memory of the believers. Zayd ibn Thabit, one of the close companions of the Prophet, copied onto sheets of parchment whatever information he could find and gave them to the caliph Umar.

When Umar died, this collection passed to his daughter Hafsah.[10] However, other copies of the Quran were circulating, too. Agreement on a standard text became necessary. Caliph Uthman (r. 644–656) commissioned Zayd ibn Thabit and other scholars to work toward this end. By using Hafsah's sheets, by correlating them with "the hearts of the people," and by adopting (for purposes of pronunciation) the dialect of the Quraysh, Muhammad's tribe, these men produced an authoritative text known as the Uthmanic recension.

Arabic Script and Exegesis

The earliest surviving fragments of the Quran date from the first quarter of the eighth century. Initially written on vellum in an Arabic script known as *kufic*, these early versions lacked the diacritical marks and vowel signs which were used later on to clarify the meaning of the text. Without such literary aids, as many as seven variant readings of the Quran were possible. As written texts of the Quran became more common, the need for exegesis became evident. (Exegesis is a learned explanation or critical interpretation of a text. In Arabic it is called *tafsir*.)

The first scholar to attempt an overall critical analysis of the Quran was the historian and theologian al-Tabari (d. 923). He was followed more than 300 years later by al-Baydawi (d. 1286), who shortened an earlier work by Zamakhshari (d. 1143), and by numerous other exegetes who will not be mentioned here in the interest of brevity.

The Limitations of Quranic Exegesis

As we shall see, reformers of the nineteenth and twentieth centuries were well-aware of the need for new interpretations of the Quran to help Muslims adjust to the

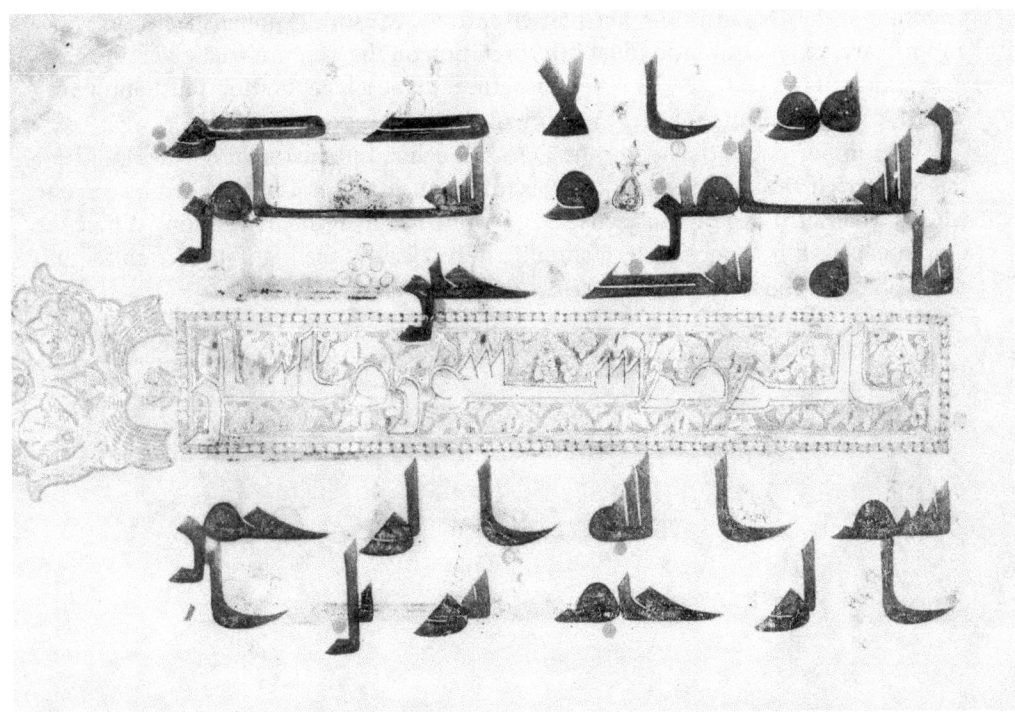

Folio from a large-format copy of the Quran, produced in North Africa or the Near East in the ninth century and used in readings at a mosque during the month of Ramadan. Calligraphy itself was considered to be an act of worship because it was a manifestation of the divine, namely, God's speech. This angular script, known as *kufic*, is especially difficult to read but since many readers knew the Quran by heart, the script served only to jog their memory. The text shown here is taken from *sura* 38, verses 87–88, and *sura* 39, verse 1. These verses read: "This is an admonition to mankind; in a while you shall learn its truth. This Book is revealed by God, the Mighty, the Wise One." (Freer Gallery of Art, Smithsonian Institution, Washington, D.C. Purchase, F1930.60.)

demands of modern times.[11] Reformers today are likely to draw distinctions between the "core" religious concepts of the Quran, on the one hand, and the less-vital ideas which are a function of the historical environment in which Islam developed, on the other.

The recent rise of Islamic fundamentalism, however, suggests that this process will not be a painless one. Just as many "born-again" Christians are dead-set against what they see as diabolical efforts to whittle away the literal truths of the Bible, so, too, will many conservative Muslims resist any bold new advances in Quranic exegesis *if these seem to threaten the veracity of the Quran itself*.

The orthodox position on the *inherent nature* of the Quran has been aptly summarized by the Swedish scholar Helmer Ringgren. In its essence, he says, the Quran is "left untouched by criticism; as the infallible world of God it cannot have been influenced by the circumstances under which it was revealed, it can contain no mistake, and it cannot be superseded by any new discovery."[12]

Fortunately (from the point of view of Muslim reformers, at least) the *inter-*

pretation of the Quran is another matter entirely. Muslim rationalists always were, and still are, in favor of individual interpretation on the grounds that given the eternal validity of the text, i.e., its inherent nature, that each generation must apply reason to it to seek out its specific meaning in the contemporary context.[13]

The importance attached to the Quran is echoed in customary "rules" on how the book itself should be treated. For example, it should not be touched by anyone who is unclean in a religious sense, e.g., women during menstruation. When the Quran is placed in a bookshelf, it should always occupy the highest place so that no other book is "above" it.[14]

Part Two

The Growth of Islamic Learning

Chapter IV

Islam Becomes the Dominant Faith of an Empire (632–873)

Historical Background

According to the Sunnis, Muhammad did not designate a successor before his death in 632, a fact which eventually led to the Sunni-Shiite schism. (Shiites believe that the Prophet designated Ali ibn Talib as his successor.) Muhammad was succeeded by his close companion Abu Bakr, whose short tenure as caliph (Abu Bakr died only two years later) was marked by "the wars of apostasy" (riddah). These occurred because some of the Arabian tribes, believing that their commitment to the umma (the Islamic community) expired with the death of Muhammad, sought to regain their former independence. Abu Bakr kept them in the Muslim fold by a judicious mixture of military force and by offering hopes of plunder from raids against neighboring states.

To bring these hopes to fruition and to strengthen the weak economic base of Islam, the second caliph, Umar I (r. 634–644), invaded Iraq, Syria and Egypt. Jerusalem fell (peaceably) to the Muslims in 638. It would become the third holiest city of the Islamic world, after Mecca and Medina. Muslim forces subsequently defeated the Persian Empire, conquered Cyprus and Tripoli, and set up Islamic rule in Iran, Afghanistan and Sind (Pakistan).

In 656–661 and again in 680–692, Islam was torn by four civil wars (fitnahs) which led to the schism between the Sunnis and the Shiites that is still evident today. In the early eighth century, Muslim armies continued the conquest of North Africa and later set up an Islamic kingdom in Spain. Damascus was the capital of the Ummayad caliphs.[1]

Baghdad became the new capital of the next dynasty (the Abbasid dynasty) in 762 and reached a cultural high point under the caliphate of Harun al-Rashid (786–809). His rule formed an early part of a golden age which witnessed the rise of a truly Islamic culture and growth of Islam into a far-flung religion. The expansion of Islam was so successful that by 873, when al-Kindi, the "philosopher of the Arabs," died, many people in the lands ruled by Islam had become Muslims.

The First Great Islamic Monument: The Dome of the Rock (Completed 691/692)

We shall now consider some of the high points of Islamic learning, beginning with Jerusalem's Dome of the Rock (Qubbat al-sakhra), which was finished 59 years after Muhammad's death.[2] Although this is not the most beautiful Islamic building in the world (that honor belongs to India's Taj Mahal), it was the first great Islamic monument and is the oldest Islamic monument which has survived, basically intact, in its original form.

Probably the first major artistic endeavor of the Umayyad dynasty, the aesthetic appeal of the Dome of the Rock is the result of a precise geometrical design which is enhanced by carefully balanced, harmonious proportions. It is the crowning glory of the most impressive structure in that part of Jerusalem known as the Old City — a huge masonry platform covering about 36 acres. This platform has many names. In Arabic, it is known as the Haram al-Sharif ("the Noble Sanctuary," the name commonly used by Muslims) or as Bait al-Maqdis ("the Holy House"). In Hebrew it is called "Har ha-Moriyya" ("Mount Moria"), Har ha-Bayit ("the Temple Mount," the name commonly used by Jews) or Beth ha-Maqdas ("the Holy House").

By whatever name we choose — the Haram or the Temple Mount — this platform is of enormous importance to Muslims and Jews alike. For Muslims, it holds two of the great sites that are centers of Islamic piety. The first and most important of these is the Dome of the Rock. Previously and incorrectly known as the Mosque of Umar, this is not in fact a mosque for public worship but is technically a *mashhad*, that is, a shrine for pilgrims. With its great dome symbolizing the heavenly vault, it is the sacred center of the Muslim pilgrimage to Jerusalem.[3] The other great Islamic site is the Aqsa Mosque. (The Aqsa Mosque was first completed in 715 but was destroyed in an earthquake of 747. Its structural history since then has been complex. However, because this mosque has been restored so thoroughly so many times, most recently in 1938 and 1942, its relatively simple, modern interior totally lacks the historic

The Dome of the Rock today.

and aesthetic interest of the Dome of the Rock. For this reason, the Aqsa Mosque will not be discussed in any detail here.)

The exteriors of both buildings can be seen simultaneously and to good advantage from the Mount of Olives, which lies to the east of the Old City, on the other side of the narrow Valley of Jehoshaphat. From this elevated vantage point, by the light of the rising sun a visitor can get an unobstructed view of much of the Haram, with the golden Dome of the Rock to the north and the gray-domed Aqsa Mosque south of it. Behind the Haram rise the functional but visually less appealing modern buildings of Jerusalem. A more dramatic view of the Dome of the Rock alone can be had from one of the narrow archways of the Old City.

For Jews, the Temple Mount is the site of their long-destroyed temples and contains the Western (Wailing) Wall, sacred to Judaism. Politically, this ancient platform still constitutes the fault line between the Palestinians and Israel. In the year 2000, for example, it sparked a Palestinian *intifada* (uprising) which still continues at this writing. For Muslims, Jerusalem is extraordinarily important, too, because of Muhammad's miraculous Night Journey.

Building the Dome of the Rock

The ninth caliph, Abd al-Malik, built the Dome of the Rock for two reasons. First, his political opponent Ibn al-Zubayr was then in power in Mecca. Abd al-Malik hoped to diminish his rival's influence by luring the *hajj* (pilgrimage) away from Mecca and encouraging pilgrims to come instead to this impressive new monument in Jerusalem, which would serve as a near-replacement for the Kabah. If they were to flock to Jerusalem, it might eventually grow into a religious and a political center which would equal, if not necessarily surpass, Mecca itself.[4]

The second reason was that building the Dome of the Rock underscored the victory of Islam over Judaism, symbolically achieved in 638 when the Muslims captured Jerusalem, which was then held by the Byzantines. (This victory over Byzantium was of paramount importance: Byzantium was the imperial rival of the caliphate.) The Dome of the Rock also provided some weighty visual competition to the Christian sanctuaries of Palestine, especially the Church of the Holy Sepulcher (completed in 336), which lies only 550 yards to the west of the Dome of the Rock.[5]

The Dome of the Rock includes part of the Western Wall, the last remnant of the First Temple of the Jews, which was destroyed in 587 B.C.E. The holy rock itself, located in the middle of the Dome of the Rock, measures about 57 feet by 42 feet and projects about 5 feet above the present paving. In the past, the Jews considered this rock to be the Foundation Stone, marking the exact center of the world and lying above a bottomless pit. Tradition has it that on this rock Abraham, the first patriarch of the Jewish people, was prepared to sacrifice his son.

The Muslims elaborate this sacred geography even further. Tradition has variously defined the rock as being the center of the world; as being supported on a palm tree watered by the river of Paradise; as the place where the spirits of the dead await the Day of Judgment; as the site where, on that last day, the Kabah will miraculously come to Jerusalem from Mecca; and where God's throne will be set up.

Muslim tradition also tells us that when Muhammad prayed on the rock immediately before his visit to heaven, the rock itself tried to follow him upward as he ascended. Visitors are still shown Muhammad's footprint on the rock and the deep indentations made in it by Gabriel as he restrained the rock with his hand. The American writer Mark Twain, who visited the Dome of the Rock in 1867, joked good-humoredly that "Very few people have a grip like Gabriel—the prints of his monstrous fingers, two inches deep, are to be seen in that rock today."[6]

In the past (but not at present, due to political considerations, i.e., the Israeli occupation of Jerusalem after the 1967 war), Muslims often visited this shrine in preparation for the great pilgrimage to Mecca. The Dome of the Rock could hold up to 3,000 worshippers and was said to have cost the sum of seven years' revenue (a symbolic number indicating a staggering sum of money) from the province of Egypt. This income was piled up in gold in the adjacent Dome of the Chain while the Dome of the Rock was under construction. When work was finished, there was just enough gold left to guild the dome. No expense was spared in maintaining the Dome of the Rock, either. It was washed down with water suffused with the scent of roses, musk and saffron. The interior was lighted by hanging lamps burning fragrant oils. Tradition tells us that clouds of incense, mingling with smoke from fires fed with aromatic woods, drifted slowly heavenwards.

During Abd al-Malik's time, the Dome was coated with gold and the holy rock was surrounded by a balustrade of ebony.[7] Between its pillars hung curtains woven with gold. A large administrative staff was necessary to keep this establishment in first-class condition. Workers included attendants to burn incense and anoint the rock with precious perfumes; 10 gatekeepers for each of the shrine's gates; 40 guards; and a number of Jews and Christians to clean the interior, make glass for lamps and goblets, and prepare wicks for the lamps. The architectural historians Richard Ettinghausen and Oleg Grabar invite us to imagine "the thousands of lights which supplemented the meagre illumination of the windows, making the mosaics glitter like a diadem crowning a multitude of columns and marble-faced piers around the sombre mass of the black rock surmounted by the soaring void of the dome."[8]

These same authors conclude that the Dome of the Rock, set as it was on a traditional holy site and drawing its inspiration from methods of construction and decoration used in the lands conquered by the Muslims, "created an entirely new combination of artistic conceptions to fulfill its purpose. It is a most splendid and singular achievement."[9]

The Dome of the Rock Today

The Dome of the Rock is a concentric, circular monument built of local limestone and is about 176 feet in diameter.[10] It is topped by a large wooden dome about 60 feet in diameter, consisting of two wooden shells guilded on the outside. The dome is set on a high, richly-decorated drum (in architecture, a drum is a circular or polygonal wall supporting a dome) about 67 feet in diameter and is supported by 4 tiers and 12 columns. It also has an octagonal arcade of 24 piers and columns plus outer octagonal walls about 60 feet wide by 36 feet high. The thick walls are pierced by numerous windows.

An Israeli scholar, Myriam Rosen-Ayalon, has pointed out that

> [The Dome of the Rock is] a magnificent and exciting building.... Despite several renovations in later periods, it preserves intact the original seventh-century design concepts with respect to the use of space, solution of construction problems, and proportions. Many engineering-oriented analyses have treated the various measurements of the different parts of the structure, and the relation of the architectural elements to each other.
>
> An instructive example of the wonderful architectural design of the Dome of the Rock is that the diameter of the dome is equal to its height, making for a perfect interior space. Moreover, the length of every one of the eight sides of the octagon is virtually identical to this diameter. The measurement is 20.4 meters (66 feet ll inches) for the dome, with small differences for the walls, for example, 20.6 meters (67 feet 4 inches).[11]

Today the octagonal walls are faced with blue, white, green, black and yellow Turkish tiles bearing stylized floral motifs. These replaced tiles which were installed by Sultan Suleyman the Magnificent in 1545–1552. They carry designs showing the lily, lotus, tulip and other flowers, bordered by blue-glazed tiles. Fine panels of blue and white calligraphy contain *suras* which refute the Christian Trinity and extol the virtues of Islam. A narrow band of tiles, inscribed in Arabic in gold on a blue background, bears the opening lines of the *sura* which begins with the cryptic letters *Ya Sin*:

> *Ya sin*. I [God] swear by the Wise Koran that you are sent upon a straight path. This is revealed by the Mighty One, the Merciful, so that you may forewarn a nation who, because their fathers were not warned before them, live in heedlessness.[12]

The Dome of the Rock is an early, classic statement of what would become Islam's unique but immediately recognizable architectural and aesthetic style. As Kay Prag, a British archeologist, has explained,

> [The Dome of the Rock] is the crown of the Haram al-Sharif, built in Byzantine-Syrian architectural style, with innovations marking it as one of the first great buildings of Islamic architecture. It is a shrine of gem-like beauty, once shining with the rich colors of gold and polychrome glass mosaic both inside and out.... The empty spaces within reflect the iconoclast and monotheist traditions of Islam, enhanced by the beauty of the floral and geometric decoration which covers nearly the whole surface of the shrine.[13]

The names of the architects who designed the Dome of the Rock have been lost, but construction was supervised by Yazid ibn Salam, a resident of Jerusalem, and Raja ibn Hayweth al-Urduni al-Filastini, a theologian with close ties to the land of Palestine.[14] For the interior of this shrine they chose marble veneer paneling and lovely mosaics, consisting of millions of tiny cubes of golden or polychromed glass arranged side-by-side to form intricate designs and pictures. These mosaics decorate the walls above the piers and columns which support the structure. Many of the designs are stylized and nonfigurative, but some are devised to bring to mind the ornate imperial jewelry of the Byzantine and Persian empires.

In the fierce sun of the Middle East, entering a large cool building where light and shadow are in a constant state of play is a welcome relief. As Kay Prag describes the interior of the Dome of the Rock,

> The visitor is first aware of the spacious dimness of the interior, with subdued light reflecting from half-seen golden ornament [sic], before the eye is drawn upwards to the light from the less deeply set windows in the drum to the glories of the gold and red curving patterns in the dome. The partially screened but illuminated mysteries of the Rock, bare and quarried, but marking the ancient and long venerated point of contact between God and man, draw the visitor towards the central area beyond the ambulatories....
> The wide and gently pointed arches [of the outer ambulatory] are covered in gold and polychrome glass mosaic work, which, though much restored, date to the original structure of 691/2. The beautiful designs, with lavish rosette and floral patterns, are worked in shades of blue, green and predominantly gold, and the mosaic cubes themselves are set at projecting angles further to reflect and sparkle in the light.... The Islamic concept of filling the field with decoration, and an Eastern delight in rich color, of indigo, gold and silver with added mother of pearl, gives this Syrian mosaic school a brilliance of its own.[15]

In its long, illustrious career, the Dome of the Rock has been restored many times. The original dome of 691 collapsed in 1016. It was rebuilt in 1022 and refurbished in 1189, 1318, 1448, 1830, 1874 and 1962. In 1994, thanks to a generous personal donation from the late King Hussein of Jordan, the dome was completely renovated. The new covering is made of copper sheets coated with a fine layer of nickel and an outer layer of gold leaf. With its reguilded exterior, the Dome of the Rock has recovered all the beauty and glory it lost in 1962, when it was restored with serviceable but rather ugly plates of gold-colored anodized aluminum.

The Earliest Monumental Mosque: The Great Mosque of Damascus (Completed 715)

Also known as the Umayyad Mosque, the Great Mosque of Damascus is the earliest surviving monumental mosque. It was designed to be big enough so that the whole Muslim community of the city could worship there. Built between 705 and 715 by the Umayyad caliph al-Walid I, it is said, symbolically, to have cost the entire tax revenues of the province of Damascus for seven years.

This great mosque has a long, interesting history with many incarnations. In about 3000 B.C.E., it was an Aramean temple to the god Hadad, a deity representing the sun and thunder. By the first century C.E. it had become a Hellenic temple to

Jupiter, the god of gods. Restored by the Romans in 193–211, later, in 379, during the reign of the Christian Emperor Theodosius it served as a church of St. John the Baptist. Myth has it that the present structure contains a shrine enclosing the head of St. John himself.

After Damascus was captured by the Arabs, Caliph al-Walid pulled down the church in 706 and built a mosque alongside what had been its southern wall. Rebuilt in 1069 because of a fire, the Great Mosque of Damascus was then destroyed in 1401 by Timur the Lame (Tamerlane), the last great tribal warlord. The Arabs rebuilt it, and it continued in service until a severe fire ruined the *liwan* (prayer hall) in 1893. The Ottomans repaired the damage, but the present structure, while still visually impressive, does not retain anything like its original magnificence.

Today this great structure, laid out as a large quadrangle 515 feet by 330 feet, is still graced by a splendid open courtyard enclosed by an arcade of arched, thin columns. It is one of the few mosques with three minarets. (A minaret is a tall, slender tower of a mosque, having one or more balconies from which a *muezzin*, or crier, now often aided by a loudspeaker, issues the daily calls to prayer.) These minarets variously date from the ninth to the fifteenth centuries.

The design of this building had an important influence on later Islamic architecture. Important elements of the design include the mosque's three axial entrances, its large main aisle, and a sanctuary three aisles deep.[16] The marble grilles on the windows of the south wall are said to be the earliest examples of the geometric interlace later used widely in the Islamic world.

The walls of the mosque were once covered by more than an acre of mosaics, depicting lush scenes of palaces next to a river and a rich garden of trees, fruits and vines. These mosaics are similar to those in the Dome of the Rock and may suggest the delights of Paradise, as described in the Quran. It is possible, however, that they simply represent scenes along the Barada River of Damascus. In any case, only portions of them have survived.

The best early description of this great mosque comes from Ibn Battuta (1304–1368/1369), the far-ranging traveler of medieval Islam, who reported:

> The Cathedral Mosque, known as the Umayyad Mosque, is the most magnificent mosque in the world, the finest in construction and noblest in beauty, grace and perfection: it is matchless and unequalled. The person who undertook its construction was the Caliph Walid. He applied to the Roman Emperor at Constantinople, ordering him to send craftsmen to him, and the Emperor sent him twelve thousand of them....
>
> The mosque has four doors. The southern door, called the "Door of Increase," is approached by a spacious passage where the dealers in second-hand goods and other commodities have their shops.... The eastern door, called the "Jayrun Door," is the largest of the doors of the mosque. It also has a large passage, leading out to a large and extensive colonnade which is entered through a quintuple gateway between six tall columns.... The western door is called the "Door of the Post"; the passage outside it contains the shops of the candlemakers and a gallery for the sale of fruit. The northern door is called the "Door of the Confectioners"; it too has a

large passageway.... At each of the four doors of the mosque is a building for ritual ablutions, containing a hundred rooms abundantly supplied with running water.[17]

Intellectual Life During the Early Abbasid Dynasty (750–833)

At the Battle of the Great Zab River in 750, the Abbasids overthrew the Umayyad caliphate. They would continue to hold nominal power for more than 500 years (in time becoming puppets of the Seljuq rulers) until finally being overthrown by the Mongol invasion of 1258. In the early part of their reign—from 750 to the end of the caliphate of al-Ma'mun in 833, after which mercenary officers began to weaken imperial unity by exercising power themselves—the Abbasids vowed to build a truly Islamic state and society.

Their purpose in doing so was more political than religious. They saw the need to establish their own legitimacy by visibly basing their rule on Islam and especially on Islamic law. Toward this end, they encouraged not only commerce and industry, but also the arts, science and the law. Let us look briefly at some of the personalities in these latter fields.

THE PROPHET'S BIOGRAPHER: MUHAMMAD IBN ISHAQ (D.C. 767)

As mentioned earlier, Muhammed ibn Ishaq was a historian who wrote the first major biography of the Prophet. His work was later edited and made more accessible by Ibn Hisham, who died in 833.

Ibn Ishaq's family had close ties with the Prophet. Ibn Ishaq's grandfather, a soldier, had been captured in Iraq by Muslim troops and had been brought to Medina. There he was freed after becoming a Muslim. Ibn Ishaq's father and his two uncles lived in Medina and collected information there about Muhammad's military campaigns. Ibn Ishaq himself soon became an authority on this subject.

After studying in Alexandria, he moved to Iraq. He lived in two different regions there before finally settling in Baghdad. His biography has generally been well-received, although parts of it have been criticized by other Muslim scholars as lacking legal validity because he did not always clearly identify the informants he used. Some of these were unnamed men he had met on his extensive travels.

Although Ibn Ishaq does not draw any distinction between pious legend and historical fact, the following miracle story gives us a clear picture of what Muhammad's followers remembered about him more than a century after his death. The dramatic image of the Prophet as a religious heavyweight would be especially striking in a desert society where many men were slender and lightly built. (Tradition has it that Muhammad himself was a little above average height and of a sturdy build.[18]) Ibn Ishaq recounts how an unidentified "learned man" told him:

> [When] some of the apostle's [Muhammad's] companions asked him to tell them about himself, He said: "I am what Abraham my father prayed for and the good news of [my brother] Jesus....

"I was suckled among [the nomads], and while I was with a brother of mine behind our tents shepherding the lambs, two men in white raiment came to me with a gold basin full of snow. Then they seized me and opened up my belly, extracted my heart and split it; then they extracted a black drop from it and threw it away; then they washed my heart and my belly with that snow until they had thoroughly cleansed them. Then one said to the other, weigh him against ten of his people; they did so and I outweighed them. Then they weighed me against a hundred and then a thousand, and I outweighed them." He said, "Leave him alone, for by God, if you weighed him against all his people he would outweigh them."[19]

Codifier of Islamic Law: Abu Hanifah (699–767)

Born in 699 in Kufah, an intellectual center of Iraq, Abu Hanifah earned a modest fortune in the silk trade before taking up the study of theology and, later, of law. For some eighteen years he worked under Hammad, the most famous Iraqi jurist. When Hammad died in 738, Abu Hanifah took his place. He also traveled extensively and profited from contacts within the intellectual circles of Iraq.

Thanks to his high intelligence, scholarly background and considerable experience, he was emboldened to undertake a formidable task — developing a uniform code for Islamic law. Law had become complex and contradictory because earlier efforts to apply Muslim doctrines to law had led to many different interpretations of the law. One of Abu Hanifah's achievements was to pioneer a new approach to the relationship between legal problems, on the one hand, and legal doctrines, on the other.

Before his time, doctrines had usually been developed only when jurists were faced with specific problems which required solutions. Abu Hanifah laid down the groundwork for solving new problems that seemed likely to arise in the future. He did this by trying to discern the legal principles relevant to a case at hand. Once these principles were known, they could then be applied in future cases. The significance of this rationalist approach was that the concept of Islamic law itself was appreciably enlarged.

Abu Hanifah was famous in his own time for his learning and was known as "the Greatest *Imam*" (religious leader). One of his teachers, who himself knew by heart two thousand traditions about the Prophet, said: "Just as I know that the sun is bright, I know that learning and Abu Hanifah are doubles of each other."[20] A contemporary Islamic scholar offered this judgment:

> All men of *fiqh* [Islamic jurisprudence] are Abu Hanifah's children.... I would not have acquired anything of knowledge had not been for my [own] teacher. All men of knowledge are children of the *ulama* [the religious scholars or, more broadly, the Islamic leadership], who were the disciples of Kufa, and they were the disciples of Abu Hanifa.[21]

Abu Hanifah's carefully formulated, consistent, systematic approach to jurisprudence was so well received by his contemporaries that they said he had attained the highest level of legal thought ever achieved up to his time. Today he is remembered as the founder of the Hanafi school of jurisprudence, the first of the four great Sunni schools of Islamic law.

Known in Arabic as *madhhabs*, literally "chosen way," these four Sunni schools are: Hanafi, Maliki, Shafii, and Hanbali. Their jurists traditionally shared the tolerant belief that pious and learned thinkers could differ on scholarly issues but could still remain within the orthodox Sunni fold. The Hanafi school, which allowed more scope for *ijtihad* (independent reasoning), became the most popular school, eventually functioning as the official school of the Ottoman dynasty, which survived until the founding of modern Turkey in 1924. Today the teachings of this school are still widely applied in India, Pakistan, Turkey, central Asia, and some Arab countries.

Abu Hanifah was famous for refusing to compromise his principles. Late in life, he was imprisoned because he refused to acknowledge an aspiring political leader as the rightful caliph. He also rejected this man's proposed bribe — to make Abu Hanifah the senior judge in the land. As a result of his refusal to give in, Abu Hanifah was poisoned and died in prison at the age of 70.

Seeker of Mathematical Knowledge: Caliph al-Mansur (d. 775)

The second caliph of the Abbasid dynasty, al-Mansur, built Baghdad, beginning in 762, and made it his capital city. He sent messengers to the Byzantine emperor, asking for mathematical texts. In return he received a copy of Euclid's *Elements*. This treatise was the most famous work by the foremost Greek mathematician. It covered not only geometry but also, among other things, ratios and proportions, number theory, three-dimensional figures, and construction of Platonic solids (pyramid, cube, octahedron, dodecahedron, icosahedron) in a given sphere.[22] The Middle East Institute believes that "This single gift, more than any other perhaps, ignited a passion for learning that was to last throughout the golden age of Islam and beyond."[23]

The Indian or, as they are now called, the Arabic numerals that form the basis of the modern European number systems did not come to the West directly from India but via Islam. The earliest surviving book in Arabic that presents the Indian numerical system stresses its practical value. Writing in the middle of the tenth century, its author, al-Uqlidisi, tells us:

> Most arithmeticians are obliged to use [this system] in their work: since it is easy and immediate, requires little memorization, demands little thought.... Therefore, we say that it is a science and practice [which comprises a tool] such as a writer, an artisan, a knight needs to conduct their affairs; since if an artisan has difficulty in finding what he needs for his trade, he will never succeed; to grasp it there is no difficulty, impossibility or preparation.[24]

Another early reference to the transmission of Arabic numerals comes from a late twelfth-century Muslim source, al-Qifti's *Chronology of the Scholars*, which tells us:

[A] person from India presented himself before the Caliph al-Mansur in the year [c. 771] who was well versed in the siddhanta [Indian] method of calculation related to the movement of the heavenly bodies, and having ways of calculating equations based on the half-chord [essentially the sine] calculated in half-degrees.... This is all contained in a work ... from which he claimed to have taken the half-chord calculated for one minute. Al-Mansur ordered this book to be translated into Arabic, and a work to be written, based on the translation, to give the Arabs a solid basis for calculating the movements of the planets.[25]

It is not known whether the Arabs or the Indians invented the concept of "zero," but this was an important mathematical breakthrough. Arab scholars understood that a sign representing "nothing" or "nought" was needed because the *place* of a sign gave as much information as did its unitary value. The place therefore had to be shown, even if the sign which showed it had itself a unitary value of "nothing."[26] An Arabic source claims that the zero was first introduced by Muhammad bin Ahmad in 967.[27]

Anthologist of Arab Poems: al-Mufaddal (fl. 762–784)

Al-Mufaddal was an Arab scholar who compiled *The Examination of al-Mufaddal* (*Al-Mufad Daliyat*), an anthology of ancient Arabic poems which are important as a record of the thought and poetic art of Arabia in the pre–Islamic era known as "the time of ignorance" (*jahiliyya*). Some of these poets were "authors of whom little has survived," that is, their work had not been set down in writing before.

Since literacy had been uncommon in nomadic society, al-Mufaddal collected these poems from the remarkable memories of the professional reciters, who were treasure troves of tribal lore. Perhaps for this reason, there are gaps in the poems; some of them exist only in a fragmentary state. Of the 126 poems recorded in *Al-Mufad Daliyat*, only five or six were composed after Muhammad's time.

Most of the poems thus extol not the virtues of Islam but the *bedouin* virtues of food and shelter for the traveler, alms for the poor, courage in battle, loyalty to the tribe, and — to use an anachronistic term — "conspicuous consumption," i.e., the public display of wealth through lavish generosity. These traits have remained important characteristics of Arab culture down to our own time.

Arabic poetry has remained important down to our own time, too. As the Lebanese scholar Philip Hitti wrote in 1937,

> No people in the world manifest such enthusiastic admiration for literary expression and are so moved by the word, spoken or written, as the Arabs. Modern audiences in Baghdad, Damascus and Cairo can be stirred to the highest degree by the recital of poems, only vaguely comprehended, and by the delivery of orations in the classical tongue, though it be only partially understood. The rhythm, the rhyme, the music, produce on them the effect of what they call "lawful magic" (*sihar halal*).[28]

Builder of the Great Mosque of Cordoba (Begun 784–785): Emir Abd al-Rahman

Hailed one of the most memorable architectural achievements of medieval Europe, the Great Mosque of Cordoba was built by the Umayyad ruler Abd al-Rahman I to demonstrate Cordoba's prosperity, its international connections and its fame as a center of scholarship. Extensions in the ninth and tenth centuries virtually doubled the mosque's size, making it one of the biggest buildings in the Islamic world. A later Umayyad caliph, al-Hakam II (r. 961–976), expanded the prayer hall, added ribbed domes and asked the Byzantine emperor in Constantinople to send to Cordoba an artisan skilled in installing gold mosaic cubes, as well as the cubes themselves.[29]

The Great Mosque forms a huge rectangle measuring 590 by 425 feet and is notable for its forest of 850 pillars made from porphyry, jasper and multicolored marbles. These pillars, together with the open, horseshoe-shaped arches with alternating red and white brickwork which they support, give the viewer a feeling of infinity. Aesthetically, the result is stunning. Moreover, rows of trees planted in the courtyard (the Patio de las Maranjas, or Court of the Oranges) seem to echo the rows of columns within the mosque itself.

One of the mosque's finest pieces of decoration, surmounting a *mihrab* (prayer niche), is a block of white marble gracefully carved into the form of a shell. The walls of the *mihrab* itself are encrusted with gold and Byzantine-style mosaics.

After conquering Cordoba in 1236, King Ferdinand III of Castile turned the Great Mosque into the cathedral of Cordoba. Its Moorish design was further modified in the sixteenth century by the addition of a Gothic altar, choir area, chapels and a 300-foot-high belfry, which replaced the former minaret. It is said that the Holy Roman Emperor Charles V (r. 1519–1556) rebuked the renovators in these words: "You have built what can be seen anywhere, and have destroyed something unique in the world."[30]

Time of Cultural Flowering: Caliph Harun al-Rashid (786–806)

When Harun, the fifth caliph of the Abbasid dynasty, came to power in 786, the Muslim empire stretched from the western Mediterranean to India. "Al-Rashid" means "one who follows the correct path." This was a title bestowed on him as a result of a successful military campaign to the Bosporus. Under his rule, a major cultural flowering took place in Baghdad and other cities of the Abbasid empire.

Literary criticism, philosophy, poetry, medicine, mathematics and astronomy flourished. Greek texts on philosophy and medicine were translated into Arabic, thus preserving the learning of the past. The prosperity of Baghdad at that time was immortalized in a famous series of stories, *The Thousand and One Nights*, which will be discussed later in this chapter. The modern scholar W. Montgomery Watt explains that these stories had some basis in fact because enormous wealth flowed into Baghdad after it was founded in 762.

Conspicuous consumption was the order of the day for the ruling class. Harun's wife, Zubaydah, would tolerate at her table only vessels of gold and silver studded with gems. Harun himself, a connoisseur of music and poetry, bestowed lavish gifts on the most accomplished musicians and poets. Indeed, one of the close friends who accompanied him when, in disguise, he wandered through Baghdad at night to check on conditions in the capital was Abu Nuwas, a famous poet (see the next action). On these nightly forays Harun was also accompanied by Masrur, his executioner: as caliph, Harun had the power of life and death and could order the immediate execution of anyone who displeased him.[31]

Poet: Abu Nuwas (c. 747–c. 813)

The most important poet of early Abbasid times, Abu Nuwas was a boon companion of Caliph Harun. Although he had a background in traditional Islamic studies (poetry, the Quran, *hadith*, and Arabic grammar), his favored themes were quite different, namely, wine and love affairs with young boys. One of his "wine songs" reads as follows:

> Ho! A cup, and fill it up, and tell me it is wine
> For I will never drink in shade if I can drink in shine!
> Cursed and poor is every hour that sober I must go,
> But rich am I whene'er well drunk I stagger to and fro.
> Speak, for shame, the loved one's name, let vain disguise alone:
> No good is there in pleasures o'er which a veil is thrown.[32]

The collected works of Abu Nuwas total about 1,500 poems, some of them devoted to hunting scenes drawn from ancient *bedouin* poetry. His formal odes (*qasidas*) were influenced by the year he is said to have spent in the desert with the *bedouin* to become familiar with their "pure" Arabic. Most of his own poems, however, are set in urban life rather than in the desert itself and reflect ironic and sophisticated urban themes. Here is an example:

> When she left me, stopped writing notes,
> My desire hurt. The thought of her
> So upset me I nearly died.
> I got Satan into a corner
> And, blubbing like a child, told him,
> "She's hooked me: tears and lack of sleep
> Cause my eyes to look like ulcers.
> Unless you make that girl love me,
> And you can, I won't write poetry,
> I won't listen to songs, and I won't
> Pickle my bones with drink. Day and night
> I'll fast, pray, and read the Quran.
> I'll follow the path He commands."
> Shamefaced she was back in a flash.[33]

Interest in Science: Caliph al-Ma'mun (r. 813–833)

The seventh Abbasid caliph, al-Ma'mun tried hard, for political reasons, to end the Sunni-Shiite split and to force upon his subjects a more rationalistic approach to Islam. Unfortunately, he failed in both endeavors. His support of learning, however, was more fruitful.

Al-Ma'mun encouraged the translation of Greek philosophical and scientific books. He founded a learned institution in Baghdad known as the House of Wisdom (*Bayt al-Hikmah*), where Muslims and Christians were set to work—primarily translating Greek texts into Arabic. The House of Wisdom was directed by three wealthy brothers who were skilled mathematicians and who were known as the *Banu Musa* ("sons of Musa"). Al-Ma'mun also imported rare manuscripts from the Byzantine Empire and built observatories where Muslim scientists could study the heavens.

The caliph had a personal interest in scientific questions. A medieval historian tells us that when al-Ma'mun wanted to know the size of the earth,

> [H]e inquired into this and found that Ptolemy mentioned in one of his books that the circumference of the earth is so-and-so many thousands of stades. He asked the commentators about the meaning of the word stade, and they differed about the meaning. Since he was not told what he wanted, he directed Khalid ibn Bad al-Malik, Ali ibn Isa, the instrument maker, and Ahmad ibn Bukhturi, the surveyor, to gather a group of surveyors and skilled artisans to make the instruments they needed.
>
> He transported them all to a place in the desert near Sinjar (in Syria). Khalid and his party headed north, and Ali and Ahmad headed south. They proceeded until they found that the maximum altitude of the sun at noon increased, and differed from the noon altitude which they had found at the place they had separated, by one degree, after subtracting from it the sun's declination along the path of the outward journey.
>
> There they put arrows. Then they returned to the arrows, testing the measurement a second time, and so found that one degree of the earth was 56 miles, of which one mile is 4,000 black cubits. This is the cubit adopted by al-Ma'mun for the measurement of cloth, for surveying fields, and for spacing waystations along the roads.[34]

Given the technical limitations of the time, such calculations were passably accurate. One of the scholars who worked at the al-Ma'mun's House of Wisdom was al-Khwarizmi (discussed later in this chapter). He concluded that the earth's circumference was about 27,000 miles, which was not too far from the figure we use today (24,902 miles).

To try to modernize his caliphate and make it more flexible, in 827 al-Ma'mun endorsed the Mutazili movement, which urged Muslims to adopt the rationalistic approaches of the Greek philosophers in order to counter the influence of Manichaeism, a dualistic religion originating in Iran. The Mutazili movement was noted for its belief in free will; for its teaching that reason is the equal of revelation in the search for truth; for its call for full responsibility by men and women; for its refined concept of God; and for its insistence that the legitimacy of the caliphate depended on the exemplary behavior of the caliph himself, not on his dynastic connections. Even more radically, the movement held that the Quran was a "created" work, that is to say, it was not, as traditionalism taught, the uncreated eternal word of God Himself.

Early in 833, al-Ma'mun required all his subjects to adhere to this movement. After assigning this task to Baghdad's chief of police, al-Ma'mun left the city to lead an expedition against the Byzantines. The chief of police set up what amounted to an inquisition. He tried, but failed, to convert the *qadis* (judges) and the *hadith* experts to Mutazili beliefs.

One of these *hadith* experts was Ahmad ibn Hanbal (discussed later in this chapter), who categorically refused to consider the Quran a created work. For this offense he was to have been brought before al-Ma'mun for punishment and was reprieved only when the caliph himself died on the Byzantine expedition.

Father of Arab Chemistry: Jabir ibn Hayyan (c. 721–c. 815)

Our word *chemistry* has its roots in *alchemy*, which in turn comes both from Arabic (the article *al*) and from Greek (*khymeia*, literally "fusion," i.e., the art of melting gold and silver). More than one hundred monumental treatises, twenty-two of them on alchemy, are attributed to the Iraqi scholar Jabir ibn Hayyan, now known as the "father of Arab chemistry."

Many of his works were issued by the Shiite community of the Ismailis[35] under his own name. But Jabir was also famous in Europe during the Middle Ages, a time when alchemy was much in vogue. Indeed, he was so well-known in Europe that in the fourteenth century a Spanish alchemist frequently signed his own treaties with the name "Gerber," the Latin form of Jabir's name, thereby widening their commercial appeal.

Jabir himself knew that the Greeks had believed that everything is composed of only four elements—fire, earth, water, and air. His own theory was that all these elements combined to produce mercury and sulfur. Metals, he thought, simply consisted of different proportions of these two substances. Since a red compound known as cinnabar is produced when mercury and sulfur are combined, Jabir hoped that if the proper proportions of these substances could be discovered, the end result would not be cinnabar, but gold. This theory became quite popular and had an effect on early chemistry.

Jabir's real achievement lay in the importance he attached to systematic experimentation. This led to practical advances in the applications of chemistry. In fact, it is said that the development of chemistry in Europe can be traced directly to him.[36] As Hamed Abdel-reheem Ead, Professor of Chemistry at the University of Cairo, tells us,

> Jabir describes processes for the preparation of steel and the refinement of other metals, for dyeing cloth and leather, for making varnishes to waterproof cloth

and to protect iron, for the preparation of hair-dyes and so on. He gives a recipe for making an illuminating ink for manuscripts from "golden" marcasite, to replace the much more expensive one made from gold itself, and he mentions the use of manganese dioxide in glass-making. He knew how to concentrate acetic acid by the distillation of vinegar, and was also acquainted with citric acid and other organic substances.[37]

Legal Scholar: Muhammad al-Shafii (767–820)

As mentioned earlier, the legal scholar al-Shafii reconciled early local variations of the *sunna* (the set of traditional social and legal customs of the Muslim community) and founded the Shafii school of law. These achievements are important enough to merit a word of explanation.

Little hard information on al-Shafii's early life has survived. He seems to have been a prudent and self-effacing man. It is said that when asked a question about Islam, he would never answer immediately. Upon being asked why he was not answering, he would reply, "Not until I know which is better: to keep silent or to speak."[38] Al-Shafii traveled widely (to Medina, Yemen, Syria, Baghdad and Cairo), studied at many of the great centers of jurisprudence, and mastered their teachings. This gave him a strong background from which to address one of the key legal and theological questions of his day: what should be the relationship between the *sunna* and the law itself?

Al-Shafii's answer was that the *sunna* had what amounted to a holy quality because these customs reflected the actual living-out of the Prophet's teachings as they were expressed in the Quran. Islamic law, al-Shafii maintained, should be based on *both* the Quran and the *sunna*. Indeed, the expression "the Quran and the *sunna*" thus came into scholarly use to define the two fountains of doctrinal authority for Sunni Islam. These insights, included in Al-Shafii's major work, the *Risalah (Prophethood)*, have led some scholars to consider him to be the father of Islamic jurisprudence.

Polymath: Muhammad ibn Musa al-Khwarizmi (c. 800–c. 850)

Al-Khwarizmi, a mathematician, astronomer, and geographer, was the greatest polymath (a person of encyclopedic learning) in the House of Wisdom in Baghdad. He is said to have influenced mathematical thought to a greater extent than any other medieval writer.[39] His achievements are worth recording.

After his book on elementary algebra, entitled *The Compendious Book on Calculation by Completion and Balancing (al-Kitab al-mukhtasar fi hisab al-jabr wal-muqabala)*, was translated into Latin in the twelfth century, it gave rise to our word *algebra*, from the Arabic *al-jabr* ("transposition"). To refer to the quantity being sought, al-Khwarizmi used the Arabic word *shay* ("thing"). Translated into Spanish, this was eventually abbreviated as x, the algebraic symbol which still stands for the unknown factor.[40]

Another work by al-Khwarizmi introduced to the West the Hindu-Arabic numbering system and its arithmetic. This work, "Concerning the Hindu Art of Reckoning," now exists only in a Latin translation. One word of its title (*algoritmi*, the Latinized version of al-Khwarizmi's name) gives us our own word *algorithm*.

A third important book was his *Book of the Description of the Earth* (*Kitab surat al-ard*), which was probably inspired by Ptolemy's work on geography. Al-Khwarizmi's book gave the coordinates of places in the known world and improved estimates of the length of the Mediterranean Sea. Finally, al-Khwarizmi also compiled astronomical tables based on Indian and Greek sources. This book, too, was translated into Latin.

Immortal Stories: The Book of the Thousand and One Nights (Alf Layla wa Layla, Ninth Century)

Also known as *The Arabian Nights*, this fictional work has something for everyone. At an elementary level, it is a lively mixture of humor, love, sex, violence, poetry and slapstick. On a deeper level, it contains subtle and profound reflections on philosophy, psychology, power and morality, all brought to life in some of the most famous stories ever told. These stories recount the pleasures, adventures and risks of human relationships, especially those between men and women.[41] They have reappeared in our own day in the form of literature, music, film, television, computer software and illustrations. Although many Western readers think of *The Arabian Nights* simply as tales for children, they were in fact written for mature readers.

The two main characters of *The Thousand and One Nights* are King Shahrayar and a young woman named Shahrazad (Scheherazade). Discovering that during his absences his wife had been unfaithful to him, the king killed her and vowed to marry — and then murder — a new wife each day. Shahrazad, the elder of the two daughters of the king's vizier (chief minister), thought of a clever way to save herself and the other women of the kingdom. She insisted that her father give her to the king in marriage. This done, every evening she told the king a new, extremely interesting story, purposively leaving it incomplete and promising to finish it the next night if the king let her live. The king was so captivated by these stories that at last he abandoned his murderous policy. Later, it is said, having learned to love and trust Shahrazad, by whom he had three children, he married her and made her his queen.

The Thousand and One Nights is a composite work with no single author. It truly has an international provenance. The text is Arabic, laced with thirteenth-century colloquial expressions from Syria, Egypt and Iran. The framework of the book is Indian. The two main characters are Iranian. The lesser characters are Arabs. The stories themselves (and the stories within stories) are folk tales, that is, fables, fairy tales, romances, comic relief and historical anecdotes, all of which were originally recited aloud. They come from Arabia, India, Iran, Iraq and Turkey.

The first written reference to *The Thousand and One Nights* is a ninth-century fragment. The following excerpt is from the definitive edition of the Arabic text in a fourteenth-century Syrian manuscript now in the Bibliothèque Nationale in Paris.

This manuscript covers 271 nights and, of course, the same number of stories.⁴² (The expression "The Thousand and One Nights" is meant to suggest a large number of stories, not 1,001 exactly.) The modern translator and editor of the text used here, Husain Haddawy, thought that this work has been so popular for so long because it weaves the unusual, the extraordinary, the marvelous, and the supernatural into the fabric of daily life. The most remarkable events are highlighted by a wealth of down-to-earth and almost-believable detail. A female demon, for example, is described as a snake as thick as the trunk of a palm tree, but the male demon is as thin as a spear and as long as two spears. A transparent curtain provocatively shielding a lovely girl in a bed is decorated with red dots. Another seductive girl goes to the market to buy ten pounds of mutton. A pious gardener purchases two flagons of wine for two mysterious lovers.⁴³

Rather than paraphrasing one of these 271 stories and thus lose the flavor of Haddawy's excellent translation, it seems better here to quote from the preface to the first story which Shahrazad tells the king, plus the first line of that story. Since, as mentioned earlier, these stories were originally transmitted orally, let us pretend that we are *listening to* rather than reading this one:

> At nightfall the vizier took Shahrazad and went with her to the great King Shahrayar. But when Shahrayar took her to bed and began to fondle her, she wept, and when he asked her, "Why are you crying?" she replied, "I have a sister, and I wish to bid her goodbye before daybreak [when Shahrazad would be killed]." Then the king sent for the sister, who came and went to sleep under the bed. When the night wore on, she woke up and waited until the king had satisfied himself with her sister Shahrazad and they were by then now all fully awake.
>
> Then Dinarzad [the sister] cleared her throat and said, "Sister, if you are not sleepy, tell us one of your lovely little tales to while the night away, before I bid you good-bye at daybreak, for I don't know what will happen to you tomorrow." Shahrazad turned to King Shahrayar and said, "May I have your permission to tell a story?" He replied, "Yes," and Shahrazad was very happy and said, "Listen":
>
> "It is said, O wise and happy King, that once there was a prosperous merchant who had abundant wealth and investments and commitments in every country."

Shahrazad then continues this story, which recounts the merchant's adventures with a demon. Just before she finishes the story, however, the reader is told: "morning overtook Shahrazad, and she lapsed into silence, leaving King Shahrayar burning with curiosity to hear the rest of the story."⁴⁴

Compier of Hadith and Founder of a School of Law: Ahmad ibn Hanbal (780–855)

The most dramatic aspect of the life of Ahmad ibn Hanbal, an Arab theologian and jurist, was the great courage he showed when he was tortured, on the orders of

Caliph al-Ma'mun (see previous section), for adhering to his orthodox beliefs and refusing to endorse the rationalism and other doctrines of the Mutazili movement, which the caliph favored. In 833 the caliph had begun what became a widespread, long-running inquisition to force the *ulama* (the religious scholars who were responsible for deciding how much rationalism should be applied in jurisprudence and theology) to subscribe to the Mutazili doctrine that the Quran was "created," i.e., that it was not the uncreated eternal word of God. The caliph had Ibn Hanbal chained, repeatedly flogged and held in prison for two years. Still, Ibn Hanbal never took refuge in the doctrine of dissimulation (*taqiyah*), which permits a Muslim, under great duress, to pretend to agree to a false doctrine while secretly maintaining his former orthodox beliefs.

When Caliph al-Ma'mun died, the new caliph, al-Mutasim, continued to persecute Ibn Hanbal, but Ibn Hanbal reiterated that he would never change his traditionalist beliefs unless confronted with truly authoritative reasons to do so, drawn from the Quran or from the *sunna*. These the caliph could not supply. It is said that a later caliph, who continued the persecution, had Ibn Hanbal beaten by 150 floggers, each of whom struck him twice. Ibn Hanbal survived this ordeal but carried to his grave the scars of the wounds he received in it.

When he finally died of natural causes at the age of 75, tradition has it that he was so revered that 800,000 men and 60,000 women came to his funeral. The great legal scholar al-Shafii is reported to have said of him: "I left Baghdad and did not leave behind me anyone more virtuous, more learned, more knowledgeable than Ahmad ibn Hanbal."[45]

In terms of Islamic learning, Ibn Hanbal could take pride in two achievements. First, pious legend has it that he had memorized "a million *hadith*," from which and from other sources he compiled the *Traditions of the Prophet Muhammad*. Known as the *Musnad*, this was a collection of about 29,000 of the most authoritative *hadith*, i.e., those whose chain of transmission (*isnad*) was considered to be reliable, unbroken and could be traced all the way back to the Prophet himself. The purpose of this canonical collection was to give Islamic scholars and jurists access to the soundest traditions which, together with the Quran itself, they could use to pass judgment on the issues of the day.

Second, Ibn Hanbal founded the Hanbali school of law, the most strictly traditionalist of the four Islamic schools of law. Though much smaller than other schools of law, the Hanbali school was eloquent and influential in upholding traditionalist patterns of thought against the inroads of rationalism. (In Islamic jurisprudence, traditionalism means interpreting the Quran by means of the *hadith*, i.e., the "traditions," whereas rationalism means applying one's reason to both the Quran and the *hadith*.[46])

Ibn Hanbal's personal courage and his staunch religious orthodoxy reverberated down through the years, strongly influencing other Muslim thinkers. Two such men, who will be discussed later, were the traditionalist theologian Ibn Taymiyya (d. 1328) and the puritanical reformer Abd al-Wahhab (d. 1792).

Greatest Compiler of Hadith: al-Bukhari (d. 870)

Beginning while he was still a child to learn by heart the *hadith* (the recorded sayings and actions of the Prophet), al-Bukhari made the pilgrimage to Mecca at the age of sixteen. In the Muslim world he is esteemed as one of the greatest compilers of *hadith*. Sunnis treat his work as second only to the Quran as a source of law and personal guidance. It has been an inexhaustible treasure trove for later Islamic scholars: al-Asqalani, for example, wrote seventeen volumes of commentary, and al-Ayni wrote twenty-five volumes.[47]

Al-Bukhari's first book was *The Large History* (*Al-Tarikh al-kabir*), which provided biographies of all the people who formed the living chain of oral transmission (*isnad*) stretching back to Muhammad's time. During his extensive travels, al-Bukhari gathered from his informants as many as 600,000 *hadith*, which he is said to have memorized. Over a period of 16 years, he identified 2,602 of these as the most reliable and included them in his definitive work, *The Authentic Collection* (*Al-Jami al-Sahih*).

Some *hadith* were cited more than once if they touched on more than one different theme. This famous compilation consisted of 97 books with 3,450 chapters on specific topics, supported by full *isnads*. This made it easier for the reader to find the *hadith* most appropriate to the issue at hand and to be confident of their authenticity.

Developer of an Arabic Vocabulary for Philosophy: Yaqub ibn Ishaq al-Kindi (800–873)

Rarely remembered in the West today, al-Kindi is still known in the Islamic world as the "philosopher of the Arabs." Because of his importance to Islamic learning, it is worthwhile to look at his work in some detail.

Al-Kindi, who was born and died in Iraq, was the first major philosopher of the Muslim world to draw heavily on Greek learning, especially Aristotle. (Most of Aristotle's works first became known in Europe as translations from Arabic.) Al-Kindi was one of the luminaries at the House of Wisdom in Baghdad. While he did not translate Greek works himself, he polished the translations done by other scholars in the House of Wisdom and made them important parts of his own thought. The reason was, as he explained in the introduction to one of his books,

> It is good ... that we endeavor in the book, as is our habit in all subjects, to recall that concerning which the Ancients have said anything in the past; that is the easiest and shortest to adopt for those who follow them, and to go further in those areas where they have not said anything.[48]

Al-Kindi had a truly tolerant and first-rate mind. "We ought not to be ashamed," he wrote, "of appreciating truth and of acquiring it wherever it comes from, even if it comes from races distant and nations different from us."[49] He made contributions

Aristotle teaching. Islamic scholars had such respect for Aristotle that they referred to him as the "first teacher." (By permission of the British Library, Or 2784 f. 96r.)

in many fields in addition to philosophy: in medicine, mathematics, geometry, music, optics, the manufacture of swords, astrology, and even cooking. Regrettably, only a few of the 270 short treatises he wrote have survived, some of them in Latin translations. Hardly any of them have been translated into English.

One of al-Kindi's major achievements was to develop an Arabic vocabulary for philosophic thought.[50] He played a key role in the debate over what role — if any — philosophy, that is, reason, should play in orthodox Islam. He himself called for the supremacy of reason and for greater attention to what was referred to as the "foreign science" of philosophy rather than the traditional "Arab science" of Quranic studies and grammar. Although he argued that the study of philosophy was in fact compatible with orthodox Islam, in the end his liberal point of view failed to carry the day. As we shall see, it was the traditionalist religious scholar al-Ghazali (d. 1111) who ultimately won the reason versus revealed religion debate.

Kiki Kennedy-Day, a modern scholar of Islam, explains the gist of al-Kindi's arguments in his metaphysical treatise, *On First Philosophy* (*Fi al-Falsafa al-Ula*):

> By the study of philosophy, people will learn the knowledge of things in reality, and through this the knowledge of the divinity of God and his unity. They will also learn human virtue. Throughout many of his treatises, al-Kindi emphasizes the importance of the intellect (*aql*) and contrasts it to matter....
>
> Other aspects of his position include emphasis on the absolute unity of God, his power — particularly as creator — and creation ex nihilo ["out of nothing"]. The Eternal, that is, God, is not due to another; he has no cause and has neither genus nor species. There is no "before" for the Eternal. The Eternal is unchanging, immutable and imperishable. In human terms, death is the soul's taking leave of the body, which it employed during life. For al-Kindi, the intellect continues.... He reiterated in his ethical treatise the idea that humans must choose the world of the intellect over the material world.[51]

In another treatise, *On the Art of Averting Sorrows* (*Fi al-hila li-daf al-ahzan*), al-Kindi urges his readers to maintain their inner equilibrium by avoiding an excessive attachment to worldly goods. If too much attention is paid to such goods, he warns, a person is courting unhappiness. He cites a story from Plutarch's *On Moral Virtue* to make this point:

> In that story, Nero [the Roman emperor] receives a gift of a gorgeous, elaborate crystal tent, with which he is obviously smitten. A philosopher who is present in the crowd advises him that he has already been impoverished through his keen attachment to this object. If Nero were to lose it, the philosopher says, he will suffer because it is irreplaceable. Later, when the rare object is lost at sea during transport, Nero is devastated.[52]

Chapter V

The Flowering of Islam (873–1041)

Historical Background

The years 873–1041 were a time of cultural florescence and political fragmentation. Most of the people living in the lands under Islamic control had become Muslims. Under the Abbasid dynasty, Baghdad retained its cultural prestige, and the Abbasids would remain in power there, if only nominally, until the Mongol invasion in 1258. In the period discussed here, the life of the mind continued to flourish and some Muslims began to speak New Persian, a language of high culture. Cultural creativity was so widespread that this period has been referred to as the "renaissance" of Islam.[1]

Politically and economically, Islam continued to expand, sometimes by conquest but more often through trade. At the same time, separatist tendencies were evident in many regions. In 929, Andalusia (Spain) declared its independence when the Umayyad ruler claimed the title of caliph. In 969 the army of the Fatimid dynasty, conquering the Nile valley, Palestine and southern Syria, set up a new capital, Cairo, to rival Baghdad. (Cairo, then known as Fustat, had originally been one of the garrison towns of the Arab conquest.) The Buyids came to power in 945. In 1041, however, the pastoralist Seljuq Turks began to surge out of their homeland in eastern Iran, thus ushering in a great new wave of tribal expansion and conquest.

Assembler of an Encyclopedic Guidebook to Sunni Life: Muslim ibn al-Hajjaj (c. 817–875)

Referred to as "Muslim," the scholar was as eminent as al-Bukhari, but much less seems to have been written about him in English. He, too, assembled a canonical collection of *hadith*. Known as the *Salih* ("true" or "genuine"), it provides an encyclopedic guide to Sunni life. It begins with an explanation of the criteria used to select *hadith* and is said to have been compiled from 300,000 *hadith*, which Muslim himself gathered in Arabia, Egypt, Syria and Iraq.

Muslim's findings generally parallel those of al-Bukhari to the extent that *hadith* approved by both men are accepted by believers as "agreed" (*muttafaq*). Although there are six collections of *hadith* accepted as canonical by orthodox Islam, the works of al-Bukhari and Muslim have by far the greatest prestige.

Translator and Mathematician: Thabit ibn Qurra (836–901)

Thabit ibn Qurra was a mathematician, astronomer, physician and philosopher who became the leading intellectual and translator (he knew Syriac and Greek as well as Arabic) on the staff of the House of Wisdom in Baghdad. It has aptly been said that in this institution, "men of enormous intellect and productivity rose to prominence."[2]

Any listing of Thabit ibn Qurra's major achievements is impressive.[3] He extended the concept of traditional geometry to include geometrical algebra, and he put forward several theories which contributed to the later development of non–Euclidean geometry, spherical trigonometry, integral calculus and real numbers. He devised a clever way to find amicable numbers, i.e., a pair of numbers in which each number is the sum of the set of proper divisors of the other number.

In astronomy, he revised Ptomely's views, studied the movements of the sun and the moon, and wrote treatises on sundials. In mechanics and physics, he studied conditions of equilibrium of bodies, beams, and levels and is recognized as a founder of statics, the mechanics dealing with the relations of forces that produce equilibrium among material bodies.

Thabit ibn Qurra translated the Greek mathematicians Euclid, Archimedes, Apollonius of Perga, and Ptolemy. He summarized the work of Galen of Pergamum and Hippocrates (both physicians) and of the philosopher Aristotle. Some of his work was later translated into Latin and Hebrew, thus becoming available in the West. He also wrote over seventy original works on a wide range of subjects. Toward the end of his life he was named court astronomer for the seventeenth Abbasid caliph, al-Mutadid.

Quranic Scholar and Historian: al-Tabari (839–923)

Revered by Muslims today as one of the major *mujtahid imams* (that is, a religious leader authorized to use independent thought to find new solutions to legal and other problems), al-Tabari consolidated Sunni thought by distilling the knowledge of preceding generations of Muslim thinkers.[4] Working primarily in Baghdad, he laid the groundwork for rigorous Quranic and historical studies through two massive works, the *Quran Commentary* and the *History of Messengers and Kings* (*Tarikh al-Rusul wa al-Muluk*).

In a modern edition, the *Quran Commentary* runs to 15 volumes of about 500 pages each. The *History* consists of 5 volumes with the same number of pages, plus a 500-page appendix. Lengthy as they are, legend has it that al-Tabari limited these works to this total only out of compassion for his students: it is said that he had originally intended to write 300 volumes of each book.

Al-Tabari's enormous productivity can be seen from a comment made by a contemporary linguist, who remarked that al-Tabari "spent forty years writing forty pages a day."[5] This account is surely illustrative, but if al-Tabari had indeed done this, he would have produced 584,000 pages of handwritten Arabic script. Perhaps because of his prodigious output, he was labeled by a later Islamic scholar as "the master of *hadith* scholars" and is also known as the "Fountain of all True Knowledge."[6]

In his *Commentary*, al-Tabari went painstakingly through the Quran, word by word, and provided all the historical, legal and grammatical comments contained in the *hadith*, along with their chains of transmission (*isnads*). As indicated earlier, these *isnads* functioned much like modern footnotes: they provided the scholarly genealogies for the opinions contained in the *hadith*. Thus al-Tabari, like most of his scholarly colleagues, took great pains to cite every individual *hadith* along with its proper "footnote." If there were contradictory *hadith* about the same subject, the contradictions had to be cited in full, so that the reader could follow the different strands of thoughts and the different doctrines of the disputing legal and theological schools involved.

This same basic technique of citing sources is evident in al-Tabari's *History*, where he used short monographs on significant events and important people. The *History* also drew on assorted works on genealogy, poetry, tribal history, rabbinical and Christian traditions and sources, and records of the Sassanian kings. It begins with the creation of the universe and proceeds to cover the years from 622 (the date of the *hijrah*, i.e., Muhammad's migration to Medina) down to the author's own times (i.e., 915, when the *History* ends). This book clearly defines Islam's place in history by explaining that idolatry (that is, *shirk*—putting someone or something in God's place) and monotheism are both part-and-parcel of the human story. The pre–Islamic Qurayshite worship of idols, on the one hand, and Muhammad's divine revelations from one God, on the other, are simply the final manifestations of idolatry and monotheism before the Day of Judgment and the end of time.

In addition to its contribution to religious learning, the *History* had a political purpose as well: to identify and analyze the sources of imperial strength and decline in order to reverse the waning of Abbasid power in al-Tabari's own time. The essence of al-Tabari's argument here is that the ethics of monotheism would guarantee that Abbasid government and taxes were just; if so, the success of the whole imperial venture was assured. In contrast, idolatry carried the connotation of submitting reason to self-interested human authorities (the self-proclaimed spokesmen for the idols). The result would be corruption, which would ultimately undermine imperial power. Al-Tabari asserted that this is what had in fact happened to past empires. This was also the fate in store for the Abbasid caliphate, warned al-Tabari, unless it mended its ways.

There was a financial component to al-Tarabi's thought as well. Corruption was to be avoided not only because it was offensive from an ethical point of view but also because it undermined the fiscal system of the government. Unless this system worked equitably and well, the peasants could not earn a decent living, and the military could not be paid. Such developments might lead to political unrest. What we find in al-Tabari's thought, then, is not simply a call for morality *per se* but a highly practical socio-political analysis of history, couched in religious and symbolic language.

Multi-faceted Physician: Muhammad ibn Zakariya al-Razi (c. 865–930)

The greatest physician of the Islamic world, al-Razi was also skilled in mathematics, astronomy, chemistry, alchemy and philosophy. Born in Rayy (Iran), he was first put in charge of the Royal Hospital there but later moved to Baghdad, where he headed the Muqtadari Hospital for many years. He worked in other cities, too, before finally returning to Rayy, where he died in 930. Today his achievements are commemorated in the Rasi Institute near Tehran.

Al-Razi's practical, hands-on approach to medicine is shown by the following story. When he had to select a location in Baghdad where a new hospital was to be built, he did so by hanging up pieces of meat in different quarters of the city. He chose as the site for the hospital the quarter where the putrefaction of the meat was slowest.

One of the most valuable of al-Razi's two hundred treatises was *The Comprehensive Book on Medicine* (*Kitab al-Hawi fi al-tibb*). This was a large private notebook which he used to record his own clinical cases as well as extracts from earlier authors discussing diseases and the cures for them. The U.S. National Library of Medicine in Bethesda, Maryland, has the oldest recorded copy of the part of this book which deals with gastrointestinal complaints: an unnamed scribe finished copying it on 30 November 1094. This is the oldest volume in the National Library of Medicine and the third oldest Arabic medical manuscript preserved today.

Al-Razi was known in Europe by the Latin version of his name, i.e., Rhazes, and many of his works were translated into Latin. The *Hawi* is an important source for modern knowledge of Greek and Indian writings as well as for early Arabic writings that are now lost. Another treatise, the *Book of Medicine Dedicated to Mansur* became one of the most widely read medieval medical manuals in Europe. A third work by al-Razi, this one on smallpox and measles, was not the earliest monograph on this subject but was the most influential, being twice translated into Latin, the last time as late as the eighteenth century.[7]

Synthesizer of Reason and Revelation: Abu al-Hasan al-Ashari (873/874–935)

An Iraqi theologian, Abu al-Hasan al-Ashari wrote between two hundred and three hundred treatises. In his work *Theological Opinions of the Muslims* (*Maqalat al-Islamiyin*), he produced a synthesis of reason and revelation which became the orthodox Sunni theological position.[8] It also gives good insights into the earliest days of Muslim theology.

Initially al-Ashari was part of the Mutazili movement and described its reason-oriented views fully in the first volume of this treatise. At the age of 40, however, he abandoned this school of thought because he felt it had become too sterile. Specifically, it is said that al-Ashari decided to leave the Mutazili movement when his mentor failed to resolve a question al-Ashari put to him about the alleged divine obligation to abandon the good for the sake of the better.[9] Al-Ashari's later work, *The Luminous Book* (*Kitab al-Luma*), reflected his new and, ultimately, more traditionalist beliefs.

After moving from Basra to Baghdad, he gathered disciples and formed a new school of theology there which included among its later members the luminaries al-Ghazali and Ibn Khaldun, both of whom are discussed later in this chapter. Known as the Asharite school, this drew on both Mutazili and Hanbali (traditionalist) lines of thought.

To defend himself against charges that too much reliance on reason could result in heretical conclusions about the nature of God, al-Ashari fell back on a traditional defense. Rather than asking *why* revealed truth (the Quran) is true, he argued that believers must simply accept its veracity on faith alone.[10] The reason is that, as a modern Muslim commentator puts it, "Allah knows best."[11] Al-Ashari thus defended the orthodox theological position that stressed the importance of the divine revelation and the limited scope of human reason and human will.[12]

The "Second Master": Abu Nasr al-Farabi (c. 878–c. 950)

One of the greatest Muslim philosophers of all time, the scholar Abu Nasr al-Farabi was known to the Arabs as the "Second Master"—the first master being Aristotle himself. In the European Middle Ages, al-Farabi was known as "Alfaribi," "Abunaser," or "al-Pharabius." Few details about his life have been preserved, but his philosophic legacy looms so large that Western philosophers have dubbed him the "Father of Islamic Neoplatonism."[13] (The Neoplatonic school of philosophy was founded by Plotinus, who died in 270. It was the last school of Greek philosophy.)

Al-Farabi is said to have written 160 treatises. He was an expert not only in logic and philosophy but also in music and political science. The philosophic positions he took on metaphysics, i.e., the nature of reality, and on epistemology, i.e., theories of knowledge, are too detailed to be presented here. In general, he argued that the destiny of humanity is to cultivate reason. Reason should be used to regulate behavior and feelings so that the soul can be purified and reintegrated into a spiritual reality.[14]

The modern scholar Ira Lapidus has termed al-Farabi "the premier political philosopher in the philosophic tradition."[15] Al-Farabi called for harmony between the ideals of religion and the goals of the state. In his treatise on political science, entitled *The Virtuous City* (*al-Madina al-fadila*), the concept of happiness lies at the heart of his political philosophy. He taught that the "virtuous society" is one in which people work together to achieve happiness. The "virtuous city" is one where such cooperation occurs. The "virtuous world" can come about only when all its countries collaborate in the pursuit of happiness.

Al-Farabi postulates that from the Divine Being, i.e., God, there emanate ten Intellects. The Tenth, or Active, Intellect constitutes a bridge, as it were, between heaven and earth. The highest type of human happiness can be achieved by an ideal ruler who is spiritually in tune with this Active Intellect.[16] It is interesting to note that for al-Farabi one goal of knowledge is political power. He tells us:

> To be a truly perfect philosopher one has to possess both the theoretical sciences [philosophy] and the facility for exploiting them for the benefit of others according to their capacity. Were one to consider the case of the true philosopher, he would find no difference between him and the supreme ruler.... It follows, then, that the idea of Imam, Philosopher and Legislator is a single idea.[17]

Great Poet Who Lacked Common Sense: al-Mutanabbi (915–965)

Finest of the classical Arabic poets, al-Mutanabbi wrote exuberant poems of elaborate praise, using an ornate style marked by unusual metaphors. They are said to be impossible to translate into adequate English but they aroused the greatest enthusiasm among native speakers of Arabia. Al-Mutanabbi's influence on Arabic poetry was enormous and lasted until the nineteenth century.

His life was as colorful as his poetry. He lived with the *bedouin* for a time. Then, claiming to be a prophet, he led a revolt in Syria, which failed. "al-Mutanabbi" is a nickname; it means "he who pretends to be a prophet." His real name was Abu al-Tayyid Ahmad ibn Husayn. After spending two years in prison, he became a wandering poet and then joined the household of a poet prince in Syria.

Political problems forced al-Mutanabbi to leave Syria for Egypt, where he managed to offend his patron, the ruler of Egypt, by writing satirical verses about him. Al-Mutanabbi was thus forced to flee to Iran, where he became court poet in Shiraz. There, too, he made enemies and found it necessary to move on to Baghdad. His unfailing pride and arrogance, however, led to his death: on this journey he was attacked and murdered by bandits because, it was said, "bravado got the better of common sense."[18]

Al-Mutanabbi excelled at writing poems to mark special events. Following is one he wrote when his patron, the Hamdanid prince Sayf al-Dawla, was leaving Antioch (Turkey):

> Whither do you intend, great prince? We are the herbs of the hills, and you are the clouds;
> we are the ones time has been miserly towards respecting you, and the days cheated of your presence;
> Whether at war or peace, you aim at the heights, whether you tarry or hasten.
> Would that we were your steeds when you ride forth, and your tents when you alight!
> Every day you load up afresh, and journey to glory, there to dwell;

and when souls are mighty, the bodies are wearied in their quest.
Even so the moons rise over us, and even so the great seas are unquiet;
and our wont is comely patience, were it with anything but your absence that we were tried.
Every life you do not grace is death; every sun that you are not is darkness.[19]

Epistle by the Brethren of Purity (c. 969)

We have little firm information about the Brethren of Purity (*Ikhwan as Safa* in Arabic) except that its members lived in Basra (Iraq), met once a week to debate and take notes on intellectual issues, and then compiled their notes into 52 epistles. These works, collectively known as the *Epistles of the Brethren of Purity* (*Rasa'il e Ikhwan as Safa*), are quite liberal in their approach. Two passages are especially relevant here:

> Know that the truth is found in every religion and is current in every tongue. What you should do, however, is to take the best and transfer yourself to it. Do not ever occupy yourself with imputing defects to the religions of people; rather try to see whether your religion is free from them.
> Acquire knowledge, any type of knowledge — philosophical, legal, mathematical, scientific or divine. All that is nourishment for the soul and life for it in this world and the hereafter.[20]

The epistles cover a wide variety of subjects—mathematics, astronomy, geography, theology, ethics, music, and biology — and form an unusual and creative synthesis of Islamic and Greek philosophical themes. In one of them, for example, translated as *The Case of the Animals versus Man Before the King of the Jinn* [spirits], the animals bring the humans to court to account for their cruelties and atrocities.

In this allegory, the animals charge that humans have unjustly usurped and exploited the balanced, orderly natural world in which all living beings have a place, a form and a function that is perfectly adapted to the environments in which they live. At the end of a complex, energetic debate, the humans ultimately manage to defend their privileged position, arguing that they are the vice-regents of Allah because they have the ability to reason, but they are forced to agree to respect the rights of the animals and, as stewards of the earth, to respect the planet as a whole.[21]

The Most Important Islamic University: al-Azhar (founded c. 970)

Situated in Cairo and formerly also located with the great al-Azhar Mosque, this is the oldest and still the most important Islamic university in the world. Al-Azhar University has taught Islamic law, theology and Arabic for more than 1,000 years. The first recorded seminar was held in 975, when chief justice Abu El-Hassan sat in the courtyard of the university and, reading from a book on jurisprudence written by his father, instructed students in the intricacies of Shiite law. (In the twelfth century al-Azhar became, and still is, a Sunni university.)

In the early days of the university, courses in philosophy and medical studies were offered, but these were later withdrawn because it was feared that they might encourage independent thinking. Philosophy was reintroduced at the end of the nineteenth century. In more recent times (1961), new faculties have been added: medicine, agriculture, engineering, an affiliated Islamic Girls Faculty, and an Academy of Islamic Studies. Today, we are told, "These newly introduced faculties [which are spread out over several campuses in different cities] are not duplicates of their counterparts in other universities since they combine both the empirical as well as the religious sciences."[22]

Al-Azhar now has about 90,000 students. Its academic reputation, however, rests entirely on its past glories: the university is now controlled by the government of Egypt, which uses highly conservative political considerations in selecting the professional staff. The result is predictable.

> [The American writer Graham Fuller has deplored] the stultified and closed nature of political and intellectual life in large parts of the Muslim world today where either the state or conservative Islamic establishments intimidate and crush most new Islamic thinking. Egypt represents the heart of the problem: al-Azhar University — a renowned center of Islamic learning — has grown extremely cautious and narrow in its interpretations, rivaled in intolerance and restrictiveness by Islamist[23] groups that seek to embarrass the state for alleged insufficient vigilance in maintaining the purity of Islam.[24]

A modern Syrian scholar, Aziz al-Azmeh, who will be discussed later, also took a negative stand on intellectual conditions at al-Azhar in recent years:

> What modernism there is in modern Sunni Islam in the Arab world is ambiguous, hesitant, apologetic, defensive, and manifestly very vulnerable to attack both from traditionalists and radicals (the two currents presently converged, for instance, in the Azar, which had traditionally been traditionalist, paying lip-service, under Nasser ... to modernism).[25]

Ismaili Qadi (Judge): al-Numan (d. 974)

The Ismailis constitute a branch and community of Shiite Islam. The era of the Fatimid caliphs (909–1171) was a high point in their history. Teaching and learning were very important to them. Indeed, the Ismailis originally called their doctrine the "summons to truth" (*dawat al-haqq*).[26] Within the Ismaili community, the teacher and propagator of the faith, known as "the summoner," was second in importance only to the imam himself. As Muhammad Hassanali, a modern student of Ismaili thought, tells us, the Ismaili idea of knowledge, learning and teaching is this:

> Knowledge means life; learning means resurrection from the death of ignorance. Knowledge is a good entrusted by Allah to human beings, who must not selfishly keep it to themselves but instead pass it on. Learning and teaching are

a divine mission: the person who is spiritually resurrected through learning has a duty to bring others back to life as well.[27]

Considered one of the greatest Ismaili legal scholars and theologians of this era, al-Numan wrote more than forty treaties on jurisprudence, history and religion. He rose to become the highest judicial official in the Fatimid state. Not much is known about the personal side of his life. He is now remembered as the founder and greatest exponent of Ismaili jurisprudence. A contemporary Muslim historian paid him a graceful tribute.

> [This great qadi was] a man of the highest abilities, deeply versed in the Quran, fully acquainted with the meaning of the expressions contained in that book, skilled in jurisprudence, well informed respecting the conflicting opinions entertained by the legists learned in Arabic philology, in poetry of the higher class, in the history of the battle-days of the people [the Arabs of Muhammad's time], and distinguished for intelligence and equity. He composed for [the Fatimids] some volumes containing thousands of leaves; they were drawn up with great talent and in a style remarkable for the beauty of its cadences and rhymes.[28]

Islamic Humanist: Abu Sulayman Muhammad al-Sijistani (c. 932–c. 1000)

One of the great figures of the humanist movement in tenth-century Baghdad, al-Sijistani was known as "the Logician." He gathered around himself a circle of philosophers and literary figures who met to discuss philosophy, religion and linguistics. Few of al-Sijistani's works have survived, but his student al-Tawhidi took excellent notes on his teachings. These notes remain our primary source of information; it has been said that "we have to look at his teachings through the window of his pupil's writings."[29]

Al-Sijistani's thought, influenced by Aristotelian and Neoplatonic themes, focused not only on philosophy but also on politics, aesthetics and friendship. Rather than trying to force a marriage between faith (i.e., religion) and reason (philosophy), he held that the two are independent entities and cannot be reconciled. Indeed, their techniques and goals are quite different: religion aims at proximity to God, while philosophy aims at contemplation.[30]

Al-Sijistani not only criticized contemporary attempts to harmonize religion and philosophy but also criticized Muslim theologians who pretended that their methodology was rationalist when in fact it was merely "false rationalism." Moreover, al-Sijistani also taught that "through reason we overcome all obstacles to reach God through the intellect, which is the medium between human beings and the supernatural world."[31]

"The Jerusalemite": Muhammad ibn Ahmad al-Muqaddasi (or al-Maqdisi) (c. 946–c. 1000)

Al-Muqaddasi was an encyclopedic scholar who spent twenty years traveling in order to study the religious and political institutions of Islam. He was originally from al-Quds (Jerusalem) and thus was surnamed "the Jerusalemite." He felt great affection for his native city, but he could see its faults, too. When his travels brought him back to Jerusalem, he reported that life there was so agreeable that the city must be close to Paradise. At the same time, however, he noted that it was something of an intellectual backwater. "The Mosque is empty," he complained. "There are no scholars, no savants, no disputations, and no instruction."[32]

In 985 al-Muqaddasi produced a well-regarded work, *The Best of Classification for the Knowledge of the Regions* (*Ahsan al-taqasim fi marifat al-aqalim*), which is usually known by a shorter title, *The Description of the Muslim Empire*. This was based on his travels through the Islamic world and was full of firsthand knowledge. Unlike other "geographies" of the time, his book tries to understand and to explain clearly the practical foundations and the functioning of societies in different Muslim countries.[33] Among the topics he covers are water management, fiscal issues and finance, weights and measures, city and urban developments, local diets, clothing, and pre–Islamic customs.

On this last point, al-Maqaddasi's account of Egypt just after the Muslim conquest is worth mentioning here. He tells us that the local farmers explained to their new ruler the process by which they assured the annual rise of the Nile, which was essential to replenish the fertility of their fields. They said: "O Prince, regarding this Nile of ours there is a practice embedded in tradition without which it will not flow. On the twelfth night of this month we select a virgin girl who is the firstborn of her parents, and we recompense them both. We dress her in jewelry and raiment the best there are, then we cast her into the river."

The prince told them that "because Islam supersedes what was before it," this custom would no longer work. As a result, the farmers did not sacrifice a virgin but waited for the new religion of Islam to make the river rise. After two months, however, this still had not happened, and they were on the point of emigrating. The prince then wrote to Umar bin al-Khattab (the second Muslim caliph, who reigned from 634 to 644) for advice and was told that his understanding of Islam was indeed correct.

The caliph sent the prince a slip of paper and ordered him to throw it into the Nile. This slip of paper read:

> From the servant of God, Umar, Commander of the Faithful, to the Nile of Egypt, now then! If you flow by your own power alone, then flow not! If, however, it be the One God, the Conqueror, that causes you to flow then we ask Him — exalted be He — to make you flow.

The prince threw the paper into the river. When the farmers woke up the next morning, they saw that "God had caused the river to flow so that it reached a height of sixteen cubits." The moral al-Muqaddasi drew from this incident was that "God had thus prohibited that evil custom among them to this day."[34]

Cairo's House of Knowledge (1005)

Founded in Cairo in 1005 by the sixth Fatimid caliph, al-Hakim, who was known as the "Mad Caliph" because of his many cruelties and eccentricities, the House of Knowledge (Dar al-Ilm) is not to be confused with the earlier House of Wisdom established in Baghdad by Caliph al-Ma'mun more than a century before. A firsthand account of the founding of the House of Knowledge has fortunately survived and is worth reading. Written by al-Musabbihi, al-Hakim's court chronicler and his intimate friend, and quoted by the Egyptian historian al-Maqrizi (discussed in the following chapter), it states that:

> On this Saturday [24 March 1005] ... the so-called House of Knowledge in Cairo was inaugurated. The jurists took up residence there, and the books from the palace libraries were moved into it. People could visit it, and whoever wanted to copy something that interested him could do so; the same was true of anyone who wanted to read any of the material kept in it. After the building was furnished and decorated, and after all the doors and passages were provided with curtains, lectures where held there by the Qur'an readers, astronomers, grammarians and philologists, as well as physicians. Guardians, servants, domestics and others were hired to serve there.
>
> Into this house they brought all the books that [the caliph] ordered to be brought there, that is, all the manuscripts in all the domains of science and culture, to an extent to which they had never been brought together for a prince. He allowed access to all this to people of all walks of life, whether they wanted to read books or dip into them ... he granted substantial salaries to all those who were appointed by him there to do service — jurists and others.... He also donated what people needed: ink, writing reeds, paper and inkstands."[35]

The most important scientific achievement of the House of Knowledge was an astronomical chart with comparative data about stars and planets. After al-Hakim mysteriously disappeared one night in 1021 (his donkey was found with its tendons cut and al-Hakim's bloodstained clothes were discovered in a nearby pond, but the mystery of his death was never solved), the House of Knowledge itself began to go downhill and eventually came to a sorry end.

It played no significant role during the reigns of the next two caliphs. As Cairo itself slipped into political chaos, the caliph's officials and soldiers were not paid. As a result, the great libraries in the caliph's palace and in the House of Knowledge were both plundered in 1068. This is what a contemporary account tells us:

> From [the library in the caliph's palace] 18,000 volumes on antique sciences were robbed; in addition 24,000 Qur'an manuscripts with gold and silver illumination; all these were hauled away by the Turkish soldiers.... In the month of Muharram, twenty-five camels loaded with books made their way on a single

Teaching taking place in a well-stocked library. (Bibliothèque Nationale, MS. Arabe 5847, folio 5v. A67/276.)

day from the palace to the house of the vizier.... [He and the former vizier] divided up these books in their two houses [as compensation] for their services, for which [the finance department] owed them and their employees money. The share of the vizier ... was valued at 50,000 dinars, but was in reality worth more than 100,000 dinars....

The library of [the House of Knowledge] was also emptied.... The Berbers [who lived as nomads on the western edge of the Nile Delta and in present-day Libya, Tunisia, Algeria and Morocco] acquired countless indescribably beautiful books through purchase or robbery and took them with them. Their slaves and maids used the covers to make sandals for their feet; as for the leaves, they burnt them because they came from the palace; for they believed they contained the religious doctrines of the Orientals [the Ismailis], which contradicted their own [Sunni] religious doctrines. The ashes formed great hills in the province of Ibyar [in the Nile Delta], which are even today called the "Hills of Books" (*tilal al-kutub*). Many books were thrown into the river or were otherwise destroyed, but many of them reached the great metropolises [of other countries].[36]

Famous Surgeon: Abu al-Qasim al-Zahravi (936–1013)

Known in the West as Abulcasis, this Spanish physician was one of the most famous surgeons of the Muslim era and was physician to King al-Hakam II of Spain.[37] His thirty-volume medical encyclopedia (*al-Tasrif*) covered different aspects of surgery based on operations he had performed himself. These included cauterization; dental work; removal of a stone from the bladder; dissection of animals; surgery of eye, ear and throat; removal of a dead fetus; and amputations of limbs. Al-Zahravi is said to have been the first to describe in detail the disease of hemophilia. His medical encyclopedia continued to influence the medical world for 500 years.

Author of a National Epic: Firdawsi (c. 935–c. 1020)

Firdawsi's *Shahnama* (*Book of Kings*) has been considered the national epic of Iran ever since its completion in 1010. The author was said to have spent 35 years composing this long poem, which has nearly 60,000 couplets. It draws on an earlier Persian work that covers legendary times down to the end of the reign of Khosrow II in 628. Firdawsi added new material to carry the story up to the victory of the Arabs over the Sassanians in the mid-seventh century.

The *Shahnama* has been popular for so long because it glorifies Iran's past, chronicling tales of pre–Islamic Iranian kings and their victories over the enemies of their country. Many of its dramatic scenes have inspired Iranian miniaturists. One illustrated copy of the *Shahnama*, for example, shows the dying hero Rustam killing his treacherous half-brother Shaghad by shooting him with an arrow loosed with such force that it first penetrates the trunk of a tree before hitting Shaghad.[38]

Oleg Grabar, a modern historian of Islamic art, describes the *Shahnama* in these laudatory words:

> It is an astonishing fresco winding its way through myths and history, marked by many repetitions and formulas, carrying an absolutist and imperial ideology, a limitless passion for an Iranian-centered idea of what is good and beautiful,

but also animated by its eloquent spirit, its sometimes staggering images, and its entrancing rhythmic language.[39]

Despite its age, this epic can easily be understood by Iranians today because it is written in pure Persian with only touches of Arabic. Iranians consider Firdawsi and Hafiz (discussed in the next chapter) to be their greatest poets.

Ismaili Propagandist: Hamid al-Kirmani (d. c. 1021)

In the eleventh century, Ismaili literary activity reached a peak with the authors of the Fatimid era. One of the leading lights was al-Kirmani, an Ismaili religious and political propagandist.

Propaganda was a useful tool in the tenth century because conflict arose between the Fatimid and the Abbasid caliphates. Neither side could win militarily, so a period of cold war set in, during which propaganda became the major weapon. Al-Kirmani was chosen by the Fatimids to infiltrate the Abbasid caliphate and try to weaken it by propaganda. Because this was a secret mission, classical historians of Islam rarely if ever mention him.[40]

His date and place of birth and death are not recorded, but al-Kirmani worked in Iraq, Iran and Egypt. He distinguished himself in Cairo in about 1015 by combating the heresy of an emerging Muslim community known as the Druzes, who were originally Shiites. In 1020 al-Kirmani produced one of the great achievements of Ismaili thought, the *Peace of the Intellect* (*Rahat al-aql*). This work reflects his understanding not only of contemporary Muslim philosophers but also of Aristotelian and Neoplatonic philosophy.[41] A contemporary said of him: "Had the Ismaili *dawa* [reformist missionary program] produced no philosopher except Kirmani, that would have been enough."[42]

"Universal Genius": Ibn Sina (980–1037)

The brilliant Iranian philosopher and physician Ibn Sina was the most influential thinker of his time. He has been described as "a sort of universal genius."[43] Known in the West as Avicenna, he had an enormous impact on the medieval scholars of the West. His *Canon of Medicine*, written in about 1020, was used until modern times and remains one of the most famous books in the history of medicine.

Ibn Sina's intelligence and energy level were both extraordinarily high. He had memorized the complete text of the Quran and a good deal of Arabic poetry by the age of 10. Easily outstripping his teachers, he went on to study, on his own, logic, Greek philosophy, law and medicine. He began to study medicine at the age of 13 and was treating patients and teaching medicine when he was 16. By the time he was 21 he had mastered all branches of the learning of his day and had an enviable reputation as a successful physician.

Later in his life, after a specialist in Arabic philology had criticized him for not having mastered this subject, too, he studied it for three years, wrote several letters imitating precisely the prose styles of the greatest Arabic writers, and produced a massive book entitled *The Arabic Language* (*Lisan al-arab*).

The death of his father and political upheavals in Iran forced Ibn Sina to earn his living as a roving courtier, serving first at one court, then at another. At no time, however, did he need much sleep. During the day, he worked both as a court physician and as an administrator. At night, he taught students, discussed philosophy and science with them, rounding off the evenings with music and conviviality which lasted until the early hours of the next day. His students liked and respected him so much that they accorded him the honorific title of "Leader among the wise men" (*al-Sheikh al-Rais*).

Ibn Sina wrote about 450 works, of which about 240 have survived. The first of his books was the *Book of Healing* (*Kitab al-shifa*), a huge encyclopedia which covered logic, the natural sciences, psychology, geometry, astronomy, arithmetic, music and metaphysics. In fact, this may have been the most ambitious encyclopedia ever produced by one person. It was partially translated into Latin early in the twelfth century.

Ibn Sina's greatest single achievement, however, was *The Canon of Medicine* (*al-Qanun fi al-tibb*), written in about 1020 and now considered to be the most famous single book in medical history. It, too, is an encyclopedia, running to about one million words. Drawing heavily on the Greek medical knowledge known during the Roman imperial age, it describes 760 drugs, as well as Ibn Sina's own experiences as a physician. The *Canon* was translated into Latin, in full, in 1187. The practical tone of the *Canon* is evident from this excerpt from its introduction:

> Medicine considers the human body as to the means by which it is cured and by which it is driven away from health. The knowledge of anything, since all things have causes, is not acquired or complete unless it is known by its causes. Therefore in medicine we ought to know the causes of sickness and health. And because health and sickness and their causes are sometimes manifest, and sometimes hidden and not to be comprehended except by the study of symptoms, we must also study the symptoms of health and disease.... Of these causes there are four kinds: material, efficient, formal, and final....
>
> One ought to attain perfection in [medical research]; namely, how health may be preserved and sickness cured. And causes of this kind are rules in eating and drinking, and the choice of air, and the measure of exercise and rest; and doctoring with medicines and doctoring with the hands. All this with physicians is according to three species: the well, the sick, and the medium of whom we have spoken.[44]

Perhaps not surprisingly for one gifted with such a fine mind, Ibn Sina claimed that God is pure intellect and that knowledge consists of the mind grasping the intelligible. "It is important to gain knowledge," he tells us. "Grasp of the intelligibles determines the fate of the rational soul in the hereafter, and is therefore crucial to human activity."[45]

This is how Seyyed Hossein Nasr, a modern Islamic scholar, sums up Ibn Sina's achievements:

> [Translations into Latin] spread the thought of Avicenna far and wide in the West. His thought, blended with that of St. Augustine, the Christian philosopher

and theologian, was a basic ingredient in the thought of many of the medieval Scholastics, especially in the Franciscan schools. In medicine the Canon became the medical authority for several centuries, and Avicenna enjoyed an undisputed place of honor equaled only by the early Greek physicians Hippocrates and Galen. In the East his dominating influence in medicine, philosophy, and theology has lasted over the ages and is still alive within the circles of Islamic thought.[46]

The Father of Modern Optics: Ibn al-Haytham (c. 965–c. 1040)

One of the most outstanding mathematicians and astronomers of his time, al-Haytham made important contributions in optics and in the use of scientific experiments.[47] His Arabic name has traditionally been Latinized as Alhazen.

Educated in Baghdad, he was not only brilliant but also prudent. When asked by Caliph al-Hakim to devise a way to control the annual rise and fall of the Nile, al-Haytham carefully studied the flow of the river near the southern border of Egypt but decided that this task was beyond his powers. Fearing the wrath of al-Hakim, however, he then pretended to be mad and arranged to be confined to his own home, where he earned a modest living copying manuscripts until the caliph died in 1021.

Al-Haytham is thought to have written 92 works, of which about 55 have survived. His most important book, *Optics* (*Kitab al-Manazir*) shows, correctly, that the eyes passively receive light rays reflected from objects, rather than actively darting out light rays themselves. This book also discusses reflection and refraction. The latter is accurately explained by the fact that light moves more slowly in a dense medium. In the words of a modern commentator, Al-Haytham offers the reader "experimental proof of the specular reflection of accidental as well as essential light, a complete formulation of the laws of reflection, and a description of the construction and use of a copper instrument for measuring reflections from plane, spherical, cylindrical, and conical mirrors, whether convex or concave."[48] Thanks to these groundbreaking analyses, he has been praised as the father of modern optics.

In addition, al-Haytham stated and solved (by means of conic sections) what has become known as "Alhazen's problem." First formulated by the Greek mathematician Ptolemy in the year 150, this problem can be stated as follows:

> Given a light source and a spherical mirror, find the point on the mirror where the light will be reflected to the eye of an observer.[49]

In modern times this has also been known as Alhazen's Billiards Problem. In this latter case, it is cast in terms of finding the point on the boundary of a circular billiards table at which the cue ball must be aimed if it is to hit the black ball after one bounce off the cushion.[50]

Another famous work by al-Haytham, *On the Configuration of the World* (*Hayat al-alam*), contains a nonmathematical description of how Ptolemy's astronomical work could be understood by the application of the natural philosophy of al-Haythan's day. In Latin translations, both the *Optics* and the *Configuration* had a major influence on Western thinkers and scientists in the Middle Ages and thereafter.

Chapter VI

Population Movements and Islamic Cities (1041–1453)

Historical Background

The military and political history of the mid-eleventh through the mid-fifteenth century is quite complex. In overview, however, it can be said that those three centuries were characterized by two major trends: the movement of peoples and the growth of Islamic cities.

The Movement of Peoples

Both Easterners and Westerners were on the move. In the east, Turkic peoples (Seljuqs and Mongols) flowed into the eastern reaches of the Islamic world for about 400 years, beginning in 1041. In 1258 the Mongols, led by Hulegu, a grandson of the great conqueror Genghis Khan, sacked Baghdad, killing 800,000 people and ending its primacy as the largest city in the Arab world. The warlord Timur began his ruthless conquests in Iran in 1383: whole cities were laid waste and towers were built of the skulls of their inhabitants. He sacked Delhi in 1398, occupied Damascus in 1401, captured Smyrna in 1402, and had set out on an expedition to China when he fell ill and died in 1405.

After Timur's death, political power began to shift from the migrating populations to the sedentary peoples living in centralized empires. One of the most important events of this era was the Ottoman conquest of Constantinople in 1453 and, with it, the end of the Eastern Roman Empire, known as the Byzantine Empire. Constantinople was promptly renamed Istanbul. By 1520 the Ottomans controlled almost all of the Arab world.

In the west, Pope Urban II launched (at the Council of Clermont in 1095) the First Crusade, the first of what would eventually become the eight "numbered" or papally sponsored Crusades to "liberate" the Holy Land (Palestine, especially Jerusalem) from the control of the "infidels" (Muslims). These "pilgrimages in arms," as they were termed, would last for 200 years and would involve millions of men, women and children in many different theaters of war.

From the Western, i.e., Christian point of view, the First Crusade was a dramatic, unqualified success. The crusaders captured Jerusalem in 1099, put the inhabitants to the edge of the sword, and thus cleared the way for large numbers of Christian pilgrims to visit the holy sites of Palestine.

Although the words "crusader" and "Crusades" may still evoke a positive response in the West, especially in the United States, in point of fact the crusaders' aggressiveness and fanaticism poisoned relations between Muslims and Christians for many centuries to come. Sir Steven Runciman's definitive three-volume History of the Crusades, published between 1951 and 1954, remains the standard work on the subject, and it is worth repeating his conclusion here:

High [crusading] ideals were besmirched by cruelty and greed, enterprise and endurance by a blind and narrow self-righteousness; and the Holy War itself was nothing more than a long act of intolerance in the name of God.[1]

THE GROWTH OF ISLAMIC CITIES

From its modest beginnings in the towns and deserts of Arabia in 610, Islam had spread with enormous speed over vast regions and had evolved into an international urban religion. One sign of its success is that before the Black Death, which reached Constantinople in mid–1347 and then spread, Baghdad may have had as many as 840,000 inhabitants during its Abbasid heyday. Cairo probably had somewhere between 300,000 and 450,000 people in the fourteenth century. The cities of the Islamic world were thus much bigger than their European counterparts: Paris had only 210,000 people, Venice 180,000, and London 40,000.[2] *Islamic cities would continue to be the nursery of Islamic learning.*

A Chessboard Problem: al-Biruni (973–1048)

A German scholar, E. Sachau, once referred to al-Biruni, an Islamic thinker and scientist born in Turkmenistan, as "the greatest intellect on this earth." Another German scholar, F. Krenkow (1872–1953), felt that this was perhaps an overstatement but nevertheless readily admitted that al-Biruni "was a most remarkable man and in advance of his time."[3]

What is clear is that al-Biruni had a truly encyclopedic range of knowledge. He knew Turkish, Persian, Sanskrit, Hebrew, Syriac and Arabic. He excelled in a number of different fields—the chronology of history and history itself and the reckoning of time and astronomy, medicine, mathematics, physics, geography, and determination of the specific gravity of precious stones and metals.

In terms of religious beliefs, al-Biruni was nominally a Shiite but—remarkable in an age of faith—he was known to incline toward agnosticism. He never married and spent most of his life in the pursuit of knowledge.[4] A modern biographer records that it was rumored that al-Biruni "never raised his head from reading books and went out only twice a year on festival occasions, to procure provisions for himself."[5] One of his favorite sayings was: "The fact that Allah is omniscient does not justify ignorance."[6]

Al-Biruni was a prolific writer, producing some 146 treatises containing the equivalent of roughly 13,000 printed pages of modern book. His major works include

Chronology of Ancient Nations (Athar al-baqiyah), which outlined the chronology, history and geography of these nations.

The Masud Canon (Al-Qanun al-Masudi), a treatise on astronomy dedicated to Sultan Masud. This work put forward new theorems dealing with astronomy, trigonometry, and the movements of the sun, the moon and the planets.

A History of India (Tarikh al-Hind), the first Arabic compendium on Hindu civilization. Often using original Sanskrit sources, al-Biruni discussed India's religion, philosophy, caste system, marriage customs, systems of writing and numbers, geography, astronomy, astrology, and calendar.[7]

A History of Drugs Used by Physicians (Kitab al-Saydalah).

Book of Gems (Kitab al-Jawahir), which accurately measured the specific gravity of nine gems and nine metals by using hydrostatic principles.

In physics, al-Biruni showed that springs of water flow forth in accordance with the principles of hydrostatics. In geography, he theorized that, given its stratigraphy and the fossils it contained, the Indus valley of India must once have been the bed of an ancient sea. He developed a new method of measuring the circumference of the earth based on observing the horizon from the top of a mountain. By climbing a peak in the Punjab (Pakistan), measuring the dip of the horizon and applying trigonometry, he decided that one degree was in fact equal to the figure used by the surveyors working for Caliph al-Mamum in the ninth century (discussed previously).[8]

What he is best known for today, however, is a famous chessboard problem. Sayyed Hossein Nasr, a contemporary historian who is a leader of what can be termed "the Islamization of science," describes the problem in these words. Al-Biruni asked the king that he be given "the amount of grain which would correspond to the number of grains on a chessboard, arranged in such a way that there would be one grain in the first square, two in the second, four in the third, and so on up to the sixty-four squares. The ruler first accepted but soon realized there was not that much grain in his whole kingdom."[9]

This problem can be stated in mathematical terms as $\Sigma^{64} 2^{n-1} = 2^{64} - 1$ or a total of 18,446,744,073,709,551,615 grains of wheat would be needed to fill the chessboard in this manner.[10]

Lover of Difficult Rhymes: al-Ma'arri (d. 1057)

Blinded by smallpox at the age of four in his native Syria, al-Ma'arri became a poet when he grew up. He is considered to be the finest Arab writer of philosophic poetry.[11]

After first serving as a poet in the Hamdanid court in Aleppo (Syria), he became an ascetic and a teacher at the age of 35, explaining that

> Men of acute mind call me an ascetic, but they are wrong in their diagnosis. Although I disciplined my desires, I only abandoned worldly pleasures because the best of these withdrew themselves from me.... I was made an abstainer from mankind by my acquaintance with them and my knowledge that created beings are dust.[12]

Al-Ma'arri's best-known work is *The Necessity of That Which Is Not Necessary* (*Luzum ma la yalzam*), which takes its name from his own commitment to use very difficult rhymes. He also challenged the established political order and, as a freethinker, even flirted with heresy by extolling the virtues of reason. Here are two selections from another work of his, entitled *Meditations*.

> You've had your way a long, long time,
> You kings and tyrants,
> And still you work injustice hour by hour.
> What ails you that you do not tread a path of glory?
> A man may take the field, though he love the bower [an attractive
>   dwelling or retreat].
> But some hope a divine leader with prophetic voice
> Will rise amid the gazing silent ranks.
> An idle thought! There's naught to lead but reason,
> To point the morning and evening ways.

Here is the second poem:

> Had they been left alone with reason,
> they would not have accepted a spoken lie;
> but the whips were raised to strike them.
> Traditions were brought to them,
> And they were ordered to say,
> "We have been told the truth";
> If they refused, the sword was drenched with their blood.
> They were terrified by scabbards of calamities,
> and tempted by great bowls of food,
> Offered in a lofty and condescending manner.[13]

"Hardened Literalism": Ibn Hazm (994–1064)

Sometimes known in the West as Abenhazam, this writer, historian, jurist and theologian was one of the luminaries of Islamic Spain. He is said to have produced 400 treatises (some 80,000 pages of writing) on a wide range of subjects, including on the art of love. *The Dove's Neck-ring* (*Iqd al-Hamama*), a treatise on the concept and nature of love, is perhaps his most famous work. Ibn Hazm was a leading voice in the Zahiri ("literal") school of law, which emphasized a simple piety based the literal truths of the Quran and the *hadith*, in contrast to the complicated "hidden" (esoteric) meanings that Ismaili scholars purported to find in them.

Ibn Hazm applied these literal truths to theology in such an excessively logical manner, however, that he soon reached the point of absurdity. As an example, a modern Islamic scholar, G.F. Haddad, cites a *hadith* which states: "Let no one urinate in still, non-running water and then use it to bathe in." Haddad tells us that from this *hadith* Ibn Hazm drew the following conclusions:

The interdiction about bathing applies only to the person who urinated; anyone else is free to use that water to bathe in.

This *hadith* applies only if one urinates directly into the water. If the urine has reached the water indirectly — for example, by running off the ground or by being poured out of a container — the water can still be used for bathing.

The *hadith* applies only to urination. Therefore, water that has been used to clean oneself after defecation can still be used for bathing.

Haddad quotes approvingly another Islamic scholar, al-Nawawi, who said: "All this which Ibn Hazm held is in contravention of the consensus of the scholars [*ijma*], and is the ugliest example of hardened literalism reported from him."[14]

In Search of Learning: Nasir-i Khusraw (1004–c. 1092)

Traveler, poet, theologian and Ismaili missionary, Khusraw was one of the greatest writers of Iranian literature. His most famous book is the *Diary of a Journey through Syria and Palestine* (*Safarname*), also known as *The Book of Travels*. It records a seven-year journey he made after a pilgrimage to Mecca.

Khusraw was a relatively objective observer and was less swayed by popular superstitions than many other travelers of his time. He reports, for example, that at Jerusalem's Valley of Gehenna (a Hebrew word for hell) "the common people say that anyone who goes to the edge of the valley can hear the voices of the people in hell." But he candidly admits to his readers: "I went there but heard nothing."[15] He reported more favorably on the beauty of the Dome of the Rock. "When the sun strikes this," he tells us, "the rays play so that the mind of the beholder is absolutely stunned."[16]

Khusraw had a very active, inquiring mind. He was always in search of learning; as he said of himself, "No knowledge remained in the world from which I was not benefited more or less."[17] One of his poems, entitled "The Candle of the Intellect," reflects this same search:

> Kindle the candle of intellect in your heart
> and hasten with it to the world of brightness;
> If you want to light a candle in your heart,
> make knowledge and goodness its wick and oil.
> In the path of the hereafter, one should not walk
> on foot but with the soul and the intellect,
> and for provisions you must fill the tablecloth
> of your heart with obedience and knowledge.

> Oh son, your mind is the garden of intellect,
> turn it not into a furnace with fumes of wine;
> your heart is the blessed mine of knowledge,
> why have you planted a perverse hardness in it?
> Let your heart become soft because a shirt of
> dusky soft silk does not befit a heart of stone;
> cast away ignorance from your mind because
> celebration does not befit a house of lament.
> Comprehend well the wise poetry of the [wise man],
> for it is elevated and powerful like Mount Qaran,
> and with the needle of reflection, prick his
> excellent words in your subtle heart and soul.[18]

Independent Reasoning: Abu Hamid al-Ghazali (1058–1111)

This widely traveled theologian was a logician, a jurist, a Sufi mystic, and a member of the Asharite school of theology, which advocated a synthesis of rationalism and traditionalism. Although he was vehemently opposed by the Hanbali school of law for introducing rationalist philosophy into Sunnite theology, he was nevertheless revered in his own time as an outstanding religious authority. Over 400 treatises are ascribed to him, although this figure is thought to be too high. Al-Ghazali helped to define Sunni Islam and was a proponent of the right of *ijtihad*, that is, the authority to use independent reasoning to resolve legal and religious problems. For this reason, we shall look at his thinking in some detail.

AL-GHAZALI AND THE ROBBER

Legend has it that al-Ghazali was so dedicated to his scholarly pursuits that when he was robbed during a journey, he begged the thief to take anything—but not his books. Hearing this, the thief asked him, "How can you claim to really *know* these books when, by taking them, I can deprive you of their contents?" Al-Ghazali interpreted these words as a rebuke from God and spent the next three years memorizing the notes he was taking for another book, so that he would really *know* it.[19]

When he abandoned a brilliant academic career to become a monastic mystic, he won many followers and not a few critics. Some modern Western scholars, for their part, have studied al-Ghazali's writings in detail because they are interested in the autobiographical accounts of his own spiritual development. He is remembered today as being the last great figure of the classical period of Sufism and, arguably, as the most influential Muslim after Muhammad himself.

AL-GHAZALI AND SUFISM

Sufism is a term which comes from the Arabic word *suf* (wool) and originally referred to the light, coarse woolen robe worn by early ascetics. We saw in Chapter I that a full scholarly understanding of Islam would have to include four interdependent disciplines: philosophy, theology, jurisprudence, and Sufism. The first three disciplines are relatively straightforward and have already been touched on here, but Sufism, the mysticism of Islam, is more opaque. Historically, however, it has been (and still is) an important part of Islamic learning and thus merits our attention.

Mysticism itself can be defined as "a personal spiritual quest for union with the divine." It is not irrational or antirational but seeks instead a kind of knowledge that cannot be adequately expressed in words alone — if, indeed, it can be expressed at all. What Sufism demanded from its Muslim adherents was not *objective* learning (for example, the learning needed to trace the chain of transmission of a *hadith*) but *intuitive* learning—that is, the esoteric learning needed to get in touch with the divine. Such learning was often full of surprises. As one Sufi poet put it, "I sought Him [God] for thirty years; I thought that it was I who desired Him, but no, it was He who desired me."[20]

Sufism constitutes much of the ethics and practical philosophy of Islam. Guided by a master (*shaykh* in Arabic), an aspirant tries to refine his knowledge and morals through initiation into Sufi learning and rituals. The goal is to experience God at first hand and to have one's intellect enlightened by the light of divine reason. Progress toward this goal is made by passing through several spiritual "stages," each representing inner spiritual growth. Spiritual enlightenment is intensified by the love for all living things that the Sufi experiences along the path toward God. This enlightenment is the essential ingredient of justice. Sufis believe that one must constantly seek justice for one's neighbor without the slightest consideration of personal gain or loss.

The first Sufis were pious ascetics protesting against the worldliness of the early Umayyad dynasty (661–749). It was a famous woman mystic, Rabia al-Adawiyah (d. 801), who introduced into Sufi thought the concept of a pure love of God that was totally disinterested.[21] In other words, the worshiper was supposed to love God only for His own sake, not because of any personal hope for paradise or any fear of hell. Later, Sufi orders, that is, religious fraternities centered around a revered scholar, came into being and sponsored a great deal of Sufi preaching and missionary activity in India, central Asia, North Africa and West Africa.

Death and the Afterlife

Al-Ghazali's own contribution to Sufism was his great four-volume work *The Revival of the Religious Sciences* (*Ihya ulum al-din*), written in the last decade of the eleventh century and consisting of forty "books." This work was so highly acclaimed by his contemporaries that al-Ghazali was awarded the honorifics of "Proof of Islam" (*Hujjat al-Islam*) and the "renewer" (*mujaddid*) of his age.[22]

The Revival became the most frequently cited Islamic text after the Quran and the *hadith*. Its great achievement was to bring orthodox Sunni theology and Sufi mysticism together in a useful, comprehensive guide to every aspect of Muslim life and death. Al-Ghazali wrote it because he had become convinced that the *ulama* (religious scholars) of his day were pursuing religious learning only as a way to advance their own careers.[23] He was convinced that the true purpose of study is not to better oneself in this world but to know God.

The Sufi Shaykh al-Baghdadi (d. 1209) preaching in a mosque. Women and children are relegated to a separate room. (Bodleian Library, Ms. Ouseley Add 24, folio 55 verso.)

Here, for example, is an excerpt from *The Revival* which enjoins the believer to focus on the certainty of his own death and on the Quran's promise of paradise:

> When the righteous bondsman is laid in his tomb he is surrounded by his righteous acts, such as his prayer, his pilgrimage, his engagement in the Holy War, and the charity he used to distribute. Then the Angels of Chastisement approach him from the direction of his feet, but are told by Prayer, "Get back from him, you have no authority over him, for upon those [feet] he stood in me at length for the sake of God."
>
> Then they approach from the direction of his head, but Fasting says, "You have no authority over him, for in the world's abode he thirsted at length for the sake of God." Next they draw near to him from the direction of his trunk, but Pilgrimage and Holy War say, "Get back from him, for he exhausted himself and wearied his body when he accomplished the Pilgrimage and the Holy War ["struggle" is actually a better translation here] for the sake of God: no authority do you have over him."
>
> Then they approach him from the direction of his hands, but Charity says, "Back! Retreat from my master, for many an act of charity issued from those two hands to fall into the hand of God, while he acted only for His sake; no authority do you have over him."
>
> Then he shall be told, "Rejoice! Good you have been in life and in death!" Next, the Angels of Mercy come, and spread a heavenly cloth and resting-place for him, and his grave is widened around him for as far as the eye can see. A candle is brought from Heaven, and from it he has light until God resurrects him from the grave.[24]

HISBA: THE DUTY OF CITIZENS

In *The Revival*, al-Ghazali also gave believers a definitive guide to *hisba*, that is, the primary duty of every Muslim to "promote what is right and to prevent what is wrong" (*Al-amr bi al-maruf wa al-nayhy an al-munkar*).[25]

In practice, *hisba* in al-Ghazali's time meant that upright citizens were supposed to condemn the petty offenses which were common in public places, such as markets, baths and mosques. These offenses included house balconies that extended over narrow alleys, blocking the light; protruding shop benches that restricted the flow of pedestrian traffic; pack animals carrying sharp-edged loads that tore people's clothing; adolescent boys leering at respectable women on their way to or from the baths; and loud, overzealous religious services at mosques.[26]

While trying to prevent such abuses, al-Ghazali took great pains to limit the application of *hisba* to prohibit any infringement on the rights of law-abiding citizens. He specified, for example, that the offense had to be one which all orthodox jurists would consider objectionable; that *hisba* should not be applied in doctrinal matters over which there was disagreement; that the offense had to be *in progress* and could not be punished retroactively; that it had to be visible, not hidden; that searching a house or spying on someone was forbidden; and that people could not be questioned about the behavior of their neighbors.[27]

To make his point about the need to protect privacy, al-Ghazali cited the example of Caliph Umar II, who, it is said, climbed up the front wall of a man's house, looked down into the interior and found him drinking wine and engaging in forbidden sexual activity with a woman. The caliph began to berate the man, but this fellow stoutly defended himself, saying,

> Granted that I have committed an offence, but you have committed three offences: God said, "Do not spy," and you have spied; and He said, "Enter houses through their doors," and you have come in through the roof; and He said, "Do not enter other people's houses without first asking their permission and saluting them [Quran *Sura* 24:27}," and you have failed to do so.[28]

At what point, according to al-Ghazali, might brute force be used in the pursuit of *hisba*? The highest and last of the eight stages of al-Ghazali's doctrine on *hisba* was that the *muhtasib* (a local official who was both the supervisor of the markets and the guardian of public morality) could call for armed assistance if he could not carry out his duties unaided.[29] Unless applied with the utmost care, however, this provision could easily lead to street fighting. For if the *muhtasib* rounded up a posse, the offender was likely to ask his own friends to arm themselves, too, and come to his aid.

Al-Ghazali's solution to this dilemma was to restrict armed intervention to the few symbolic offenses which were held to be so serious that, if left unchecked, it was feared that they would undermine the solidarity of the Muslim community as a whole. Examples of such offenses were drinking wine, fornication and failure to pray.[30]

IJTIHAD: INDEPENDENT REASONING

A further explanation of the important concept of *ijtihad* is needed before we see what al-Ghazali has to say about it. *Ijtihad* can be divided into complete *ijtihad*, defined by Muslims as "the ability to discern Allah's rulings in all areas of Islamic law" and partial *ijtihad*, "the ability to do so only in certain areas of the law." Formerly, many Muslim and Western scholars believed that, at least by the twelfth century if not earlier, a consensus had been reached by Sunni scholars that "the gate of *ijtihad*" was closed.

What this actually meant in practice was a matter of learned dispute. At minimum, the "closure of the gate" meant that no new schools of legal thought could henceforth emerge in Sunni Islam.[31] At maximum, it meant that, subsequently, no original thought was permitted on major doctrinal issues. Instead, Sunni scholars were supposed to rely on the past decisions of eminent legal authorities rather than using their own reason. For their part, senior Shiite leaders, e.g., the ayatollahs of Iran who have earned a special title—*marja-e taqlid*, literally "a good precedent to follow"—from the Shiite Jafari school of law were allowed to interpret the holy texts themselves.

According to James Piscatori, a modern specialist in Islamic thought, these conventional understandings of both the Sunni and Shiite positions are overstated. The current academic view is something of a half-way house between them:

The door in Sunni jurisprudence was never tightly shut and it was always open to some extent; and the door in Shi'i jurisprudence — supposedly wide open — did not preclude following precedent (*taqlid*).[32]

In any case, some traditions recount Muhammad's personal approval of using original thought. Islamic scholars, for example, can cite a *hadith* that runs along the following lines:

> Before the Prophet sent one of his followers to Yemen, he asked him on what he would base his judgment. "In accordance with the Book of Allah [the Quran]," the man replied. Muhammad asked him: "But what if you don't find it there?" The follower answered that he would decide "according to the *sunna*." Muhammad persisted: "But what if you don't find it there, either?" In that case, said the follower, "I will exert my own opinion." Muhammad then put his hand, approvingly, on the man's chest and said: "Thank God for assisting His Apostle [Muhammad himself] with what he loves."[33]

CLOSING THE GATE OF INDEPENDENT REASONING?

Al-Ghazali was a leading member of the conservative Asharite school of theology. In a book entitled *The Incoherence of the Philosophers* (*Tahafut*), he asserted that the philosophers contradicted themselves, that they did not abide by the Quran and were even heretical, and that a transcendent divinity could not be known by reason alone. He believed that, guided by the divine enlightenment achieved through Sufi practices and knowledge, continuous *ijtihad* was the best way to keep Islam alive and well. At the same time, however, he was also against an undisciplined recourse to *ijtihad*: he feared that, if left unchecked, this practice could jeopardize Islamic orthodoxy. Al-Ghazali's point of view on this important issue is alleged to have reflected the "closure of the gate" of independent reasoning.

There is still a vigorous scholarly debate about whether al-Ghazali himself closed the gate of *ijtihad*, whether he was simply carrying out a long-established policy followed by earlier thinkers, or whether the gate was ever closed entirely and is thus still open today. Because of its importance to the future of Islamic learning, we will revisit this issue later on.

Author of Tales About a Confidence Man: Al-Hariri (1054–1122)

Author, scholar of the Arabic language and government information officer in Iraq, al-Hariri is now remembered chiefly for his treaties known as the *Maqamat* (*Assemblies*). This is a series of anecdotes ("assemblies") that recount the fictional adventures of a confidence man, Abu Zayd of Saruj, as related by the merchant-narrator al-Harith, who displays all the literary abilities of al-Hariri himself.

In the first "assembly," for example, al-Harith, who is down-and-out in Yemen and is looking in vain for a handout, wanders into the marketplace. There he finds a wailing crowd and recounts that:

> Then I entered the thicket of the crowd to explore what was drawing forth tears. And I saw in the middle of the ring a person slender of make [Abu Zayd]; upon him was the equipment of pilgrimage, and he had the voice of lamentation. And he was studding cadences with the jewels of his wording, and striking hearings [sic] with the reproofs of his admonition. And now the medley of crowds had surrounded him, as the halo surrounds the moon or the shell the fruit. So I crept toward him, that I might catch of his profitable sayings, and gather up his gems.[34]

After witnessing how Abu Zayd's eloquence stimulates the crowd to bestow generous alms on him, the narrator follows him to the cave where Abu Zayd lives. Despite his public claims of misfortunes and abject poverty, Abu Zayd is in fact living rather well there: his servant has prepared for him a meal of white bread, roast kid and date wine. When the narrator asks him to explain this contradiction, Abu Zayd is furious first but then relents and cheerfully confesses:

> I don the black robe [of a mendicant] to seek my meal, and I fix my hook in the hardest prey: And of my preaching I make a noose, and steal with it against the chaser and the chased. Fortune has forced me to make way even to the lion of the thicket by the subtlety of my beguiling.... Now if Fortune were just in its decree it would not empower the worthless with authority.[35]

Al-Hariri's book was extremely popular among the educated bourgeoisie of the Arab lands because of its linguistic brilliance and its punning style. Moreover, as the Lebanese scholar Philip Hitti concluded in 1970,

> In these *maqamat* of al-Hiriri [sic] and other writers there is much more than the elegant form and rhetorical anecdote which most readers consider the only significant feature. The anecdote itself is often used as a subtle and indirect way of criticizing the existing social order and drawing a wholesome moral. Since the days of al-Hamadhani [969–1008, who created this art form] and al-Hiriri [who perfected it] the maqamat has become the most perfect form of literary and dramatic presentation in Arabic, a language which has never produced real drama.[36]

Mathematician and Author: Omar Khayyam (1048–1131)

An Iranian mathematician and astronomer, Omar Khayyam was, according to one of his fellow students, "endowed with sharpness of wit and the highest natural powers."[37] He should really be remembered in the West for his scientific accomplishments, but thanks to the English writer Edward FitzGerald's translation of the nearly 600 quatrains (short four-line poems) ascribed to Khayyam, which was published in 1859 as *The Rubaiyat of Omar Khayyam*, he is now known as a poet instead.

There is no little injustice here. In the first place, in the annals of Iranian poetry the *Rubaiyat* is not considered to be a masterpiece. It is famous in the West only because it was one of the earliest poems to be translated into English — at a time when fascination with the Orient was in vogue. Second, some scholars doubt that Khayyam himself ever wrote any poetry: his poems were never mentioned by his contemporaries. Other scholars think he wrote only 120, not 600, quatrains. Finally, FitzGerald's translations are very free and do contain errors. For example, the most famous quatrain translated by FitzGerald is

> Here with a Loaf of Bread beneath the Bough
> A flask of Wine, and Book of Verse — and Thou
> Beside me singing in the Wilderness —
> And Wilderness is Paradise enow.[38]

Alas, the word translated by FitzGerald as "Book" is not *kitab* ("book") but *kabab* ("roast meat"). The two words look much alike in Persian. *Kabab* is not only the correct reading but intuitively makes more sense. *Kitab* usually refers to the Quran itself — hardly appropriate reading matter together with a flask of wine and a beloved![39]

Khayyam's mathematical reputation is more solidly based. It rests on his famous *Treatise on Demonstration of Problems of Algebra* (*Risalah fil-barahin ala masail al-jabr wal-muqabalah*). The work solved cubic equations by the use of intersecting conic sections. Khayyam also devised ways to extract the nth roots of numbers for arbitrary whole numbers n.

The Seljuq sultan Malik-Shah invited Khayyam to come to Esfahan, a leading center of Islamic scholarship, to work on improving the calendar. By making astronomical observations at a new observatory, Khayyam produced what was known as the Jalali calendar. This was more accurate than the Gregorian calendar, having an error of only one day in 3,770 years versus the Gregorian error of one day in 3,330 years.

Khayyam's other achievements include critiques of Euclid's theories of parallels and of proportion. He also accurately computed the length of the year (as 365.24219858156 days) and taught philosophy, law, history, mathematics, medicine and astronomy.

Quran Commentator: Zamakhshari (1075–1144)

Zamakhshari was a philologist and grammarian who was born and died in Turkmenistan but who spent so much time in the holy city of Mecca that he was dubbed the "Neighbor of God." His main achievement was a c. 1130 commentary on the Quran entitled *The Discoverer of Truth* (*al-Kashaf an Haqaiq al-Tanzil*), which attained an almost canonical reputation.

In the preface to this work, Zamakhshari outlined the challenges presented by the Quran:

> Of all the sciences, that which abounds with the most difficulties, which demands the greatest effort in spirit, which offers the largest number of problems capable of fatiguing the strongest intellect, I mean those extraordinary

subtleties from which it is difficult to extricate oneself, which are locked as if in vaults, whose thread is cut and difficult to regain — that science is the interpretation of the Qur'an. It is a science for which ... no savants are fitted, and to which they devote their lives without hope of complete success.[40]

Zamakhshari also wrote a set of edifying maxims for the faithful known as the "Golden Necklaces." This is one of them:

When you go to the mosque, walk with reverence; and when you pray, fill your heart with humility. Think of the power of the glorious King [Allah], and do not forget what is written concerning the temptations of the devil. Consider before what all-powerful sovereign you kneel, and what deceitful enemy you have to combat. Verily, no one can maintain himself on a firm foundation in this difficult world, except it be the man who is loyal to noble principles and fortified by his profession of faith; the faithful who sighs in fear of chastisement, contrite, repentant, eager in the pursuit of reward, who spurs his horse into the areas of obedience, and disciplines his spirit in the practice of submission.[41]

The Book of Roger: al-Idrisi (1100–1165/1166)

Al-Idrisi, a Moroccan geographer, worked in Palermo for the Norman king of Sicily, Roger II, who was keenly interested in geography himself. Al-Idrisi's own travels took him throughout North Africa and to Spain, Portugal, France, England, and Asia Minor. His chief work, *The Pleasure Excursion of One Who Is Eager to Traverse the Regions of the World* (*Kitab nuzhat al-mushtaq fi ikhtiraq al-afaq*), is also known as *The Book of Roger* (*Al-Kitab al-Rujari*). It remains one of the most famous works of medieval geography.

In al-Idrisi's time, Palermo was a crossroads for far-ranging sailors, merchants, pilgrims, Crusaders, explorers and scholars. It is not surprising, then, that Roger and his court saw the merits of making use of so much knowledge by producing a book about the world and a map of the world as well.[42] According to the fourteenth-century Arab scholar al-Safadi, Roger therefore invited al-Idrisi to come to Palermo, reminding him that

You are a member of the caliphal family. For that reason, when you happen to be among Muslims, their kings will seek to kill you, whereas when you are with me you are assured of the safety of your person.[43]

When al-Idrisi agreed to stay in Palermo, Roger was so pleased that it is said he gave him a pension fit for a king.

Roger and al-Idrisi then proceeded to choose "certain intelligent men" and some skilled draftsmen. These teams were sent out to travel much of the known world. When they returned to Palermo, al-Idrisi listened to their reports and included the information thus obtained in his book and maps.[44] The book and maps, which took fifteen years to finish, constitute some of the most voluminous, most valuable and most detailed geographic work undertaken during the twelfth century.

In his book, al-Idrisi described the earth as a globe 22,900 miles in circumference (as noted earlier, we now use the figure of 24,902 miles) which hangs immovably in space. He considered it to be "stable in space like the yolk in an egg." He divided the earth's surface into seven climatic zones and then subdivided each one into ten longitudinal sections. Each of the 70 sections was carefully described and was illustrated by a map.

When all these maps were assembled in 1154, the result was a large rectangular map of the world. A copy of this map was also engraved on a big silver tablet measuring about 12 feet by 5 feet. The silver tablet has been lost (it was broken up by a mob in 1160), but the maps themselves and *The Pleasure Excursion* have survived and were later republished.

Chronicler of Cultural Frictions: Usama ibn Munqidh (1095–1188)

The Syrian author, diplomat and warrior Usama ibn Munqidh was one of the most distinguished Arabs to chronicle the Crusades. He fought with Saladin against the Crusaders but later became friends with some of them. (Saladin, sultan of Egypt, Syria, Yemen and Palestine, was the founder of the Ayyubid dynasty. He is the most famous of Muslim heroes because of his recapture of Jerusalem in 1187.)

Usama ibn Munqidh himself bore the title of emir (prince) and, since he lived in Palestine, personally knew most of the leaders of Jerusalem after its capture by the Crusaders in 1099. An ambitious intriguer and an unscrupulous plotter, he was accused of arranging the assassinations of a Fatimid caliph and an Egyptian vizier to further his own ends.[45] His autobiography, which is the ultimate source of the following cited passage, was written in about 1175. It shows him to have been a gifted observer with a fine eye for detail.

With Jerusalem occupied by the Crusaders, cultural clashes between Muslims and Christians were inevitable. Although Usama ibn Munqidh himself got along very well with the Franks (literally the French, but by extension foreigners in general), one experience he had in Jerusalem in about 1140 was so remarkable that it must have confirmed the Muslim belief that all the Franks were savages. As Usama ibn Munqidh tells the tale,

> This is an example of Frankish barbarism, God damn them! When I was in Jerusalem I used to go to the Masjid al-Aqsa [al-Aqsa Mosque], beside which is a small oratory which the Franks have made into a church. Whenever I went into the mosque, which was in the hands of Templars [a knightly order which protected the unarmed Christian pilgrims] who were friends of mine, they would put the little oratory at my disposal, so that I could say my prayers.
>
> One day I had gone in, said the *Allah akhbar* ["God is great"— the beginning of the Muslim sequence of prayers] and risen to begin my prayers, when a Frank threw himself on me from behind, lifted me up and turned me so that I was facing the east. "That is the way to pray!," he said. Some Templars at once intervened, seized the man and took him out of my way, while I resumed my prayer. But the moment they stopped watching him he seized me again and forced me to face the east, repeating that this was the way to pray.

Again the Templars intervened and took him away. They apologized to me and said: "He is a foreigner who has just arrived today from his homeland in the north, and he has never seen anyone pray facing any other direction than east." [Many medieval Christians faced east when they prayed.] "I have finished my prayers," I said, and left, stupefied by the fanatic who had been so perturbed and upset to see someone pray facing the *qibla* [the direction of prayer, i.e., toward the Kabah in Mecca, which lies southeast of Jerusalem].[46]

One of Usama ibn Munqidh's best features was his broadmindedness. He was quick to recognize that even the Franks were capable of learning good manners once they saw them being practiced by their Muslim betters. "Among the Franks," he explains to his readers, "we see some who have settled down among us and who cultivated the society of Muslims. These Franks are much superior to those who have come only recently to the territories they occupy. But they constitute the exception and cannot be treated as a rule."[47]

"The Commentator": Ibn Rushd (1126–1198)

Known in the West as Averroës, this Spanish religious philosopher tried to meld Islamic religious traditions with classical Greek thought. His work, more of which has survived in Latin and Hebrew than in Arabic, influenced such Jewish and Christian thinkers as Maimonides, Thomas Aquinas and Albert the Great. Where Aristotle was known as "the Philosopher" by medieval philosophers, by the same token Ibn Rushd was called "the Commentator." A contemporary Muslim commentator said of him:

> He excelled in the Law, heard *hadith*, mastered medicine, and embraced speculative theology and philosophy until his erudition became proverbial in the latter. He authored works together with intellectual brilliance and diligent work night and day. He authored numerous works in jurisprudence, medicine, logic, mathematics, [and] theology.[48]

Ibn Rushd came from a family of judges and as a young man studied astronomy, law, theology, medicine, Arabic grammar and poetry. By 1153 he was making astronomical observations at Marrakesh in Morocco. About ten years later, he met the caliph Abu Yaqub Yusuf, who commissioned him to write commentaries on most of Aristotle's works, as well as on Plato's *Republic*. (These books had already been translated into Arabic.) Ibn Rushd's penetrating, incisive explanations of Aristotle, written between 1169 and 1195, helped Jewish and Christian scholars to understand this philosopher better.

Ibn Rushd was appointed as senior judge (*qadi*) of Cordoba and of Seville, as well as personal physician to the caliph and his son. Of greatest relevance here, however, was the heroic if ultimately unsuccessful campaign he waged to establish philosophy, i.e., reason, as a valid tool for the study of revealed religion. Refuting the conservative doctrines of al-Ghazali (see previous section), he insisted that philosophy and religion did in fact share the same goal. In about 1190 Ibn Rushd wrote

[T]he business of philosophy is nothing other than to look into creation and to ponder over it in order to be guided by the Creator — in other words, to look into the meaning of existence. For the knowledge of creation leads to the cognizance of the Creator, through the knowledge of the created. The more perfect the knowledge of creation, the more perfect becomes the knowledge of the Creator. The Law encourages and exhorts us to observe creation ... the Law urges us to observe creation by means of reason and demands the knowledge thereof through reason.[49]

He also cited a number of passages from the Quran extolling the use of reason. Here are two of them:

Will [men] not ponder upon the kingdom of the heavens and the earth, and all that God created...?[50]

Do [men] never reflect on the camels, and how they were created? The heaven, how it was raised on high? The mountains, how they were set down? The earth, how it was made flat?[51]

Ibn Rushd's philosophic works, written between 1179 and 1180, include the *Decisive Treatise on the Agreement between Religious Law and Philosophy* (*Fasl al-Makal*); the *Examination of the Methods of Proof Concerning the Doctrines of Religion* (*Kashf al-Manahij*); and *The Incoherence of the Incoherence* (*Tahafut al-Tahafut*), a refutation of al-Ghazali's views.

Ibn Rushd's spirited defense of reason made him enemies in both the Islamic and Christian worlds. Muslim thinkers rejected his works because he argued that only the philosophers, who are skilled in logic (syllogisms), are competent to interpret the *sharia*. Such a point of view automatically excluded the religious conservatives, who relied on dialectical arguments instead of on logic. (Dialectical arguments use commonly held beliefs as their premises. There is no logical guarantee, however, that such beliefs are in fact true.)

Christian thinkers, for their part, denounced Ibn Rushd as an archenemy of Christianity. This was not only because of his reliance on reason but also his teaching that, at death, all men are reunited into an amorphous "unity of the intellect." This latter view contravened the Christian doctrine of individual salvation and individual immortality.

Despite — or, in fact, because of — his intellectual achievements, Ibn Rushd eventually got caught up in a political controversy which led to his exile. The caliph, his patron, was at that time fighting a *jihad* against the Christians in Spain and desperately needed the support of the powerful Islamic theologians. Because Ibn Rushd had repeatedly crossed swords with these conservatives, he was declared a heretic and was exiled in 1195. His works on logic and metaphysics were burned. As soon as the political climate improved, however, the caliph, who personally liked and admired Ibn Rushd, restored him to favor.

Ibn Rushd is said to have written more than 20,000 pages, most of which dealt with philosophy, jurisprudence and medicine. Eighty-seven of his books are still extant. On medicine alone he is reported to have written twenty treatises. He has been hailed as one of the greatest thinkers and scientists of the twelfth century. Ibn Rushd's books were included in the syllabi of Paris and other universities until the age of modern experimental sciences.[lii]

Islamic College: The Mustansiriyya (Founded in 1233)

In the early days of Islam, the mosque was not only the place of worship but was also the schoolroom. Students sat on the floor in a circle in front of a lecturer, who was also sitting on a dais or cushion, his back resting against one of the mosque's columns. The more advanced a student was, the closer he was seated to the instructor.

By the eleventh century, colleges of Islamic (strictly Sunni) studies, known as *madrasas*, had been set up in major cities. Some of these were termed *nizamiyyas* in honor of the vizier Nizam al-Mulk (1018–1092), who established and endowed the first one in Baghdad in 1057.[53] It served as the model for a widespread network of similar institutions in the Middle East: for example, in that era Cairo had 75 *madrasas*; Damascus, 51; and Aleppo, 44.[54] These institutions were often near, but were not part of, the main mosque. The *madrasas* taught theology and jurisprudence, usually including *hadith* and Quranic exegesis but not mathematics or the sciences, which could be studied independently, outside the *madrasas*. Financed by rulers or by charitable foundations, *madrasas* were used both for study and for prayer. Accommodations for students and faculty were also provided.[55]

It must be noted that as a modern scholar, Sayyed Hossein Nasr, has pointed out, in marked contrast with traditions of learning in the West,

> The transmission of knowledge [in Islam] has always had a highly personal aspect, in that the student has sought a particular master rather than an institution, and has submitted himself to that teacher wholeheartedly. The relation that has always existed between the teacher and the student has been a highly intimate one, in which the student reveres the teacher as a father and obeys him, even in personal matters not concerned with his formal studies....
>
> In even the most formal type of learning, oral teaching accompanies the written text and the importance of actually hearing a teacher and receiving an ijazah [a permit to teach] from him personally keeps alive a chain of transmission [from the Prophet Muhammad to the student] which is of paramount importance in preserving and perpetuating the Islamic educational tradition.[56]

A contemporary Muslim chronicler, Ibn al-Fuwati, has left us a memorable account of the festive inauguration of the great Mustansiriyya *madrasa* in Baghdad on 6 April 1234. Founded a year earlier by the caliph al-Mustansir as a school for the four orthodox branches of law, it prepared students for prestigious careers as lawyers, teachers or scholars.

> [While the caliph watched quietly from a private window,] the deputy vizier came to the college with all the governors, chamberlains, qadis [judges], teachers,

religious notables, controllers of the household, Sufis, preachers, Koran readers, poets, and foreign merchants. Each of the four orthodox schools chose sixty-two representatives.... Each of the professors was presented with a black gown and a blue mantle, as well as a riding mule with complete equipment ... while each of the assistant professors was presented with a heavy tunic and a red turban.... Then a banquet was prepared in the courtyard of the College, and the tables loaded with all kinds of food and drink. After the company had feasted, further presents were distributed, ... and poems were recited in honor of the occasion. Next, accommodation in the building was allotted to the four schools.... Sufficient allowance for their upkeep was made in accordance with the provisions of the founder.[57]

Palace and Walled Fortress: The Alhambra (Built 1238–1358)

In 714 Spain was conquered by a Muslim army and later became an intellectual center of Europe. One of the finest examples of Islamic secular architecture is the Alhambra, a lovely complex of buildings set at the foot of the Sierra Nevada on a plateau that overlooks the city of Granada. Begun by the Nasrid dynasty, this was the palace and the walled fortress of the Moorish rulers of Spain. Its name comes from the Arabic *al-Hamra*, "the red," referring to the color of the sun-dried *tapia* (bricks) of clay and gravel used to build its outer walls.

The Alhambra, the most popular tourist destination in Spain, has been declared a national monument and was added to UNESCO's World Heritage list in 1984. In its own time, though, it was less esteemed. A Spanish ambassador to Timur's court was much more impressed by Timur's own pavilions of gold cloth, studded with jewels and surrounded by lush gardens and clear streams.[58] Now much restored, the Alhambra is a remarkable piece of work. The buildings around the Patio de los Leones (the Court of the Lions, so-named for its alabaster, light-reflecting water fountain supported by twelve white marble lions, symbolizing strength and courage) are richly decorated in geometric, botanical and calligraphic designs. The latter include excerpts from the Quran and poems by a local courtier. These inscriptions suggest that the Lion Court is meant to echo classical Islamic descriptions of paradise. The courtyard itself is surrounded by a gallery supported by 124 tall, slender white marble columns. Light playing on the Alhambra inspired the fourteenth-century court poet Ibn Zamrack to proclaim:

> And how many arches rise up in its vault supported by
> columns which at night are embellished by light!
> You would think that they are the heavenly spheres whose orbits revolve,
> overshadowing the pillar of dawn when it barely begins
> to appear after having passed through the night.[59]

The Alhambra's interior designs make strong use of symmetric (repeating) patterns. In mathematical terms, a pattern is symmetric if there is at least one symmetry that leaves the pattern unchanged. Technically, there are four plane symmetries:

rotation (turning an object around), translation (moving an object without rotating or reflecting it), reflection (producing a mirror image of an object), and glide reflection (combining a reflection with a translation along the direction of the mirror line). Examples of symmetry abound in the Alhambra — in wallpaper patterns, also used in carved wood ceiling panels; tiled friezes or strip patterns; and rosette patterns.[60]

Writer of an Encyclopedia of Sufi Mysticism: Ibn al-Arabi (1165–1240)

Ibn al-Arabi, a famous Spanish Sufi philosopher, gave Islamic mysticism its first definitive philosophic expression by creating a theosophical system, that is, an approach that deals with the relationship of God and the world, based on a "Unity of Being."

Al-Arabi is remembered for two major works. The first was *The Meccan Revelations* (*Al-Futuhat al-Makkiyyah*) of thirty-seven volumes, which has long been controversial. Islamic conservatives have denounced it as pantheistic and therefore heretical; indeed, it was banned in Egypt as recently as 1979.[61] The second book is entitled *The Bezels of Wisdom* (*Fusus al-Hikam*) and contains only twenty-seven chapters. (In this context, "bezels" are the oblique sides or the faces of cut gems.) This book is a summary of the teachings of twenty-eight prophets, who taught different kinds of spirituality. It is the fullest and most mature expression of al-Arabi's mystical philosophy.

Educated in Seville, where he studied under a number of mystic thinkers who were struck by his spiritual sensitivities and his high intelligence, al-Arabi traveled widely in Spain and North Africa. In one famous encounter, while still a young man, he met with the celebrated thinker Ibn Rushd (see previous section), who asked him about his mystical experiences.

As al-Arabi described the interview, Ibn Rushd put to him two very difficult philosophical questions: "How did you find the situation in unveiling and divine effusion [sic]? Is it what rational consideration gives us?" Al-Arabi replied cryptically: "Yes and no. Between the yes and the no spirits fly from their matter and heads from their bodies."[62] It is said that this reply made Ibn Rushd turn pale and tremble. It implied that al-Arabi had attained a degree of mystical knowledge exceeding that attainable by reason alone, i.e., his learning was divinely inspired.

In 1198 al-Arabi had a vision which impelled him to leave Spain and travel to Mecca and other lands of the east. It was in Mecca that he said he received a command from God to begin his major work, *The Meccan Revelations*, which he completed years later in Damascus. Running to 37 volumes (560 chapters), this opus was an encyclopedia of Islamic mysticism and a record of al-Arabi's own spiritual development. It, was also in Mecca that he fell in love with a beautiful young girl who was a scholar, too. He wrote a series of love poems for her and used her to personify "wisdom."

After further travels in Egypt and Turkey, al-Arabi finally settled in Damascus, where he was revered as the greatest spiritual master of his age. His profound esoteric commentaries on the Quran and on *hadith* have been praised by Francis Robinson, a modern scholar of the Islamic world, as "a masterly synthesis of Sufi, philosophic, and Neoplatonic thought."[63]

Poet and "Perfect Master": Jalal al-Din al-Rumi (1207–1273)

The greatest mystical poet in the Persian language, Rumi is said by his followers to have attained the level of a "perfect master" because he lived on a spiritual plane inaccessible to most mortals. He is still famous for his lyrics and for his epic *Spiritual Couplets* (*Masnavi-ye Manavi*).

Rumi was a "drunken Sufi," that is, a Sufi given to waves of the most intense religious ecstasy. His writings about wine and love have often been mistranslated or misinterpreted as referring, literally, to love of alcohol and sex. In fact, Rumi was only using these as metaphors for the mystic's sublime relationship with the divine. The Sufi poetic theme of "the cupbearer" pouring golden wine into the lover's cup to the point of overflowing is a metaphor for God letting the light of divine knowledge fill the intellect of the Sufi.[64] As Rumi tells us in one of his poems,

> What is to be done, O Muslims? For I do not recognize myself...
> I am not of the East, nor of the West, nor of the land, nor of the sea;
> I am not of Nature's mint, nor of the circling heaven....
> I have put duality away. I have seen that the two worlds are one;
> One I see, One I know, One I call.
> He is the first, He is the last, He is the outward, He is the inward....
> I am intoxicated with Love's cup, the two worlds have passed out of my ken;
> I have no business save carouse and revelry....
> I will trample on both worlds, I will dance in triumph for ever....[65]

A chance encounter in Syria in 1244 with a wandering holy man who called himself the "Sun of Religion" (Shams al-Din) led Rumi ever deeper into mysticism. These two men lived together and became so close that Rumi neglected his own family and his disciples. This caused a scandal that was resolved only when Shams al-Din was murdered in 1247—if not by them then certainly with the knowledge of Rumi's sons.

Rumi dealt with this loss by signing Shams al-Din's name to most of the 24,660 verses and quatrains he wrote thereafter. These works, composed by Rumi when he was in an ecstatic state induced by repetitive sounds (notes from a reed flute, drum beats, the hammering of goldsmiths, the turning of a water mill), are now known as *The Collected Poetry of Shams* (*Divan-e Shams*). Persian-speaking mystics still rank this book as second in importance only to the Quran itself.

Not long after the death of Shams al-Din, Rumi became spiritually attached to a local goldsmith and then, after the goldsmith's death, to Husam al-Din Chelebi, who became the inspiration for the nearly 26,000 verses of Rumi's chief work, *The Spiritual Couplets*. These reflect the full range of Sufi thought in the thirteenth century.

After Rumi's death in 1273, one of his disciples founded the Mawlawiyah order, known in the West as the Whirling Dervishes because of their stately spinning dance, which is used to induce a mystical trance. A website devoted to the memory of Rumi describes this dance as follows:

> The dervishes turn timelessly and effortlessly. They whirl, turning round on their own axis and also moving in orbit. The right hand is turned up toward heaven to receive God's overflowing mercy which passes through the heart and is transmitted to earth with the down-turned left hand. While one foot remains firmly on the ground, the other crosses it and propels the dancer round. The rising and falling of the right foot is kept constant by the inner rhythmic repetition of the name of "Allah-Al-lah, Al-lah...." The ceremony can be seen as a great crescendo in three stages: knowing God, seeing God and uniting with God.[66]

One of Rumi's most moving descriptions is of a reed cut from the reed bed to be used as a flute. This poem opens the *Spiritual Couplets*. Rumi uses the image of the cut reed to evoke a soul which has been emptied of ego and refilled with the divine spirit:

> Hearken to the Reed forlorn,
> Breathing, even since 'twas torn
> From its rushy bed, a strain
> Of impassioned love and pain.
> The secret of my song, though near,
> None can see and none can hear.
> Oh, for a friend to know the sign
> And mingle all his soul with mine!
> 'Tis the flame of love that fired me,
> 'Tis the wine of Love inspired me,
> Wouldst thou learn how lovers bleed,
> Hearken, hearken to the Reed!"[67]

Traditional Seer: Nasr al-Din al-Tusi (1201–1274)

An excellent example of the traditional Islamic *hakim* ("wise man"), who encompasses within himself all the different aspects of the sage, i.e., scholar, medical healer and spiritual guide, al-Tusi was an outstanding Iranian philosopher, scientist, mathematician, logician, astronomer, theologian and diplomat. He wrote at least fifty-six and perhaps as many as sixty-four treatises.[68] He also seems to have been good at trimming his sails to catch the prevailing winds.

Brought up as a member of the Twelfth Imam school[69] (a main branch of the Shiite faith), al-Tusi moved to the mountain stronghold of an Ismailite ruler in about 1227 to escape the advance of the Mongols and later converted to the Ismailite faith. Believing that reason alone could not answer the ultimate metaphysical questions of life, he took comfort instead in the Ismaili doctrine of following the teachings of an infallible Imam who could provide spiritual guidance.[70]

When the Mongols came to power, al-Tusi was involved in negotiations which resulted in the surrender to them of the Grand Ismaili Master. The Mongols invited al-Tusi to serve them as a scientific adviser — an offer he accepted with alacrity. He stood in high favor with them not only because of his intellectual achievements and negotiating skills but also because, it was rumored, he may have been a secret agent who passed to them information on local defenses.

Al-Tusi married a Mongol woman and was given a senior position in the Mongol administration as the official in charge of charitable endowments. He was with the Mongols when they sacked Baghdad in 1258. Later, he took advantage of the Mongol leader's interest in astrology and persuaded him to build a major observatory in Azerbaijan (northwestern Iran) in 1262. This institution included an excellent library and a staff of Islamic and Chinese scholars under al-Tusi's direction.

A man of extraordinarily wide learning, al-Tusi wrote some 150 treatises in three different languages (Arabic, Persian and Turkish). He edited the definitive Arabic editions of Greek texts by Autolycus, Aristarchus, Euclid, Apollonius, Archimedes, Hypsicles, Theodosius, Menelaus and Ptolemy. Al-Tusi also made important contributions to astronomy, mathematics and Ismailite theology. He was the first to establish trigonometry as a mathematical discipline in its own right (not just as a tool of astronomy). Using earlier Arabic translations, al-Tusi presented Euclid's proof of the Pythagorean theorem, which is used to calculate the relationship between the legs and angles of a triangle. He was also the first to describe the whole system of plane and spherical geometry.[71]

He is most remembered today for his *Treasury of Astronomy* (*al-Tadhkirah fi'ilm al-haya*), which introduced what is now referred to as the "Tusi couple." The Tusi couple resolves linear motion into the sum of two circular motions. Its purpose was to remove all parts of Ptolemy's model of the planetary system that were not based on the principle of uniform circular motion. Al-Tusi's work may well have inspired the heliocentric astronomical model of Nicolaus Copernicus (1473–1543).

Corrector of Greek Medical Knowledge: Ibn al-Nafis (1213–1288)

For centuries, the verdict of the famous Greek doctor Galen was accepted without question: in the human body, blood flows directly from the right side of the heart to the left side. The Syrian physician and jurist al-Nafis, however, proved him wrong. As the first chief of the al-Mansuri Hospital in Cairo and dean of its medical school, al-Nafis studied the anatomy of the heart and found that

> [T]he blood from the right chamber of the heart must arrive at the left chamber, but there is no direct pathway between them. The thick septum of the heart is not perforated and does not have visible pores as some people thought or invisible pores as Galen thought. The blood from the right chamber must flow through the vena arteriosa (pulmonary artery) to the lungs, spread through its substance, be mingled with air, pass through the arteria venosa (pulmonary vein) to reach the left chamber of the heart.[72]

Al-Nafis was also the first person to describe coronary circulation accurately. As he put it, "the nourishment of the heart is from the blood that goes through the vessels that permeate the body of the heart."[73] His discoveries do not appear to have been known in Europe at the time. Although some of al-Nafis's work was translated into Latin in 1547, it was not until the twentieth century that scholars brought all his findings to light.

Poet of Human Kindness, Humor and Resignation: Sa'di (c. 1213–1291)

The real name of this Iranian poet was Musharrif Od-din Muslih Od-din, but he is known by his pen name, Sa'di, which he borrowed from the name of his patron, a local prince. Sa'di acquired the traditional learning of Islam at the Nezamiyeh College in Baghdad, but due to the unsettled political conditions following the fall of Baghdad to the Mongols in 1258, he spent most of his life wandering abroad, not all of it in pleasant surroundings.

Captured in North Africa by the French, he was forced to labor for years in the clay pits near the fortress of Tripoli. Eventually, a Syrian acquaintance discovered him there, paid ten *dinars* for his release, took him to his home in Aleppo, and made him marry his daughter, to whom he gave a dowry of a hundred *dinars* for this purpose. The marriage was not, alas, a happy one. Sa'di says of his wife:

> She was a woman always scowling, disobedient and growling; she began to give me plenty of her shrewish tongue, and made life wholly miserable for me.... Once in a torrent of abuse she said, "Are you not that man whom my father bought back from the Franks?" I said, "Yes, I am that man whom your father bought back from the Frankish chains for ten *dinars*, and delivered into your bondage for a hundred *dinars*.[74]

Sa'di is remembered today chiefly for two works. The first was the *Bustan* (*The Orchard*). Written 1257, this philosophical and epic poem is a compilation of maxims and stories, each one representing a flower of a figurative garden. Sa'di described his book thus:

> I traveled in many regions of the globe and passed the days in the company of many men. I reaped advantages in every corner, and gleaned an ear of corn from every harvest. I regretted that I should go from the garden of the world empty-handed to my friends, and reflected: Travelers bring sugar-candy from Egypt as a present to their friends. Although I have no candy, yet have I words that are sweeter. The sugar that I bring is not that which is eaten, but what knowers of truth take away with respect.[75]

The other book for which Sa'di is famous is the *Gulistan* (*The Rose Garden*). Written in 1258, this is a collection of poems documenting the author's travels. In the *Gulistan*, Sa'di sang the praises of the free and simple lifestyle he followed:

> Astride a horse I am not, not camel-like carry a load,
> Subjects I have none, nor follow any sultan's code.
> I worry not for what exists, nor fret for what is lost,
> I breathe with extreme ease, and live at very little cost.[76]

Sa'di wanted to make the *Gulistan* an echo of paradise. Just as paradise was thought to have eight entrances, so, too, the *Gulistan* has eight chapters. These address a broad swath of subjects: the manners of kings; the morals of dervishes; the virtues of contentment and silence; love, youth, weakness, and old age; education; and rules for personal conduct in life. These poems appealed to a wide range of people (from youths to grandparents) because they are full of witticisms and common sense that everyone could readily understand. Here is an example from the *Gulistan*:

> One of the *ulama* [religious scholars] had been asked that, supposing one sits with a moon-faced beauty in a private apartment, the doors being closed, companions asleep, passion inflamed, and lust raging, as the Arab says, the date is ripe and its guardian not forbidding, whether he thought the power of abstinence would cause the man to remain in safety. He replied: "If he remains in safety from the moon-faced one, he will not remain safe from evil speakers."
>
> > If a man escapes from his own bad lust
> > He will not escape from the bad suspicions of accusers.
> > It is proper to sit down to one's own work
> > But it is impossible to bind the tongues of men.[77]

Sa'di's work also became popular with intellectuals in nineteenth century Europe and influenced the American transcendentalists Ralph Waldo Emerson and Henry David Thoreau. In more recent times, the United Nations has honored Sa'di's memory by engraving upon the entrance to the Hall of Nations in New York these four lines from his poetry:

> Of one Essence is the human race,
> Thusly has Creation put the Base;
> One Limb impacted is sufficient,
> For all Others to feel the Mace.[78]

Controversial Traditionalist: Ibn Taymiyya (1263–1328)

A member of the late Hanbali school of traditionalist legal thought, Ibn Taymiyya has always been an intensely controversial figure. He was convinced that religious truth could never be attained by use of logic alone: the intellect had to submit to revelation. He was strongly opposed to any deviation from tried-and-true Sunni traditions.

Ibn Taymiyya detested, for example, the liberal, emotional "popular Islam" advocated by the Sufis, not to mention the unorthodoxies of the Shiite and other creeds.

In fact, he accused them of idolatry, which is a serious breach of the monotheist covenant: he asserted that the Sufi *shayks* and the Shiite *imams* had become human beings worshipped as gods.[79]

His opinions were so extreme that they appalled the great traveler Ibn Battuta (see the following section), himself a man of far more moderate religious views. Ibn Battuta has left us the following firsthand report:

> One of the principal Hanbalite doctors at Damascus was Taqi al-Din Ibn Taymiya [sic], a man of great ability and wide learning, but with some kink in his brain. The people of Damascus idolized him. He used to preach to them from the pulpit, and one day he made some statement that the other theologians disapproved of; they carried the case to the sultan and in consequence Ibn Taymiya was imprisoned for some years....
>
> Later on his mother presented herself before the sultan and interceded for him, so he was set at liberty, until he did the same thing again. I was in Damascus at the time and attended the service which he was conducting one Friday, as he was addressing and admonishing the people from the pulpit. In the midst of his discourse he said "Verily God descends [from heaven] to the sky over our own world in the same bodily fashion that I make this descent," and stepped down one step of the pulpit....
>
> [Other theologians, who strongly objected to this anthropomorphic heresy,] carried the matter before the principal amir [prince], who wrote to the sultan about the matter and at the same time drew up a legal attestation against Ibn Taymiya for various heretical pronouncements. This deed was sent on to the sultan, who gave orders that Ibn Taymiya should be imprisoned in the citadel, and there he remained until his death.[80]

Whether because of the "kink in his brain" or for some other reason, Ibn Taymiyya seems to have made more enemies than friends. He angered his fellow Sunni scholars, for example, by denouncing the four orthodox Sunni schools of jurisprudence as stagnant, sectarian, and unduly influenced by Greek logic and Sufi mysticism.[81] He considered those Sufi *shayks* who claimed divine authority for themselves as constituting the greatest single threat to the Muslim community, both intellectually and politically. In place of these schools and these religious leaders, he called instead for a total reliance on the Quran and the *sunna* as the only sure path toward a revival of Islam. His outspokenness cost him many years in jail, both in his native Syria and in Egypt.

Because of his seminal role in the history of Islamic fundamentalism, however, it is important to look at Ibn Taymiyya's ideas in some detail. His teachings have give inspiration to at least three fundamentalist trends: the Wahhabi movement, which began in Saudi Arabia late in the eighteenth century and which is still critically important there today; the Muslim radicals who assassinated Egyptian President Anwar Sadat in 1981; and Osama bin Laden's Al Qaeda terrorist network.[82]

Ibn Taymiyya's hard-line stance is evident from his uncompromising views on innovation and on *jihad*. He begins with the premise that the chief duty of human beings is *to serve God*— not to know Him or speculate about Him (these are the mistaken goals of theology) or to love Him (which is the mistaken goal of Sufism). Ibn Taymiyya sternly warns his followers,

> The religion of Islam turns on these two principles: worshipping God and worshipping Him by what He prescribed. He is not served by innovation [i.e., Sufi *shaykh*-worship, Shiite *imam*-worship, or even blind adherence to the masters of a given law school].... It is not permissible when guilt has been established by proof or witness to suspend the legal punishment, whether by remitting it or by substituting a fine or any other thing: the hand of the thief must be cut off, for the application of the punishments is one of the acts of religion like the *jihad* in the Way of God.[83]

In his *Governance According to God's Law in Reforming Both the Ruler and His Flock* (*al-Siyasa al-shariyya fi Islah al rai'i wa al-ra'iyya*), he is no less forthright on the absolute necessity of *jihad*:

> The command to participate in *jihad* and the mention of its merits occur innumerable times in the Koran and the Sunna. Therefore it is the best voluntary [religious] act that man can perform.... *Jihad* implies all kinds of worship, both in its inner and outer forms. More than any other act it implies love and devotion for God, Who is exalted, trust in Him, the surrender of one's life and property to Him, patience, asceticism, remembrance of God and all kinds of other acts [of worship] [sic].... Since lawful warfare is essentially *jihad* and since its aim is that the religion is God's entirely and God's word is uppermost, therefore according to all Muslims, those who stand in the way of this aim must be fought.[84]

Both Ibn Taymiyya's friends and foes agreed that he claimed to be a *mujtahid*, that is, a scholar with the right to use independent reasoning (*ijtihad*) to find solutions to doctrinal or legal questions. One contemporary admirer described him in these glowing words:

> Our shaykh, master, and imam between us the Allah Almighty, the master of verification, the wayfarer of the best path, the owner of the multifarious merits and overpowering proofs which all hosts agree are impossible to enumerate, the Shaykh, the Imam and faithful servant of his Lord, the doctor in the Religion, the Ocean, the light-giving Pole of spirituality, the leader of imams, the blessing of the Community, the sign-post of the people of knowledge, the inheritor of Prophets, the last of those capable of independent legal reasoning, the most unique of the scholars of the Religion, Shaykh al-Islam ["Chief of Islam," an honorific title].[85]

A contemporary critic, however, had much less flattering things to say about Ibn Taymiyya:

> He used to bring up in one hour from the Book [the Quran], the *sunna*, the Arabic language, and philosophical speculation, material which no one could bring up in many sessions, as if these sciences were before his very eyes and he was picking and choosing from them at will. A time came when his companions took to over-praising him and this drove him to be satisfied with himself until he became conceited before his fellow human beings. He became convinced

that he was a scholar capable of independent reasoning (*mujtahid*). Henceforth he began to answer each and every scholar great and small, past and recent, until he went all the way back to Umar [Umar ibn al-Khattab, the second of the four "rightly-guided" caliphs] and faulted him in some manner. This reached the ears of [the local ruler] who reprimanded him. Ibn Taymiyya went to see him, apologized, and asked for forgiveness."[86]

G.F. Haddad, a modern Islamic scholar, tells us that despite his brilliance, Ibn Taymiyya's disparaging manners alienated even his admirers. His debating technique was simply to overwhelm his opponents with a barrage of quotes and citations. Upon close examination, however, these often turned out to be dubious, either in terms of Islamic doctrine or of the soundness of the chain of transmission from the Prophet.[87]

There is one last point to be made here. Even though the conquering Mongols and their rulers had converted to Islam, Ibn Taymiyya still referred to them as "unbelievers." Applying such an epithet to fellow Muslims was traditionally and strictly forbidden. Perhaps this, too, was a sign of "some kink in the brain."

The Greatest Traveler of Medieval Islam: Ibn Battuta (1304–1368/69)

The Moroccan scholar Ibn Battuta tells us,

I left Tangier, my birthplace, on Thursday, 2nd Rajab 725 [14 June 1325], being at that time twenty-two years of age, with the intention of making the Pilgrimage to the Holy House [in Mecca] and the Tomb of the Prophet [in Medina]. I set out alone, find no companion to cheer the way with friendly intercourse, and no party of travelers with whom to associate myself. Swayed by an overmastering impulse within me, and a long-cherished desire to visit these glorious sanctuaries, I resolved to quit all my friends and tear myself away from my home.[88]

Unlike most other medieval travelers, who journeyed for such practical reasons as trade, pilgrimage or education, Ibn Battuta traveled chiefly for the joy of meeting new people and learning about new lands. As a learned man (he had received a traditional legal and literary education), he was known as "the traveler of Islam" and was welcomed by the great and the good wherever he went. Making it his policy never to travel any road twice, in 29 years he covered about 75,000 miles in journeys to almost all Muslim countries, ranging as far afield as Mali, India, China and Indonesia.

He described his adventures, generally accurately, in a famous book entitled *Travels* (*Rihlah*), which still makes good reading today. Here, for example, is his description of Jerusalem, which he visited in 1335:

We then reached Jerusalem (may God ennoble her!), third in excellence after the two holy shrines of Mecca and Medina and the place where the Prophet was caught up into heaven. Its walls were destroyed by the illustrious King Saladin and his Successors, for fear less the Christians should seize it and fortify themselves in it.... The Dome of the Rock is a building of extraordinary beauty, solidity, elegance, and singularity of shape.... Both outside and inside the decoration is so magnificent and the workmanship is so surpassing as to defy description. The greater part is covered with gold so that the eyes of one who gazes on its beauties are dazzled by its brilliance, now glowing like a mass of light, now flashing like lightning. In the centre of the Dome is the blessed rock from which the Prophet ascended to heaven, a great rock projecting about a man's height.... Encircling the rock are two railings of excellent workmanship, the one nearer the rock being artistically constructed in iron and the other in wood.[89]

Ibn Battuta was also a good reporter on the practical aspects of Central Asian life. Here is his account of pearl divers in the Persian Gulf:

Before diving the diver puts on his face a sort of tortoiseshell mask and a tortoiseshell clip on his nose, then he ties a rope round his waist and dives.... When he reaches the bottom of the sea he finds the shells there stuck in the sand between small stones, and pulls them out by hand or cuts them loose with a knife which he has for that purpose, and puts them in a leather bag slung round his neck.

When his breath becomes restricted he pulls the rope, and the man holding the rope ... feels the movement and pulls him up into the boat. The bag is taken from him and the shells are opened. Inside them are found pieces of flesh which are cut out with a knife, and when they come into contact with the air solidify and turn into pearls [sic]. These are then collected, large and small together; the sultan takes his fifth and the remainder are bought by the merchants who are there in the boats. Most of them are the creditors of the divers, and they take the pearls in quittance of [the divers'] debt or so much of it as is their due.[90]

Great Sufi Poet: Hafiz (1325/1326–1389/90)

Hafiz (or *Hafez*) means "someone who knows the Quran by heart." It is said that Hafiz (or, more fully, Muhammad Shams Od-din Hafiz) had memorized this holy scripture in fourteen different ways, probably by listening to recitations of it by his father, who, remarkably, was only an impoverished coal merchant.[91] Trained as a Quranic scholar, Hafiz himself wrote commentaries on theological subjects and served as a poet at the court in Shiraz (Iran).

He brought to perfection the classic lyric poem of six to fifteen couplets which is known as the *ghazal* ("love lyric"). Even in translation, the opening lines from this *ghazal* entitled "Love's Awakening" manage to evoke the feelings of love and of loss:

> Ho, saki [a poetic term for a wine-bearer], haste, the beaker bring,
> Fill up, and pass it round the ring;
> Love seemed at first an easy thing—
> But ah! the hard awakening.

> So sweet perfume the morning air
> Did lately from her tresses bear,
> Her twisted, musk-diffusing hair —
> What's heart's calamity was there!
> Within life's caravanserai
> What brief security have I,
> When momently the bell doth cry,
> "Bind your loads; the hour is nigh!"[92]

Like other Sufi writers, Hafiz uses "wine" in a figurative sense, i.e., to express the ecstasy of the believer's union with the divine. Another of his odes proclaims:

> The rose has flushed red, the bud has burst,
> And drunk with joy is the nightingale —
> Hail, Sufis! lovers of wine, all hail!
> For wine is proclaimed to a world athirst.[93]

Probably because of his Sufi beliefs and because in his later days he taught with the personal authority of someone who claims to have had a direct experience of God, the orthodox clergy would not allow Hafiz a proper Muslim burial. This posed a problem because he was very popular with the local people. To resolve this issue, it was finally decided to write out Hafiz's *ghazals* in couplets, put them into a container, and then let a young boy (so young he could not read) pull out one couplet at random. All agreed that they would treat that couplet as an oracle and would comply with its advice, no matter what it was.

The couplet chosen by the boy turned out to be a tongue-in-cheek rebuke from Hafiz to the local clergy. It read:

> Neither Hafiz's corpse, nor his life negate, wait.[94]

The Greatest Arab Historian: Ibn Khaldun (1332–1406)

Born in Tunis, Ibn Khaldun lived in turbulent times and seemed to make enemies very easily. A modern Islamic biographer tells that

> There is certainly no doubt that he behaved in a detached, self-interested, haughty, ambitious and equivocal manner. He himself does not attempt to hide this, and openly describes ... his successive changes of allegiance.[95]

Because of his troubled era and his abrasive personality, Ibn Khaldun was often on the move and held a wide variety of jobs: secretary to the Sultan of Morocco, diplomat, prime minister, leader of a military expedition, professor at Cairo's al-Azhar University, chief judge of Cairo, and author. He is important to us because he was the first Arab scholar bold enough to invent and to base his writings on a nonreligious philosophy of history. A modern scholar, Charles Issawi, tells us that "Just as

Ibn Khaldun had no known predecessors in the history of Muslim thought, so he had no worthy successors."[96]

In his most celebrated work, the *Introduction* (*Muqaddimah*) to his multivolume history of the world (*Kitab al-Ibar*), he set out to devise a new science. This he termed "the science of culture" (*ilm al-umran*) and described it thus:

> This science ... has its own subject, viz., human society, and its own problems, viz., the social transformations that succeed each other in the nature of society.[97]

Arnold Toynbee, the great twentieth century English historian, saw this as a truly remarkable and original achievement. It was, he said, "a philosophy of history which is undoubtedly the greatest work of its kind that has ever yet been created by any mind in any time or place."[98] In contrast to all earlier Islamic historians, Ibn Khaldun looked for and found a purely secular explanation for the cyclical rise and fall of dynasties. His research led him to conclude instead that a *natural* historical cycle was at work here. This cycle was based not on God's will but on human politics, psychology, history and sociology, as well as on economic and environmental factors.

In Ibn Khaldun's analysis, tribally organized migratory peoples such as the *bedouin* have a very strong *asabiyya* (*esprit de corps*, i.e., the common spirit existing among members of a group and inspiring enthusiasm, devotion and strong regard for the honor of the group). This positive outlook on communal life helps them conquer the decadent city-dweller people standing in their path. Having attained power themselves, the vigor of these tribal peoples is for a time renewed by successive "builders" (charismatic leaders) from their own group. Ultimately, however, the migrants settle down and become city dwellers themselves. When this happens, the soft life of their new sedentary existence inevitably encourages decadence, internal rivalries and jealousies.

These defects sap the military effectiveness of the troops of the ruling king. As a result, he is forced to pay ruinous wages to hardy mercenary troops because he needs them to prop up his rule. It is not long before his weakened dynasty is in turn overthrown by a new group of tribesmen who have a vigorous *esprit de corps*.[99]

Evaluating Ibn Khaldun

Remarkably, Ibn Khaldun also worked closely with and has left us a vivid account of his interviews with the Mongol conqueror Timur. In 1400 Ibn Khaldun played a key role in arranging the peaceful surrender of Damascus to Timur. We can easily imagine that in this great warlord Ibn Khaldun found his perfect example of tribal social cohesiveness.[100]

According to the *Encyclopedia of Islam*, Ibn Khaldun was the first Arab scholar to arrive at "a dynamic conception of the dialectic development of the destiny of man, and at a system of history which is retrospectively intelligible, rational and necessary. His famous cyclic schema of historical interpretation, which in itself is not particularly original, must be included, in order for its true meaning to be seen, in this general view."[101]

Ibn Khaldun's *Introduction* did not become widely known in Western scholarly circles until it was translated into French in 1863–1868. Since then, he has been hailed in the West as "a thinker who was an aberrant genius"; as a "solitary genius" whose *Introduction* represents "one of the solemn moments of human thought"; and as "arguably one of the greatest minds of all time."[102]

Despite his brilliance and his achievements, there is nevertheless a note of sadness in Ibn Khaldun's life. This is how the French scholar R. Brunschvig summed it up:

> Just as he had no forerunners among Arabic writers, so he had no successors or emulators in this idiom until the [modern] period. Although he had a certain influence in Egypt on some writers of the end of the Middle Ages, it can be stated that, in his native Barbary, neither his *Muqaddimah* nor his personal teaching left any permanent mark. And indeed the systematic lack of comprehension and the resolute hostility which this nonconformist thinker of genius encountered among his own people forms one of the most moving dramas, one of the saddest and more significant pages, in this history of Muslim culture.[103]

Leading Mathematician and Astronomer: al-Kashi (c. 1380–1429)

Little is known about the early life of this Iranian scholar. He swims into our ken only on 2 June 1406, when he is recorded as having observed a lunar eclipse; after this, the trail becomes very clear because al-Kashi was such a prolific writer. His initial treatise was an astronomical study of 1407 entitled *The Stairway to Heaven* [*Sullam al-sama*], *on Resolution of Difficulties Met by Predecessors in the Determination of Distances and Sizes* [of heavenly bodies]. This was followed in 1410–1411 by a *Compendium of the Science of Astronomy* (*Mukhtasar dar ilm-i hayat*), dedicated to the sultan of Esfahan and Fars.

The first of al-Kashi's major books, a set of astronomical tables (*Khaqani Zij*), appeared in 1413–1414 and was dedicated to the ruler Ulugh Beg, Timur's grandson, whose patronage al-Kashi sought. According to J.J. O'Conner, a historian of mathematics, this book contained "detailed tables of the longitudinal motion of the sun, the moon, and the planets. Al-Kashi also gives the tables of the longitudinal and latitudinal parallaxes for certain geographical locations, tables of eclipses, and tables of the visibility of the moon."[104]

About 100 years later, the emperor Babur (see the next chapter) said that these tables were "used all over the world."[105] They were still in use in Europe in 1665, 1767, and in the nineteenth century; indeed, as late as 1917 a Persian-Arabic glossary of the star-names in the tables was published in Washington, D.C.[106]

Two more works were forthcoming in 1416 before Ulugh Beg finally summoned al-Kashi to Samarkand (Uzbekistan). These were the *Treatise on the Explanation of Observational Instruments* (*Risala dar sharh-i alal-i rasd*) and *The Garden Excursion, on the Method of Construction of the Instrument Called Plate of Heavens* (*Nuzha al-hadaiq fi kayfiyya san'a al-ala musamma bi tabaq al-mana tiq*). In *The Garden Excursion* al-Kashi described his invention of a device (the equatorium) which was used to find the positions of the planets.

It was in Samarkand that in 1420 al-Kashi founded a famous *madrasa* which attracted sixty of the greatest scholars of his day. Four years later, he began to build a great observatory at Samarkand, which included a huge meridian arc or sextant installed in the ground.[107] Al-Kashi also began to write what would become his three most celebrated mathematical works[108]:

The *Treatise on the Circumference* (*Risala al-muh i tiyya*, 1424) computed the value of 2 *pi* to the equivalent of 16 decimal places of accuracy, setting a record that lasted almost 200 years.

The *Key of Arithmetic* (*Mifta hal-hisab*, 1427) was such a good teaching tool that numerous copies were made over the coming centuries. Modern commentators tell us that

> In the richness of its contents and in the application of arithmetical and algebraic methods to the solution of various problems, including several geometric ones, and in the clarity and elegance of expression, the voluminous textbook is one of the best in the whole of medieval literature; it attests to both the author's erudition and his pedagogical ability.[109]

The *Treatise on the Chord and Sine* (*Risala al-watar wa'l-jaib*, c. 1429) calculates the sine of 1° correct to sexagesimal places and also studies cubic equations. His approach to this latter problem has been described by modern writers as "one of the best achievements of medieval algebra."[110]

Historian Who Set the Record Straight: al-Maqrizi (1364–1442)

Al-Maqrizi was an Egyptian chronicler, a pupil of Ibn Khaldun, and the first to recognize the importance of the Fatimid dynasty in the history of Egypt and Syria. His three-volume chronicle of the Fatimids, entitled the *Admonition of True Believers: Information about the Fatimid Imam-caliphs* (*Ittiaz al-hunafa bi-akhbar al-aimma al-Fatimiyyin al-khulafa*), correctly depicts this Ismaili dynasty as the legitimate precursor of the Ayyubid and Mamluk sultanates in Egypt, rather than merely as a heretical usurper.[111]

Al-Maqrizi was able to breathe life into history. Although the tone of his description of the Black Death (bubonic plague) in Cairo in 1348 suggests that it was an eyewitness account, it was actually written many decades after the fact. Al-Maqrizi claimed that more than a thousand people a day, or a total of 900,000 people, died of the plague[112]:

> A man would sense that he had fever in his body. Then he would feel nauseated and spit blood, with death following. One after another the people of his household would go after him until all of them had perished. As everyone left alive was sure he would die of the disease, all the people prepared themselves for the end, increasing their charities, making expiation and turning to worship.... [Cairo had become so desolate that] a person might walk all the way from one end to the other without ever being jostled.][113]

In another work, *The Road to Knowledge of the Return of the Kings* (translated in 1848 by Henry Bohn), al-Maqrizi described the Seventh Crusade. In 1249, Louis IX, king of France, had sailed to Egypt with 100 ships carrying somewhere between 15,000 and 35,000 Crusaders to capture Cairo.[114] The French believed that if they could seize this capital, the Muslims would be willing to give them Jerusalem in order to get Cairo back.

Although Louis IX managed to capture the port of Damietta and the castle of al-Mansurah, floods on the Nile, an outbreak of the plague and a shortage of food prevented him from reaching Cairo itself. He was forced to retreat. In so doing, the king himself, his household, barons and bedraggled army all were captured by the Egyptians in 1250, who held them until a high ransom had been paid for their release.

Al-Maqrizi also gives us vivid details about this ransom:

> The emir Abou Ali was nominated to treat with the king of France for his ransom, and for the surrender of Damietta. After many conferences and disputes, it was agreed that the French should evacuate Damietta, and that the king, and all [French] prisoners in Egypt, should be set at liberty, on condition of paying down one half of such ransom as should be fixed on. The king of France sent orders to the governor of Damietta to surrender the town, but he refused to obey, and new orders were necessary. At last it was given up to the Muslims, after having remained eleven months in the hands of the enemy. The king paid four hundred thousand pieces of gold, as well for his own ransom as for that of the queen, his brother, and the other lords that had accompanied them.[115]

Finally, with a good eye for interesting historical detail, al-Maqrizi tells us about a clever ruse used by a Muslim soldier during the struggles with the French:

> Not a day passed without skirmishes on both sides and with alternate success. The Muslims were particularly anxious to take prisoners, to gain information as to the state of the enemy's army, and used all sorts of strategies for this purpose. A soldier from Cairo bethought himself of putting his head inside of a watermelon, the interior of which he had scooped out, and of thus swimming toward the French camp; a Christian soldier, not suspecting a trick, leaped into the Nile to seize the melon; but the Egyptian was a stout swimmer, and catching hold of him, dragged him to his general.[116]

Chapter VII

The Age of Great Empires (1453–1699)

Historical Background

Ottoman rule continued to expand into Egypt, Turkey, Syria, North Africa and Arabia after the capture of Constantinople by Mehmed II in 1453. Suleyman I (r. 1520–1566), known in the Islamic world at the "Lawgiver" and in the West as the "Magnificent," brought the Ottoman Empire to its apogee.

On other fronts, the Safavids held sway in Iran and Iraq and outlasted the Mughal Empire. Iran became the center of a major cultural flowering, expressed through the visual arts and the refinement of the Persian language. The Mughal Emperor Babar (1483–1530) and his successors governed much of India. Islam sent down deep roots in sub–Saharan Africa and in the Malaysian archipelago as well.

The British historian Marshall Hodgson reminds us that

> In the sixteenth century of our era, a visitor from Mars might have supposed that the human world was on the verge of becoming Muslim. He would have based his judgment partly on the strategic and political advantages of the Muslims, but partly also on the vitality of their general culture. Their social and political eminence leaps to the eye. In the eastern hemisphere, where lived nine-tenths of mankind, allegiance to Islam was far more widespread than any other allegiance.[1]

In this era there were two major Islamic confrontations with Europe: the Turks besieged Vienna twice, first in 1529 and then again in 1683. If, historically, the West's hostility toward Islam can be said to date from the Crusades and from the Islamic conquest of Spain, these threats to Vienna raised new fears of Islamic warriors overrunning Christian Europe.

Islamic power began to ebb, however, after the first major Ottoman reversal — the Treaty of Carlowitz (1699), which ceded Ottoman Hungary to Austria. This was the first peace signed by a defeated Ottoman Empire with the Christian West. As such, it can be considered a milestone in the military, economic and political decline of the Islamic world from its former glories.

"The Conqueror": Mehmed II (1432–1481)

This great military leader, Mehmed II, captured not only Constantinople (renaming it Istanbul) but also the lands in Anatolia and the Balkans that would form the heartland of the Ottoman Empire for the next 400 years. Seeing himself as the successor to the Byzantine emperors and wanting to create a universal empire of his own, Mehmed II built huge palaces, especially the Topkapi Palace, completed in 1478 and known as "The Palace of Felicity"; encouraged the arts; legislated new codes of law; made Turkish and Persian (rather than the Greek used by the Byzantines) the official languages of administration; and formed a new navy based on Italian designs and Greek seamanship.[2]

Although his subjects considered Mehmed II to be excessively autocratic, he was also, paradoxically, one of the most broadminded and liberal of the Ottoman rulers. He brought Italian humanists and Greek scholars to his court after the fall of Constantinople, had a credo of the Christian faith translated into Turkish, amassed a palace library of Greek and Latin works, caused the walls of his palace to be decorated with Italian frescoes, built a grand mosque and surrounded it with eight *madrasas*, and himself composed a collection of poems. Under his rule, mathematics, astronomy, and Muslim theology reached a high point in the Islamic world.

Above and opposite: The Harem (women's quarters) is the most private and most beautifully decorated part of the Topkapi Palace in Istanbul. These three photographs show the rooms of the Sultan's mother. (Photographs courtesy of André Kahlmeyer.)

7. The Age of Great Empires (1453–1699)

Renaissance Emperor of Central Asia: Babur (1483–1530)

Founder of the Mughal dynasty of India in 1526, Babur (this nickname is variously said to mean either "tiger" or "beaver") was a highly accomplished soldier, statesman, poet and diarist. He was the first Islamic leader to use primitive firearms, i.e., muskets and artillery, in battle. His autobiography, *The Memoirs of Babur* (*Baburnama*), is one of the earliest known autobiographies in the Islamic world and gives us a remarkably detailed account of Central Asian life in his day. A fine copy, illustrated by exquisite miniature paintings, was prepared for the Mughal Emperor Akbar, Babur's grandson (see the section later in this chapter). It has become a classic and will be our focus here.[3]

Having a good eye for colorful details and a ready pen, Babur was an excellent diarist. He wrote in colloquial Turkic (a dialect of northeastern Iran) rather than in the refined stilted language of the Persian court. Here are three vignettes from his travels near Fergana (close to Samarkand, Uzbekistan), Samarkand and Tashkent:

> On the flank of the Bara-koh [a symmetrical hill in Fergana] is a mosque called the Jauza Masjid [the Twin Mosque]. Between this mosque and the town, a great main canal flows from the direction of the hill. Below the court of the mosque lies a shady and delightful clover-meadow where every passing traveler takes a rest. It is the joke of the ragamuffins of Osh to let out water from the canal on anyone happening to fall asleep in the meadow.[4]

> We entered the valley [near Samarkand] and made our way up it. Many horses and camels were left on its steep and narrow roads and at its sharp and precipitous saddles. Before we covered the 25 miles to Sara-taq pass we had to make three or four night-halts. A pass! and what a pass! Never has such a steep and narrow pass been seen; never have such ravines and precipices been traversed. We got through those dangerous narrow passages and abrupt drops, those perilous heights and knife-edge saddles, with much difficulty and suffering, with countless hardships and miseries.[5]

> [The local soldiers Babur saw near Tashkent] were in Moghul caps, long coats of embroidered Chinese satin, and had Moghul quivers and saddles of green shagreen-leather, and Moghul horses adorned in their distinctive fashion. [The Mughal leader] had brought rather few men, probably somewhere between 1000 and 2000. He was a man of singular manners, a mighty master of the sword, and brave. His preferred weapon was the sword. He used to say that [other arms, e.g., the mace, saddle-hatchet and battle-axe] ... leave a mark only from the point with which they make contact. The sword, however, works from point to hilt. He never parted with his keen-edged sword; it was either at his waist or in his hand.[6]

Admiral and Poet: Sidi Ali Reis (fl. 1552–1557)

What is known as "the little book" of the Turkish admiral Sidi Ali Reis, entitled the *Mirror of Countries* (*Mirat ul Memalik*), is worth reading. It is remarkably concise

The emperor Babur, reading. Babur established the Timurid Mugahl empire in India but he is now remembered more for his literary skills than for his military prowess. (Copyright© The British Museum, 1520–66; 1921 10 11 03.)

(only thirty-three pages on the Internet), well-organized and well-written. The Turkish-to-English translation used here was done in 1917 by Charles F. Horne, who tells us in his introduction that

> [Reis was] a man of many varied accomplishments; a genuine type of the Islamic culture of his time, and a representative of that class of official and military dignitaries whose influence is chiefly due to the fact that the Ottoman Empire, extending over three continents, attained that eminent height of culture which it occupied during the reign of Suleiman the Great.[7]

Reis opens his book with a clear explanation of its purpose:

> When Sultan Suleiman had taken up his winter residence in Aleppo [Syria], I, the author of these pages, was appointed to the Admiralship of the Egyptian fleet [in 1552], and received instructions to fetch back to Egypt the ships [15 galleys], which some time ago had been sent to Basrah on the Persian Gulf. But, "Man proposes, God disposes." I was unable to carry out my mission, and as I realized the impossibility of returning by water, I resolved to go back to Turkey by the overland route, accompanied by a few tried and faithful Egyptian soldiers....
>
> Our travels ended, my companions and fellow-adventurers persuaded me to write down our experiences, and the dangers through which we had passed, an accurate account of which is almost impossible to give; also to tell of the cities and the many wonderful sights we had seen, and of the holy shrines we had visited. And so this little book sees the light; in it I have tried to relate, in simple and plain language, the troubles and difficulties, the suffering and distress which beset our path, up to the time that we reached Constantinople. Considering the matter it contains this book ought to have been entitled "A tale of woe," but with a view to the scene of action I have called it "Mirror of Countries," and as such I commend it to the reader's kind attention.[8]

An ever-resourceful man who could use his own poems to defuse difficult situations, Reis was also ready with a creative solution when the second Mughal ruler, Humayun (1508–1556), died after tumbling down a flight of steps. Humayun's son and successor, Akbar, was at that time off on a journey. Akbar was informed of his father's death but for reasons of political stability it was essential that the death not become public knowledge until Akbar could return to the capital. Reis therefore counseled the use of a double. As a result,

> The divan [council of State] met as usual, the nobles were summoned, and a public announcement was made that the Emperor intended to visit his country-seat, and would go there on horseback. Soon after, however, it was announced that on account of the unfavorable weather the trip had to be abandoned. On the next day a public audience was announced, but as the astrologers did not prophesy favorably for it, this also had to be given up. All this, however, somewhat alarmed the army, and on the Tuesday it was thought advisable to give them a sight of their monarch.
> A man called Molla Bi, who bore a striking resemblance to the late Emperor,

though somewhat slighter of stature, was arrayed in the imperial robes and placed on a throne specially erected for this purpose in the large entrance hall. His face and eyes were veiled. The Chamberlain Khoshhal Bey stood behind, and the first Secretary in front of him, while many officers and dignitaries, as well as the people from the riverside, on seeing their Sovereign, made joyful obeisance to the sound of music. The physicians were handsomely rewarded and the recovery of the monarch was universally credited.[9]

Reis was gone so long that when he got back to Turkey he found that he had been considered as killed in action and that his post of Admiral had been given to another officer. Emperor Suleyman welcomed him warmly, however, and appointed him to a high position. Reis closes his book with this advice to the reader:

He who wishes to profit by this narrative let him remember that not in vain aspirations after greatness, but in a quiet and contented mind lieth the secret of the true strength which perisheth not.... Let [the traveler] never cease to long for the day that he shall see his native shores again, and always cling loyally to his Padishah [the Ottoman emperor]. He who doeth this shall not perish abroad; God will grant him his desire both in this world and in the next, and he shall rejoice in the esteem and affection of his fellow men.[10]

The "Shadow of God on Earth": Suleyman I "the Magnificent" (1494/1495–1566)

Suleyman ruled the Ottoman Empire for forty-six years, an era widely considered to have been the golden age of the empire. Foreigners knew him as "the Magnificent" but his own countrymen preferred to term him "the Lawgiver" (*Kanuni*) because he promulgated a code of "Sultanic" law known as *kanun*. This new body of law was needed because the *sharia* could not cover all the complexities of Ottoman political, economic and social life. Although *kanun* was purely secular law, it was treated as a valid extension of religious law. The general rule was that *kanun* would be used for any purpose as long as it did not contradict the *sharia*.

Working together with the great architect Sinan (see the following section), Suleyman refurbished the Dome of the Rock in Jerusalem; built the marvelous Suleymaniye Mosque in Istanbul; and erected numerous palaces, bridges, aqueducts and other public works. Although most widely known for his military prowess (in the sixteenth and seventeenth centuries, the Ottoman army was probably the most efficient military force in the world[11]), Suleyman was something of an intellectual as well.

He wrote poems which are said to be among the best in the Islamic world. He studied the new European discoveries in navigation and geography. He supported what Richard Hooker, a modern writer, has called "an army of artists, religious scholars and philosophers that outshone the most educated courts in Europe."[12] Under his rule, both friends and foes agreed that the Ottoman state was the largest and militarily most powerful empire in the world.[13]

Topping this hill in Istanbul is the beautiful Suleymaniye Mosque, built in the 1550s by the great Ottoman architect Sinan. Below it is the Rustem Pasha Mosque, built by Sinan in 1560 for Rustem Pasha, grand vizier and Suleyman's son-in-law. (Photograph courtesy of André Kahlmeyer.)

As a world conqueror who made Europe tremble before the might of Islam, Suleyman was not shy about advertising his own greatness. This is how he defines himself in inscriptions on two monuments:

> Slave of God, powerful with the power of God, deputy of God on earth, obeying the commands of the Quran and enforcing them throughout the world, master of all lands, the shadow of God over all nations, Sultan of Sultans in all the lands of Persians and Arabs, the propagator of Sultanic laws, the tenth Sultan

of the Ottoman Khans, Sultan, son of Sultan, Suleyman Khan.

Slave of God, master of the world, I am Suleyman and my name is read in all the prayers in all the cities of Islam. I am the Shah of Baghdad and Iraq, Caesar of all the lands of Rome, and the Sultan of Egypt. I seized the Hungarian crown and gave it to the least of my slaves.[14]

Even near the age of 60, Suleyman was still an impressive figure. In 1555 the Habsburg ambassador reported that

Istanbul: the Suleymaniye Mosque at night. (Photograph courtesy of André Kahlmeyer.)

[The sultan's] dignity of demeanor and his general physical appearance are worthy of the ruler of so vast an empire. He has always been frugal and temperate, and was so even in his youth.... Even in his earlier years he did not indulge in wine or in those unnatural vices to which the Turks are often addicted.... He is a strict guardian of his religion and its ceremonies, being not less desirous of upholding his faith than of extending his domains.[15]

To conceal his bad complexion (which was probably due to an illness), Suleyman used to put red makeup on his face. The reason for this, said the ambassador, was that "he fancies that it contributes to inspire greater fear in foreign potentates if they think that he is well and strong.[16]

The Greatest Ottoman Architect: Sinan (1489–1588)

Known in Turkish as *Mimar Koca Sinan* ("Great Architect Sinan") because of his unprecedented achievements, Sinan brought the classic mosque, with all its characteristic domes and soaring minarets, to an apogee. His most famous buildings are the Sehzade Mosque and the Suleyman Mosque, both in Istanbul, and the Selim Mosque at Edirne.

As a youth, Sinan benefited from the Ottoman institution of *devshirme*—the policy of recruiting promising Christian boys throughout the empire for conversion to Islam and then for an intensive education in military and administrative skills.[17]

Watercraft plying the Bosporus bring to mind Istanbul's intellectual and strategic importance: it linked the lands of Europe and Asia. In the background is the Suleymaniye Mosque. (Photograph courtesy of André Kahlmeyer.)

Recruited during the reign of Suleyman the Magnificent, he quickly advanced from cavalry officer to construction officer and began to build bridges and fortifications. He rose to be chief of artillery and then, in 1538, he became Suleyman's chief architect.

Sinan's output over a period of fifty years was prodigious. He designed no fewer than 79 mosques, 34 palaces, 33 public baths, 19 tombs, 55 schools, 16 poorhouses, 7 *madrasas*, and 12 caravansaries, not to mention assorted granaries, fountains, aqueducts, and hospitals.[18] A total of 477 buildings, of which 196 are still standing, have been attributed to him.[19]

His first architectural success was the Sehzade Mosque, which was finished in 1548. It set the pattern for his later mosques: a large central dome is supported by a square base and is graced by half-domes and smaller domes. Sinan's most outstanding building, however, is now thought to be the Suleyman Mosque, built between 1550 and 1557. Influenced by the huge dome of the Hagia Sophia (the great Byzantine cathedral completed in 537), this mosque was the largest ever constructed in the Ottoman Empire and formed the hub of the palace complex.

Flanked by four tall minarets, its huge central dome, which is 87 feet in diameter and 174 feet high, is pierced by 32 openings. These simultaneously convey a feeling of weightlessness and bathe the vast interior in sunlight. Today the mosque complex includes religious schools, a hospital and medical college, and the tombs of Suleyman and his Russian wife, Haseki Hurrem.

The Selim Mosque was considered by Sinan himself to be his finest work. Built between 1569 and 1575, its central dome (102 feet in diameter), flanked by the four tallest minarets in Turkey (230 feet high), rests on eight piers with deep arcades. Evaluating Sinan's contribution to Islamic architecture is difficult only because this contribution was so great. The art historian Oleg Grabar summarized it very well:

> All of these buildings exhibit total clarity and logic in both plan and elevation; every part has been considered in relation to the whole, and each architectural element has acquired a hierarchic function in the total composition. Whatever is unnecessary has been eliminated.... Everything in these buildings was subordinated to an imposing central dome. A sort of cascade of descending half domes, vaults, and ascending buttresses leads the eye up and down the building's exterior. Minarets, slender and numerous, frame the exterior composition, while the open space of the surrounding courts prevents the building from being swallowed by the surrounding city.[20]

Ruler of India: Emperor Akbar (1542–1605)

The greatest Mughal emperor of India, Akbar was an active patron of religion and philosophy and was personally interested in these subjects. He was a Muslim but was quite unprejudiced, being tolerant of other faiths and arranging for vigorous debates to be held in his court between Muslims and advocates of other religions (Christians, Hindus, Sikhs and Parsis).

He liberally financed the work of artists, scholars, translators, poets and musicians. About 100 painters, many of them Hindus, worked in Akbar's court and produced the great *Book of Hamza* (*Hamzanama*) with its 1,400 illustrations.[21] This work is a unique visual collection of dramatic stories loosely based on the adventures of Hamza, Mohammed's uncle. It took nearly fifteen years to complete and is considered not only one of the great masterpieces of Mughal painting but also one of the most impressive manuscripts ever produced in the Islamic world.[22] The artists who worked on it carefully studied the European paintings brought to the court by Jesuit missionaries and then employed the European techniques of perspective and realism in their own works.

Akbar also supported state workshops that produced beautiful textiles and decorative objects. Although illiterate himself, he had the Sanskrit classics translated into Persian and gave illustrated copies to his court. He even founded a short-lived, ecumenical, mystical sect of his own — the Divine Faith (*Din-e Ilahi*), in which he played a central but controversial role. In 1579, for example, he gave a sermon which ended with the familiar phrase *Allahu Akbar*. This traditional Muslim maxim usually means "God is great!" but in this context it was understood to mean instead: "God is Akbar!"[23]

Under his rule, Fatehpur Sikri, the new capital (near Agra in northwest India, begun in 1570 and abandoned in 1586) flourished as a center of culture. It remains one of the finest examples of Islamic architecture in India, being notable for its imposing mosque, the Jami Masjid, which became a model for later Mughal mosques.

Noteworthy, too, is a massive triumphal gateway, the Victory Gate (*Buland Darwazah*), built to celebrate the birth of Akbar's first son, Salim.

Akbar had an exceptionally high degree of intelligence, curiosity, tolerance and determination. A contemporary Sufi biographer, Abdulfazl Allami, considered him to be the ideal philosopher-king and the Perfect Man whom Sufis thought would appear once in every generation to give divine guidance to the faithful. Allami believed Akbar was intent on building a civilization so based on the Sufi ideals of "universal peace" and "universal love" that conflict would become unthinkable.[24]

Akbar's traits of tolerance and determination, however, led to friction with religious leaders.[25] A Sufi firebrand, Ahmad Sirhindi (d. 1625), denounced his religious pluralism as a threat to orthodoxy; called for firmer adherence to the *sharia*; and proclaimed that he, not Akbar, was the Perfect Man of the age.[26] When Akbar died, Sirhindi was thrown into prison after he had boasted to a crowd that during Akbar's reign "the sun of guidance was hidden behind the veil of error."[27]

Moreover, Akbar's interest in Christian doctrines led Jesuit missionaries to assume, incorrectly, that the emperor was ready to convert to Christianity. Muslim theologians did not like it when he forced them to accept him as arbiter on subtle points of Islamic law over which they themselves disagreed. They also disapproved of his discussions with representatives of other religions.

Nevertheless, later generations would give Akbar high marks on the cultural front. His son Salim, who became the emperor Jahangir, wrote of his father:

> He associated with the good of every race and creed and persuasion.... The professors of various faiths had room in the broad expanse of his incomparable sway. This was different from the practices in other realms, for in Persia there is room for Shias only, and in Turkey, India and Turan [an extensive plain in Kazakhstan, Uzbekistan and Turkmenistan] there is room for Sunnis only.[28]

"A Solitary Tear on the Cheek of Time": The Taj Mahal (Built 1632–1654)

Located in Agra in northern India, the Taj Mahal is the finest example of Mughal architecture. Built by the emperor Shah Jahan (r. 1628–1658) on the banks of the Yamuna River, it is traditionally said to honor his favorite wife, Arjuman Banu Begum, who died in 1631 while giving birth to the couple's fourteenth child. Shah Jahan had given her the title Mumtaz Mahal ("Chosen One of the Palace") on the day of their marriage. That title has since evolved into Taj Mahal, i.e., "the Crown of the Palaces."

This idyllic account of the Taj being intended for Mumtaz Mahal is, alas, quite untrue. As Henri Stierlin, an art historian, explains,

> With its grand scale and splendor, there can be no doubt that the Taj Mahal was intended for the emperor himself. Mumtaz Mahal happened to die before he did, so she came to be buried in this first monument to his reign.... The origin of the Taj Mahal and its intended purpose have thus been mythologized to

The Taj Mahal. (Photograph courtesy of Arendina F. Tieleman.)

satisfy a feeble desire for romance. The truth is that Shah Jahan had begun the project well before 1631 [when Mumtaz Mahal died]. His decision to erect a tomb for himself which would express the greatness of his reign was taken in 1628, and work must have started as soon as he came to the throne. It is impossible to avoid the conclusion that the Taj Mahal was not built for her.[29]

A flawless blend of Islamic, Indian and Iranian styles, the Taj was designated a UNESCO World Heritage site in 1983. Many people, including this writer, consider it to be the most beautiful building in the world. The most concise and most poetic description of this lovely white marble structure was the one provided by the Indian poet Rabindranath Tagore. He wrote that the Taj rises above the banks of the river "like a solitary tear on the cheek of time."[30]

The Taj complex, set on 42 acres, consists of five parts. These include (1) the imposing main gateway of red sandstone, which is about 90 feet high and which carries, in black marble calligraphy, the concluding lines from *sura* 89 ("The Dawn") of the Quran: "O serene soul! Return to your Lord, joyful, and pleasing in His sight. Join My servants and enter My Paradise"; (2) an elaborate garden with canals and fountains, which was designed to be an earthly reflection of the Garden of Paradise and which is now much smaller than it was in Shah Jahan's time; (3) a red sandstone mosque, topped by three white domes, where the faithful came to pray for the repose of the souls of the dead; (4) a guest house architecturally similar to the mosque; and (5) the singularly airy but at the same time substantial presence of the mausoleum itself, crafted in white marble, set on a platform of red sandstone and graced by four slender minarets.

The chief architect of the Taj Mahal may well have been Ustad Ahmad Lahori, a Muslim Indian of Iranian descent. A poem by Luft Allah Muandis, Lahori's son, states that

> He [Ustad Ahmad Lahori] was this monarch's [Shah Jahan's] head architect; his opinion was highly respected in this auspicious presence.
>
> When Agra became the encampment where the Emperor's standards flew, the Emperor heaped royal favors upon him and ordered him to build the mausoleum of Mumtaz Mahal.
>
> Later, by order of Shah Jahan, the just Emperor, Protector of the World, who brandishes his sword at the head of innumerable armies, Ahmad, wise and talented, built the incomparable fort [the Red Fort] at Delhi that has no like.[31]

We may well wonder: what did the Taj cost? A first-hand account came from the French jewel trader Jean-Baptiste Tavernier, who reported in 1679:

> Of all the sepulchers in Agra, that of the wife of Shah Jahan is by far the most splendid.... I saw this great work begun and completed; it took twenty thousand men working continuously for twenty-two years, which would lead one to believe that the cost was exorbitant. It is said that the scaffolding alone cost more than the entire edifice because, there being a shortage of wood, brick had to be used for it, as well as for the soffits of the arches, which was indeed costly and arduous.[32]

The 20,000 workers were recruited in India, Iran, the Ottoman Empire and Europe. The Taj complex is estimated to have cost the staggering sum of five million rupees—an estimate which does not include the marble itself or the semiprecious stones used so lavishly to decorate the buildings of the Taj.

The lightness and excellence of the decoration in the Taj as a whole fully equals that of the mausoleum itself. A modern art historian, Stephen Vernoit, reports that "The Taj Mahal combines perfect harmony of proportions with luxurious surface decoration comprised of carved and inlaid marble."[33] The south arch, for example, displays, in magnificent cursive, harmonious marble inlay, verses 1–21 of *sura* 36 of the Quran, *Ya Sin*. The remaining 62 verses of this *sura* appear on the other three arches.

The calligraphy is by a distinguished Iranian scholar, who signed his work inside one of the calligraphic inscriptions: Amanat Khan, 1048 (this is according to the Muslim calendar; the date corresponds to 1638/1639 C.E.). Of all the artists who worked on the Taj, Amanat Khan's name is the only one which appears on it.[34] Shah Jahan was so pleased with Amanat Khan's work that as a regal present Shah Jahan gave him an elephant.

In a stunning, lavishly illustrated book on the Taj, published in 1993, the art historian Amina Okada draws our attention to the "extraordinary delicacy of the floral motifs embellishing the marble surfaces." She describes them thus:

Depicted with the stamp of realism, yet with a soft lyricism, the stone flowers of the Taj Mahal captivate us with their grace and colorful freshness. From the floral friezes ... there emanates a delicate, serene poetry clearly inspired by a discreet symbolism. In Islamic culture flowers are often seen as symbols of the kingdom of God; the Persian poets describe them as springing forth from the waters of Paradise.[35]

Not for nothing did the court poet Abu Talib Kalim pay a glowing tribute to Shah Jahan's lapidaries. These men used an inlay technique which they called *parchin kari* and which modern art historians know as "hard stone." This consists of very thin slices of hard and semihard semiprecious stone, cut with the greatest care and shaped into tendrils and floral arabesques. Kalim says proudly of these Mughal lapidaries:

> They set stone flowers in the marble
> That by their color, if not their perfume,
> surpass real flowers.[36]

Despite its primary function as a tomb, the Taj could also be a joyful setting for a sumptuous party. Writing in 1875, the French author Louis Rousselet describes how Maharaja Scindia used the monument in just this way:

> It was a time of festivity and pleasure organized by Maharajah Scindia. This prince, the most powerful of Hindustan, had decided to hold high festival at the Taj....
> We step out of the carriages in the first court, in front of the grand portal of the garden: the maharajah's grenadiers lining the alley present arms in our honor and we pass beneath the ribbed vault, from which hang crystal chandeliers....
> The great alleys paved with marble make a dazzling sight: maharajahs and rajahs streaming with diamonds, governors, diplomats, officers bedizened with embroidery, Indian ministers, Rajput barons, and noble ladies from the court of Calcutta, forming a crowd unimaginable in any European ceremony....
> After supper there was a fireworks display on the banks of the Yamuna, which baths the foot of the Taj's terrace in a graceful sweep. A salvo of star rockets, in themselves quite ordinary, is reflected for an instant in the sheet of water. Then, in the subsequent darkness, we see descending the river a sheet of fire that soon covers it completely: thousands of floats fill with naphtha launched from the Toundlah Bridge, after having been set alight, now make a torch of the river.... This strange illumination lasts half an hour and disappears into the jungle. What must the tigers think as they see this river of fire pass by? Toward midnight English orchestras offer us a brilliant concert, then the crowd gradually disperses.[37]

Because of its great beauty and its importance as a symbol of Islamic learning, the Taj will be mentioned twice more — in the conclusions of this book and in appendix 1 (on the decorative and other arts of Islam). At this point, let us content ourselves with the judgment of M.C. Joshi, director of the Archeological Survey of India in 1993. He wrote:

The spirit of perfection here is visible not only in the structural scheme but also in the selection and utilization of building materials, the technique of construction, and the execution of details.... [W]hat is impressive about the Taj is mainly the superfine treatment and not the volume or structural form. It enchants but does not dominate.[38]

Greatest Iranian Philosopher: Mulla Sadra (1571–1640)

A key figure in an intellectual revival in Iran during the seventeenth century, Mulla Sadra has been characterized by a modern scholar, the late John Cooper, as "perhaps the single most important and influential philosopher of the Muslim world in the last four hundred years."[39] Ayatollah Ruhollah Khomeini, it is said, was so profoundly influenced by the teachings of Mulla Sadra that in his last address to the Iranian people before his death he urged them to continue to study Mulla Sadra's works, arguing that there could not be a truly Islamic revolution unless there was a spiritual reformation first.[40]

Because of Mulla Sadra's continuing fame in the Islamic world (he is still hailed by Iranian intellectuals as the greatest philosopher their country has ever produced), it is important to look at his ideas in some detail.

He advanced the Sufi *Ishraqi* ("Illuminist") school of thought to a more sophisticated level and integrated it into the intellectual perspectives of Shiism. ("Illuminism" is the belief in or the claim to a personal, esoteric spiritual knowledge which is not accessible to mankind in general.)

Mulla Sadra wrote more than forty works, the most famous of which is entitled *The Transcendent Wisdom Concerning the Four Intellectual Journeys* (al-Hikma al-muta'aliya fi'il-asfar al-aqliyya al-arba'a) but is usually referred to simply as *The Four Journeys* (*Asfar*). It runs to nine volumes in modern print and brings Shiite and other philosophic traditions together into what Mulla Sadra called a "metaphilosophy." This concept is based on both the revelation and the mysticism of Islam.

The Four Journeys contains a complete presentation of Mulla Sadra's philosophical ideas and describes the training a person must undergo to become a teacher of these mystic ways. The following paragraphs explain how Sajjad Rizvi, a specialist on Mulla Sadra and a lecturer in Islamic philosophy at Bristol University in the United Kingdom, sums up Mulla Sadra's contribution to Islamic learning[41]:

Mulla Sadra's holistic approach to philosophy includes various ways of knowing, internalizing and implementing reality through intellectual, theological and mystical means. For him, philosophy is not an ivory-tower exercise of the mind but a real engagement with reality and self-realization in order to improve oneself. Philosophy is thus a way of life and a spiritual path in itself. This approach allowed Mulla Sadra to combine theological inquiry, mystical insight and discursive reasoning.

His doctrine of being (and, indeed, of mind) teaches that everything in this cosmos is linked to everything else and, ultimately, to God. The more one improves oneself through the pursuit of knowledge and by spiritual exercises, the more one knows and understands and the more one truly "exists."

Mulla Sadra's doctrine of panpsychism (the belief that every creature is a conscious sentient being that has a relationship with other beings and with God) may have been one of the precursors of modern concerns about ecology and the environment.

Finally, Mulla Sadra taught that since all things that exist are in constant flux, metaphysics is thus about studying *processes* and *acts of being*, rather than contemplating the immutable substances postulated by Aristotle. Thus nothing remains the same. By extension, it follows from his thought that even understanding of Islam itself must undergo changes as circumstances develop.

Chapter VIII

The Impact of the West (1699–2003)

Historical Background

The Islamic world experienced many setbacks vis-à-vis the West between 1699 and 2003. The underlying problem was not that Islam itself had somehow "failed" but that the West's military, political and economic power, and its knowledge and technology, had grown exponentially, leaving most of the rest of the world lagging far behind. The modern scholar Marshall Hodgson put it very well:

> It was at this point — at the end of the sixteenth century — that the long-standing ecological and historical foundations of the greatness and creativity of Irano-Semitic culture disappeared.... Unable to keep up or to insulate themselves, most of the non–Western societies were instead undermined and overwhelmed. In the sixteenth century, the Muslim peoples, taken collectively, were at the peak of their power; by the end of the eighteenth century they were prostrate.... If it was any consolation, even the unparalleled power, wealth, and culture of the Chinese were subjected to the same fate.[1]

Under the terms of the Treaty of Carlowitz (1699), which ended sixteen years of hostilities between the Ottoman Empire and the Holy League (Austria, Poland, Venice and Russia), the Ottomans were forced — for the first time in their dealings with the West — to admit defeat. Subsequently, recognizing the potentially lethal threat posed by the West, the Islamic world made some efforts to strengthen itself.

Ottoman Sultan Ahmad III attempted the first Westernizing reforms in 1718–1730, but these failed. Reform efforts in other Islamic lands were usually no more successful. From a modern point of view, one underlying reason was that the Islamic world wanted to import only the technology of the West, not the thought processes and cultural values on which it was based.[2]

Western Europeans (chiefly the Dutch, British and French) came to wield power in many parts of the world where Muslims were numerous. Examples include

Indonesia (after 1602, when the Dutch East India Company was formed),

Bengal (the British East India Company took possession of Bengal and its surrounding lands in 1765 and subsequently colonized the entire Indian subcontinent),

Egypt (briefly occupied by the forces of Napoleonic France in 1798),

Algeria (French occupation began in 1830; Algeria eventually became part of France itself),

the coastal regions of Yemen (which came under British rule in 1839; the British protectorate in the Yemen-Oman-Persian Gulf region eventually expanded to embrace twenty-three Sultanates, Emirates, and tribal regimes),[3]

Tunisia (became a French protectorate in 1881),

Egypt again (the British occupied Egypt in 1882 because it was unable to pay its debts),

much of Africa (in 1884 the Berlin West Africa Conference effectively divided the continent among the European powers),

the Sudan (in 1898 the British general Kitchener captured the Dervish capital of Omdurman),

Libya (conquered by the Italians in 1911), and

Morocco (became a French protectorate in 1912).

By backing the losing side in World War I (1914–1918), the Ottoman Empire assured its own destruction. After the war, Britain and France set up protectorates or were given mandates over lands that became known as Syria, Lebanon, Palestine, Iraq, and Transjordan. Turkey was the only Muslim-populated region of the Middle East to emerge from the first World War as a fully independent state.

Following World War II, when the British withdrew from India (1947), Hindu-Muslim violence flared. The subcontinent was partitioned into two mutually hostile states, India and Pakistan, both of which had large Muslim populations. The establishment of the Jewish state of Israel in Palestine (1948), together with Israel's subsequent victories in the Arab-Israeli conflicts that followed, humiliated the Islamic world.

Anticolonialism and nationalism, once hailed as panaceas for the problems faced by the newly independent Islamic states, did little to improve the lot of the average man or woman in the street. The heavy hand of authoritarian governments in the Islamic world stifled the growth of political, economic, intellectual and academic freedom. Nevertheless, despite all these problems the last three centuries have been highlighted by a number of noteworthy Islamic personalities and cultural achievements. We shall see how Islamic thinkers have tried to deal with the intellectual and cultural challenges posed by the West.

Poet of the Tulip Period: Ahmed Nedim (1681–1730):

Trained as a religious scholar and teacher, Nedim was one of the greatest lyric poets of the Ottoman Turks. He was initially appointed as a librarian by the grand vizier and later became a favorite of Sultan Ahmed III. Indeed, the name "Nedim" means "boon companion."

Nedim worked during the Tulip Period (1718–1730), a time of peace, prosperity and cultural flourishing symbolized by the important role played by the tulip. Known in Anatolia since the eleventh century, this flower was not only used extensively in ornamental decoration and in the arts but Ottoman sultans even held lavish festivals in its honor. A prime tulip bulb could fetch as much as 500 golden coins.

The Tulip Period was also marked by Sultan Ahmed's plans to modernize Turkey by sending temporary ambassadors to the West and, more importantly, by importing European technology, styles and luxuries. This led to such ruinous expenditures, however, that heavy taxes had to be imposed on the sultan's subjects. The extravagances of the court became so extreme and so unpopular that widespread revolts broke out. Nedim himself lost his life. The sultan was dethroned by the Janissaries, an elite corps, selected through *devshirme*, which served the Ottoman sultans. They imprisoned him and put his nephew Mahmud I on the throne. The net result was an abrupt end to the Tulip Period.

Nedim's *qas idahs* (odes), *ghazals* (love lyrics) and *sarqis* (songs) were charming, joyful, colorful and articulate, i.e., a sharp departure from the strict formalism of classic Turkish poets. His songs are still sung in Turkey today. Nedim celebrated the pursuit of pleasure for its own sake; his talent and originality was such that no court poet after him would be his equal. Here is one of his good-humored poems:

> Get your mother's leave, say it's for holy prayers this Friday:
> Out of time's tormenting clutches let us both steal a day,
> And slinking through the secret roads and alleys down to the quay,
> Let's go to the pleasure gardens, come, my sauntering cypress.
> Just you and I, and a singer with exquisite airs—and yet
> Another: with your kind permission, Nedim, the mad poet:
> Let's forget our boon companions today, my joyful coquette—
> Let's go to the pleasure gardens, come, my sauntering cypress.[4]

Advocate of Reform: Shah Wali Allah (1702/1703–1762)

Given a traditional Islamic education in Delhi by his father, who was the principal of a *madrasa* there, Wali Allah was a bright lad who memorized the Quran at the age of seven. He graduated from the *madrasa* at the age of fifteen, became a teacher there two years later, and when his father died in 1719, he became its principal. In 1730 he made the pilgrimage to Mecca and then spent the next two years studying in the Arabian peninsula. This was to prove a critical turning point in his spiritual and intellectual development.

By the time Wali Allah had grown up, the Hindu and Sikh princes of the Deccan and the Punjab had seized a good part of Mughal India. Wanting to restore Muslim dominance, Wali Allah took upon himself the daunting task of trying to find a way to heal the sectarian splits between Indian Sunnis and help them adapt to the new experience of being governed by non–Muslims. In this campaign he was aided by what he believed were visions of the Prophet Muhammad.

As described by his biographer A.D. Muztar, in Mecca and Medina Wali Allah received visions which clarified for him three important but controversial points. These were[5]

1. After Muhammad's death, the order of succession of the four "rightly-guided" caliphs had taken place "under the will and pleasure of God." All four men were fully qualified, so the subsequent disputes between Sunnis and Shias over their respective merits "were just useless and needless. Such a controversy was apt to create hatred and disharmony among the Muslims."
2. Each of the Muslim mystic orders is equally acceptable to God. Muhammad himself would not have favored one of them over the others. Therefore "One may follow any or all of them, with the only proviso that they [are] followed for the sake of God Almighty."
3. None of the four traditional schools of jurisprudence excels its rivals. All of them are fundamentally the same and are therefore equally acceptable to God.

One of the earliest advocates of Islamic reform, Wali Allah was perhaps the first important Muslim thinker to understand that changing political and economic conditions would require changes in how Muslims interpreted their holy scriptures. When he returned to Delhi, he found that Indian Sunnis were suffering from three problems: lack of a strong faith; sectarian divisions, which produced disunity; and moral degeneration. He set about finding ways to mitigate these flaws and thereby strengthen the Muslim community.

To bolster the faith of his Indian coreligionists, Wali Allah gave them a more rational interpretation of Islam, taking pains to present rational arguments side-by-side with traditional dialectics. To deal with disunity, he sought to reconcile competing schools of law and of theology. To improve morality, he advocated "purification of the heart" (*tasawwuf*, i.e., practicing Sufism).[6] This meant putting aside base attitudes such as lust, anger and greed and cultivating in their place the virtues of repentance, fear of God, hope, abstention and love.

The modern scholar Stephen Dale finds that "Shah Wali Allah's intellectual energy contrasts markedly with the inertia of great Muslim states and the relative technological and scientific decline of the Islamic world."[7] Working to revivify Islam in India, Wali Allah compiled an annotated translation of the Quran in Persian, the *lingua franca* of the Muslim literati in the subcontinent.

This was important because, before his time, Quranic scholarship had been the exclusive preserve of scholars who were experts in Arabic. They insisted that the Quran should not be translated and should be available only in Arabic. By making the Quran more accessible, Wali Allah made it easier for nonscholars to understand it. Indeed, one of Wali Allah's supporters believed that "after being imbued with the philosophy of Shah Wali Allah, one can understand the overall message of the Quran directly from its text and can be satisfied with it without being compelled to seek any external aid."[8]

Wali Allah taught that while the principles of Islam were universal and eternal, their application must vary according to the needs of the day. His approach here was three-fold: to interpret these principles in the light of the Quran and the *hadith*; to allow *ijtihad*; and to resolve a theological dispute over the nature and extent of determinism by teaching that while the universe was indeed determined by God, believers still had the freedom to achieve their full potential through their own efforts.

Several of Wali Allah's metaphysical ideas were influenced by Aristotelian thought, but he did not try to prove the existence of God by pure reason. Instead, he followed the Quran's lead and took the position that the notion of God is one that is naturally rooted in the human experience. As such, he taught, knowledge of God is awakened in the human mind and soul by the prophets, especially by Muhammad; it is the prophets who, following divine dictates, give prescriptions for specific courses of action for human beings. Thus, for Wali Allah, divine revelations and prophetic teachings are the only reliable ways to know God.[9]

Wali Allah was a very prolific author. Part of his most important book (in Arabic) on philosophy, *Hujjat Allah al-Balighah*, was published in English in 1996 under the title of *The Conclusive Argument from God*. His works had an important impact on Muslim thought in the subcontinent and still echo there today. Indeed, both liberal Muslims and conservative Hindus distrust them because of the great importance he attaches to a simple, strong, centralized, highly personalized and *purely Muslim* state. As the modern scholar Ira Lapidus points out,

> Shah Waliallah [sic] believed that the reform [of Islam] required a Muslim state, modeled on the early Caliphate, to enforce the Shari'a.... In Shah Waliallah's view, the will of God radiates through the Caliph into the feelings and minds of his subjects.... [A] Caliph provides for the political defense of Muslim peoples and the organization of Muslim law. His duty is to enforce Islamic religious practice, collect the alms tax, promote the pilgrimage, foster study and teaching, administer justice and wage jihad. This was a program of religious consolidation in the struggle against popular Sufi Islam and in opposition to a lax Muslim regime.[10]

For its part, the South Asian Analysis Group, a research institute based in India, asserts that Wali Allah's thought has contributed to communal tensions between Muslims and Hindus. A recent article appearing on the website of this institute argued that

> [Wali Allah's] attempt to present an integrated view of the various schools of Islamic thought was ... more a tactical move for the political unity of Muslims to restore the political authority of Islam than for overall development of an integrated Indian society. His insistence [on] not diluting the cultural identity of Arab[s] in a Hindu-majority environment shows that his so-called reform of Islam was only for a political motive. His obsession [with] extreme Sunnism ... exposes the theory of Islamic modernism.... Wali Ullah [sic] may not stand the scrutiny of being a Muslim thinker for rational evaluation of Islam and its moderation.[11]

What is clear is that the ideas of Wali Allah became part of the ideological and theological foundations for the Deoband seminary and movement (discussed later in this chapter) in northern India. Its teachings eventually spread to the religious colleges of northeast India, i.e., to the region that became Pakistan. Students from these colleges were known as Taliban (in Persian, *taliban* is the plural of the Arabic *talib*, i.e., student).

Voice of Fundamentalism: Muhammad ibn Abd al-Wahhab (1703–1787)

A contemporary of Shah Wali Allah, Abd al-Wahhab was a Sunni theologian and reformer who founded the puritanical sect of Islam which is known in the West as Wahhabism and which still flourishes in Saudi Arabia today. He called for a strictly literal interpretation of the Quran and demanded that Muslim states be based exclusively on Islamic law, specifically as found in the *sunna* of the first Muslim generations. (The *sunna* is the body of customary social and legal traditions and obligations of the Muslim community, based on the life, teachings and practices of Muhammad).

Not much is known about his youth in the Najd (central Arabia), except that his religious extremism was so pronounced that his father and his brother Suleyman, both of whom were Islamic scholars, warned others against him. Suleyman, in fact, went so far as to write a book, entitled *Divine Thunderbolts*, opposing Abd al-Wahhab's opinions.[12]

Educated in Medina, Abd al-Wahhab traveled widely and taught for many years in Iraq and Iran. In 1736 he began to criticize the liberal Sufi doctrines followed by some Iranians. When he returned to the Najd, he expounded his own doctrines in his major work, the *Book of Unity* (*Kitab al-tawhid*). This book led his followers to call themselves "People of Unity" or "Unitarians" (*ahl al-tawhid* or *Muwahhidun*), names which are derived from their belief in the absolute "oneness" of God (*tawhid*). Opponents and non–Muslims alike, however, have traditionally referred to them as Wahhabis.

Abd al-Wahhab's severe doctrines drew heavily on the jurisprudence of Ibn Hanbal (d. 855) and on the theology of Ibn Taymiyya (d. 1328). He admonished his followers that on the Day of Judgment it will not be a valid excuse to tell God: "I heard people saying something, and I said it too."[13] Instead, what is needed for salvation is *genuine belief and genuine understanding*. He taught that in order to revitalize Islam and restore it to its former eminence, it is essential for the faithful to abandon heresies, idolatry and folk practices and return to the only true or genuine principles of Islam — the *earliest* principles, namely, those enunciated by the Quran and the *hadith*.

He was therefore firmly opposed to any religious innovations (*bidah*) which might interpose themselves between human beings and God. For this reason, he strongly condemned idolatry; Sufi mysticism; philosophy; the decoration of mosques, e.g., minarets; visiting tombs; venerating saints, holy rocks or sacred trees; and anything else that smacked of *shirk*, i.e., elevating someone or something to the point where this person or object encroaches upon the dignity of God. He required his followers to attend public prayers and prohibited shaving the beard, smoking tobacco, and abusive language.

The inhabitants of the Najd, however, valued their traditional practices and were so incensed by Abd al-Wahhab's strictness in forbidding them that they expelled him. He moved to Diriyah, the capital of Ibn Saud, a local chieftain. There, in 1749, he and Ibn Saud set up a fledgling government with a new and explicit division of power: Abd al-Wahhab would be the religious authority and Ibn Saud the political authority. The faithful were required to support both parties. This unique agreement was cemented by intermarriage between the two families.

Such an alliance was significant because, as the modern scholar Francis Robinson has pointed out, in the eighteenth century Muslim power had began to decline and tensions between the transmitters of knowledge, on the one hand, and the wielders of political power, on the other, were exacerbated.[14] Abd al-Wahhab and Ibn Saud solved this problem by their power-sharing agreement. In doctrinal terms, the result was (to cite Robinson again) "a shift from an Islam which was inclusive to *one which was increasingly exclusive*, and from an Islam which was otherworldly to one which was concerned *to put God's guidance into practice on earth.*"[15]

Under the unifying banner of Wahhabism, the Saud dynasty conquered virtually all of the Arabian peninsula. Ever since the eighteenth century, the Sauds' alliance with the Wahhabis has provided the religious and therefore the political legitimacy needed for the royal family to stay in power. Ironically, one of the few challenges to Sauds' political dominance has come from another religious extremist also influenced by Abd al-Wahhab — the terrorist leader Osama bin Laden, who was born and raised in Saudi Arabia.

Founder of a Sufi Brotherhood in Libya: Muhammad ibn Ali al-Sanusi (1787–1859)

Al-Sanusi, Islamic theologian and scholar, set up an important mystical movement in Libya and elsewhere, known as the Sanusiyah. A modern scholar, Knut Vikør, explains that

> [Al-Sanusi was] one of the most influential Islamic leaders of nineteenth-century North Africa. He created an organization that spread through most of central Sahara and the desert edge, and was to have a profound and lasting impact on the nomadic society of what today is Libya. His brotherhood played an important part in the resistance to the French in the Sahara and the Italians in Cyrenaica [eastern Libya], and was seen by the colonists as the arch-enemy of progress and reason. His grandson rose to become the first independent ruler of modern Libya. Indeed, the entity called "Libya" may in many ways be said to have grown out of the activities of the Sanusi order.[16]

Born in Algeria, al-Sanusi was primarily a teacher who encouraged his *bedouin* followers to be good Muslims. He himself was in favor of *ijtihad* (independent reasoning) and belonged to the Maliki school of law. His order was notable for its centralized organization and especially for its structure of lodges. The first lodge was set up in Cyrenaica in 1841. A lodge usually offered houses for officials of the brotherhood, a mosque or a *musalla* (a place of prayer), a school for children, a guesthouse, a shelter for the poor and those without families, servants' quarters, a bakery, stables, storehouses, and a garden. As Vikør describes it,

> The lodge ... was a place where the instruction al-Sanusi originally gave out in person could be spread in an organized fashion. It was a place where the brethren could perform religious duties under proper guidance; and an important part of that guidance was constructive work. Thus it was a place for piety through study, guidance and labor.... The lodge was for al-Sanusi the insertion of the religious into the mundane.[17]

Poet Caught Up in a Great Mutiny: Mirza Ghalib (1797–1869)

Ghalib was the last important poet of the Mughal era and in 1850 was appointed by the last Mughal emperor, Bahadur Shah II, to be his poet laureate. Ghalib wrote both in Persian and in Urdu and was famous for his poems, letters and prose. Most of his *ghazals* (love lyrics) focus on three basic questions of life: What is love? What is the nature of the universe and man's place in it? What is God?[18] Here are some verses from two of these *ghazals*. The first is about Ghalib himself:

> The beauty of the verse
> and the fragrance of the flower
> both from the same eternity commence.
> This blooming red rose
> is sired by the spring
> and gives tongue to my lucid eloquence.[19]

The second evokes a noblewoman walking in her garden:

> On the flower laden path
> Of the garden
> You step down
> Statuesque, vain, proud.
> Emanating from your closeness,
> The timeless constellations mirroring in its eyes,
> The sweet-smelling rose extends its stalk
> To reach to your turbaned brow.[20]

Like many other Indians of his time, Ghalib was caught up in the great mutiny of 1857 against British rule, known as the Sepoy Mutiny. This revolt was sparked by rumors that the paper cartridges for the firearm issued to Indian troops (sepoys), the 1853 pattern Enfield rifled musket, had been greased with pigs' fat or with cows' fat.

Each of these cartridges, made by women working in the Royal Arsenal's paper cartridge factory in Britain, consisted of a paper tube which had been filled with a lead bullet and a charge of gunpowder. The cartridges were then coated with a mixture of tallow and beeswax, both to waterproof them and to lubricate the bore of the rifled musket when it was fired. Easily opened at one end (which was closed only by a twist of paper held by a thread), they were bitten open immediately before use: the soldier would tear off the top of the cartridge with his teeth, pour the gunpowder down the barrel, and ram the bullet and paper cartridge home with his ramrod. A percussion cap (a tiny explosive device used to ignite the powder charge) would then be placed on the nipple of the breech and the musket was ready to fire.[21]

Since Hindu soldiers were forbidden to eat beef and Muslim solders were forbidden to eat pork, the alleged beef/pork lubrication quickly became the catalyst for a ferocious, far-reaching mutiny by both Hindus and Muslims. The modern scholar Ira Lapidus explains that

> The cartridges, however, were but a symbol of deeper cultural and political antagonisms. The Mutiny concerned not only Indian soldiers in the service of the East India Company, but the Muslim and Hindu upper classes of central and northern India. For these classes the cost of British rule had grown heavier.... [It] threatened the self-esteem, the hallowed lifestyles, and the economic and political interests of the hitherto privileged Indian elites. As the economic and cultural price of political inferiority bore down upon Mughal India, it took only the pig [and cow]-fat incident to provoke a widespread Hindu-Muslim revolt against British rule.[22]

Ghalib's own attitudes toward British rule were very ambivalent — a not-uncommon reaction among educated Indians during the nineteenth century.[23] On the one hand, he was intellectually attracted by the rationalism of the West, which seemed to offer the foundation of good government. During the mutiny he kept a diary, known as the *Dast-Ambooh*. This work mildly criticized some of the harsher aspects of Britain's colonial rule but expressed real horror at the bloody tactics of the mutineers themselves. The diary was written with an eye for publication; indeed, Ghalib planned to send a copy of it to Queen Victoria. It was thus a pro–British document.

On the other hand, however, during the mutiny Ghalib also wrote many private letters to his own friends, and these contain some of the most graphic and damning accounts of British atrocities. For example, Indian sources claimed that 27,000 people were hanged during the summer of 1857. What is certain is that, by their own account, the British publicly executed at least forty mutineers by tying them to the muzzles of cannons and then firing the cannons. A British eye-witness account in the November 1857 issue of *Blackwood's Edinburgh Magazine* reported that

> [The mutineers] were bound to the guns, their backs leaning against the muzzles, and their arms fastened to the wheels.... [A]t a signal from the Artillery-Major, the guns were fired. It was a horrid sight that met the eye: a regular shower of human fragments of heads, of arms, of legs, appeared in the air through the smoke, and when that cleared away, these fragments lying on the ground —fragments of Hindoos, and fragments of Mussulmans, all mixed together — were all that remained of those ... mutineers.[24]

What is perhaps of greater relevance to us here is that despite his Victorian prejudices, the author of this account was visibly impressed by the spiritual fortitude shown by these condemned men:

Nothing in their lives became them like the leaving of them.... They certainly died like men.... Whence had these men this strength? Their religion, bad as it may be and is, in all other points, at least befriends them well at the hour of death: it teaches them well that great and useful lesson, how to die. It is their religion that supports them, for there is no native, however low in the scale of society—however deeply sunk in vice, in debauchery, and in crime—but acknowledges and practices the form of some sort of religion. Even in the midst of his crimes he acknowledges that there is a God, and calls on that God to sustain him at the hour of his death.[25]

The Sepoy Mutiny resulted in the collapse of the Mughal Empire and the imposition of direct rule by Britain. Many of Ghalib's friends had been financially ruined, exiled, jailed or hanged. In 1858 Ghalib published his diary and gave copies to the British authorities to prove he had not supported the mutiny. The British were not impressed and told him they suspected that his real loyalty still lay with the Mughal emperor. Nevertheless, they took no action against him, and he continued writing until his death ten years later.

Islamic Reformers: The Deoband Movement (1866 to the Present)

One of the results of the Sepoy Mutiny was the resurgence of Islamic reform movements within India itself. The Deoband movement, initially established in northern India in 1866 as a lone seminary in the city of Deoband in Uttar Pradesh, was largely based on Shah Wali Allah's teachings. Known in Arabic as the "House of Sciences" (*Dar-Al-ulum*), it combined *hadith*, Islamic jurisprudence, exegesis, and philosophy with Sufism. Ultimately the Deoband movement expanded into a network of religious colleges that trained leaders charged with proselytizing, educating and making true Muslims out of Indian believers.[26]

Many of the Deoband's students came from Afghanistan, Central Asia, Yemen and Arabia, in addition to India. The movement became so popular that by 1966, its centenary, it claimed to have set up no fewer than 8,934 branch schools.[27] As mentioned previously, the Taliban regime of Afghanistan drew many of its ideas from the Deoband movement. Indeed, in the spring of 2001 the self-styled "ambassador at large" of the Taliban went so far as to claim that "every Afghan is a Deobandi."[28]

Although the Deoband seminary was strictly traditionalist in its theological orientation and was strongly committed to missionary work to advance the cause of Islam, it did not hesitate to adopt many of the secular features of nineteenth century British academic institutions. These included the school as a physical institution, an extensive library (consisting of thousands of printed books and manuscripts in Arabic, Persian and Urdu), student residences, a professional staff, a formal curriculum of study, written examinations, academic awards, affiliated colleges, and public contributions as a source of financial support.[29] It was thus a unique academic blend of East and West.

The Deoband movement is still going strong today. It has the second-largest Islamic university (after al-Azhar University in Cairo) and is active on the Internet. One website, for example, tells us that

Deoband has invariably remained as the central institution catering to requirements of religious education of the Muslim community all over [the] Subcontinent. To a certain extent, it also played the role of a unifying force for them [in its role as an advocate for an independent Pakistan in 1947.][30]

Portent for the Future? Jamal al-Din al-Afghani (1839–1897)

A fiery orator, political activist and writer, al-Afghani made a deep impact on the Islamic world of his own time and continues to be a source of inspiration — and controversy — today. Al-Afghani was one of first to sound the alarm about the ominous decline of Muslim power vis-à-vis the West. He was also one of the first to urge that Islam reform itself by becoming more modern and more rational, i.e., by permitting Muslims to use *ijtihad* (independent reasoning), as recommended by both Muhammad and the Quran.

Al-Afghani's origins (and even some of his thoughts) remain obscure.[31] He styled himself "al-Afghani" ("the Afghan"), indicating that he was from Sunni Afghanistan; his enemies, however, claimed that he was actually from Shiite Iran. In any case, he was definitely familiar with Shiite thought. He went to India in 1855 to continue his studies and was present during the Sepoy Mutiny of 1857. There he learned, at first hand, about the military might, sciences and mathematics of the West, as well as about the potential impact of religion on imperial politics. These revelations set the stage for his own intellectual development.

Al-Afghani tried to bridge the intellectual gap between the Islamic world and the West. As the modern scholar Ibrahim Kalin explains,

> [He] took a middle position between blind Westernization and its wholesale rejection by the traditional *ulama* [religious scholars]. His basic assumption was shared by the whole generation of the 19th century Muslim thinkers and activists: modern Western science and technology are essentially separable from the ethos and manners of European nations, and can and should be acquired by the Islamic world without necessarily accepting the theological and philosophical consequences emerging from their application in the Western context.... Afghani's views on science should be understood in light of this general program of Islamic "reform" or renewal (*islah* or *tajdid*).[32]

Perhaps the most productive period of his life was spent in Egypt, beginning in 1871, where he received a pension from the government and became the mentor of a group of young Egyptians who would play key leadership roles in Egyptian politics and thought later on. One of the most important of these men was the great reformer Muhammad Abduh, Grand Mufti (the senior legal counselor) of Egypt, who is discussed later in this chapter.

Al-Afghani's political activism (he was strongly opposed to Western imperialism), his religious views (he genuinely believed in Islam but his enemies considered his views heretical), and his abrasive personality often got him into trouble with the local authorities. When serving as counselor to the shah of Iran, he was suspected of heresy. The shah became very suspicious of him. In response, al-Afghani instigated a campaign of violent opposition against this ruler. The result was that the shah had al-Afghani deported from Iran in 1892. Four years later, however, al-Afghani got his revenge: he arranged for the assassination of the shah, who was murdered by one of al-Afghani's disciples.

This resort to violence was not surprising: those who knew al-Afghani well described him as a man "devoted to his convictions, obstinate, ascetic, quick to anger when honor or religion was touched, wild and untamable."[33] The British explorer and Arabist Wilfrid Blunt, who worked closely with him, declared that he was "a wild man of genius."[34] The end result of all these frictions was that al-Afghani was often on the move and had to live and work in a number of different countries.

Although he was an excellent speaker, he did not like writing and wrote only five treatises, none of which broke much new ground intellectually. However, the modern scholar Albert Hourani was able to piece together some of his thoughts, using both al-Afghani's own writings and those of his associates.[35]

Al-Afghani started from the basic premise that the Islamic world had to unite and defend itself against the relentless expansion of the European powers, especially Britain. In order to do so, he argued, Muslims had to understand Islam correctly and begin to live according to its teachings. When they did so, he asserted, they would become strong enough to fend off Europe's military, political and cultural encroachments. As we shall see, this assertion, which is clearly based more on faith than on reason, is still a familiar theme today in Muslim efforts to reform the Islamic world.

Al-Afghani recognized that the strength of Europe ultimately lay in its knowledge and in the application of that knowledge. Although he knew that the Islamic world of his time could not match these achievements, he nevertheless held out hope for the Islamic world of the future. This is evident in his reply to the French historian and philosopher Ernest Renan.

In 1883 Renan had delivered a blistering attack on Islam in a lecture and article entitled "Islam and Science." Renan claimed that Arabs in particular and Islam in general were incapable of philosophical thinking or of producing science. He did admit that a so-called "Arabic" philosophy and science existed, but he dismissed these as being Arabic only in language and in substance little more than warmed-over ideas from Greek and Sassanian times.

Al-Afghani's reply was somewhat inconsistent. On the one hand, he rebutted Renan's charges and, where Renan had been negative, he was positive. On the other, he appeared tacitly to accept one key element of Renan's argument. Al-Afghani replied in part that

> If it is true that the Muslim religion is an obstacle to the development of sciences, can one affirm that this obstacle will not disappear someday? How does the Muslim religion differ on this point from other religions? All religions are intolerant, each one in its own way. The Christian religion ... has emerged from the first period to which I have just alluded; thenceforth free and independent, it seems to advance rapidly on the road of progress and science, whereas Muslim society has not yet freed itself from the tutelage of religion.... I cannot keep from hoping that Muhammadan society will succeed someday in

breaking its bonds and marching resolutely in the path of civilization after the manner of Western society.... No, I cannot admit that this hope be denied to Islam.[36]

Al-Afghani strongly believed that the Quran should be interpreted in the light of reason: any apparent contradictions between its contents and modern knowledge must be interpreted symbolically. As Hourani puts it,

> Since reason can interpret, all men can interpret, provided that they have a sufficient knowledge of Arabic, are of sound mind, and know the traditions of the *salaf* ["Elders"], the first generations of guardians of the Prophet's message. The door of *ijtihad* is not closed, and it is a duty as well as a right for men to apply the principles of the Quran anew to the problems of their time. To refuse to do this is to be guilty of stagnation (*jumud*) or imitation (*taqlid*), and these are the enemies of true Islam just as materialism is an enemy.[37]

In summary, al-Afghani held that the weaknesses of the Islamic world of his day were not due to any defect in Islam itself but rather because Muslims had fallen away from the practice of the true faith, i.e., the earliest teachings of Islam. In the Prophet's time and immediately thereafter, he argued, the Islamic world had been strong. It had become weak only when Muslims slipped into error. However, once present-day Muslims had reformed (by going back to their roots) and had become *genuine Muslims* again, they would, al-Afghani believed, become powerful once more as well. He knew that the Islamic world had to be modernized; for him, faith in Islam was an essential component in the process of modernity.[38]

In retrospect, we can speculate that al-Afghani's policies, and especially his role in arranging the assassination of the shah, had an element of desperation in them. If so, they may have been a portent for the future. The modern religious writer Karen Armstrong sees a relevance to our own times:

> [T]he intrusion of the West into their lives raised major religious questions. The humiliation of the *ummah* [the Islamic community] was not merely a political catastrophe, but touched a Muslim's very soul. The new weakness was a sign that something had gone gravely awry in Islamic history.... How could Islamdom [sic] be falling more and more under the domination of the secular, Godless West? From this point, a growing number of Muslims would wrestle with these questions, and their attempts to put Muslim history back on the straight path would sometimes appear desperate and even despairing. The suicide bomber — an almost unparalleled phenomenon in Islamic history — shows that some Muslims are convinced that they are pitted against hopeless odds.[39]

Modernizer of Islam in India: Sayyid Ahmad Khan (1817–1898)

An Indian reformer, educator, jurist and writer, Sayyid Ahmad Khan believed that Islam was entirely compatible with modern science and wanted to found "a Muslim

Cambridge" in India.[40] He achieved this goal in 1875 by establishing the Anglo-Mohammedan Oriental College at Aligarh in Uttar Pradesh, India.

This institution, later renamed the Aligarh Muslim University, was designed to mold a new kind of leader by enabling the sons of the Muslim elite to study Western learning in India without having to sever their religious roots.[41] Sayyid Ahmad Khan's school was so successful, at least in political terms, that by the early twentieth century its alumni had become the spokesmen of Muslim opposition to British rule in India and, later, the advocates of an independent Muslim Pakistan.[42] The Aligarh Muslim University remained the mainstay of Muslim education in the subcontinent until partition in 1947. It is still going strong in India today and has an active website.

To modernize Islam, Sayyid Ahmad Khan believed it was necessary to reinterpret the Quran. He agreed the Quran had been revealed by God but stressed that its many difficult passages must be interpreted by reason—that is to say, symbolically, allegorically or analytically—in order to ferret out their true meaning. When the Quran was thus stripped of all the accretions of nonessential traditions and exegesis, it would stand revealed, he believed, as the fountainhead of a truly rational religion which was not in conflict with modern science.

In addition to enabling Muslims to study science without fear of jeopardizing their faith, Sayyid Ahmad Khan also believed that his reforms would help convince the British rulers of India that Islam was not an irrational religion and was worthy of their respect.[43] He was sure that bypassing much of the "blind imitation" (*taqlid*), which formed the stock-in-trade of orthodox Muslim scholars, was a good step toward modernizing Islam.

This step would, he felt, help the faithful get back in touch with what he called "the original religion of Islam which God and the messenger [Muhammad] have disclosed, not that religion which the *ulama* and the preachers have fashioned."[44] Independent thought (*ijtihad*) was to be encouraged. The sayings and doings of the Prophet (*hadith*) were to be examined critically and the least reliable of them must be culled. When reason and a holy text differed, reason should prevail.

Unfortunately for the reformers, however, Sayyid Ahmad Khan was vulnerable on two fronts. First, the *ulama* agreed that, never having finished his Islamic education, he lacked the academic qualifications needed to interpret the Quran and the *hadith*. Second, Muzaffar Iqbal, a modern biographer, frankly admits that "the shallowness of his knowledge of Western science and its philosophical underpinnings was apparent from his writings."[45] It seems clear, then, that Sayyid Ahmad Khan lacked the intellectual tools needed to accomplish his objectives.

Moreover, his willingness to collaborate with the British (he was knighted by Queen Victoria in 1888), his opposition to parliamentary democracy in India (which he feared would result in Muslims being dominated by the Hindu majority), and his liberal-rationalist interpretation of Islam all combined to cost him the support of the influential, highly traditionalist *ulama*. Without their backing, there was no chance that his doctrinal reforms would be put into effect in India.

Reformer and Grand Mufti of Egypt: Muhammad Abduh (1849–1905)

A liberal Egyptian religious scholar and jurist who advocated *ijtihad* (independent reasoning), Abduh is widely acknowledged as the chief architect of the nineteenth century reform movement in Islam. His teachings inspired the Salafiya (a reformist movement designed to purify Islam through a blend of traditional, modernist, and nationalistic thought) in Egypt, the Arab Middle East, and North Africa.[46] For this reason, it is important to explore his ideas at some length. As Elma Harder, a modern scholar, explains,

> Abduh's ideas were met with great enthusiasm, but also by tenacious opposition. They are still a subject of contention today ... as questions of modernism and tradition re-emerge in conflict in the Muslim world. Although he did not achieve his goals, Muhammad Abduh remains a continuing influence, and his work, *Risalat al-Tauhid* (*The Unity of Theology*) is the most important statement of his thought.[47]

Abduh was educated in the Nile Delta at the Ahmadi mosque in Tanta, the greatest center of religious learning in Egypt aside from al-Azhar University, and then, from 1869 to 1877, at al-Azhar itself, where he was awarded the degree of *alim* (scholar).[48] It was at this university that in 1871 he studied with the revolutionary preacher al-Afghani, whose teachings had such a profound influence on him that he renounced the ascetic life he had been following to that time and began to work for the renaissance of Islam and the end of the colonial domination of the Islamic world.

Financial and political frictions between Britain and Egypt culminated in the British occupation of Egypt in 1882. Abduh played a key role in the anti–British movement, echoing al-Afghani's views in numerous articles in the Egyptian press. For his pains, Abduh was exiled from Egypt for three years. Once abroad, he continued to work closely with al-Afghani. Allowed to return to Egypt in 1888, he became a judge and the next year was appointed Grand Mufti. He subsequently taught and wrote, working together with Rashid Rida, a disciple who became his biographer and who will be discussed in the next section. Abduh also organized schools, helped reform al-Azhar, learned French so that he could master modern European thought, and traveled to Europe.

His religious and political convictions were popular with Islamic liberals but not with the traditionalists or the nationalists. As al-Afghani had done, Abduh began by thinking about the problem of Islam's inner decay and thus about the need for an inner revival. A specific issue for him, as it had been for al-Afghani, was the gap between reason and faith. During the latter half of the nineteenth century, Egyptian life was changing rapidly and was becoming more secularized: its reliance on reason was growing. Abduh believed, however, that since Egyptian society was ultimately based on faith, it could never be wholly secularized. The result was, according to the modern scholar Albert Hourani, "a chasm which revealed itself in every aspect of life."[49]

Abduh set out to close or at least to narrow this chasm by strengthening Islam's moral roots. Since change could not be stopped in its tracks, he argued that it had to be accepted and could indeed be justified as being in accordance with the essence of Islam. He wanted to prove that Islam contained the rationality, social science and morality needed for a modern society. Indeed, in his autobiography Abduh indicated that the most important goal of his life was to restate *what Islam truly was*. He wrote:

> [His chief purpose was to liberate Islamic thought] from the shackles of *taqlid* [blind imitation], and understand religion as it was understood by the elders of the community before dissention appeared; to return, in the acquisition of religious knowledge, to its first sources, and to weigh them in the scales of human reason ... and to prove that ... religion must be accounted a friend to science, pushing man to investigate the secrets of existence, summoning him to respect established truths, and to depend on them in his moral life and conduct. All this I count as one matter, and in my advocacy of it I ran counter to the opinion of the two great groups of which the body of the *umma* [the Islamic community] is composed — the students of the sciences of religion, and those who think like them, and the students of the arts of this age, with those who are on their side.[50]

The fears of these two groups seem to have been well-founded. As Hourani puts it,

> Without intending it, Abduh was perhaps opening the door to the flooding of Islamic doctrine and law by all the innovations of the modern world. He had intended to build a bridge against secularism, he had in fact provided an easy bridge by which it could capture one position after another. It was not an accident that ... one group of his disciples were later to carry his doctrines in the direction of complete secularism.[51]

The traditionalists' doubts about Abduh's approach is quite evident. When a certain professor al-Khawli, inspired by Abduh, began a literary-critical study of the Quran, he was quickly removed from office by the joint forces of the conservative politicians and the *ulama* (religious scholars) of the university of al-Azhar.[52]

Abduh himself was highly critical of the *ulama*. They had, he asserted, singularly failed to distinguish between the essence of Islam, on the one hand, and its mass of intricate but less important social regulations, on the other. Such an "excess of adherence to the outwardness of the law," as Abduh described this failing of the traditionalists, gave rise to blind imitation, which was the exact opposite of the freedom he could detect in genuine Islam.[53]

The traditionalists must have been especially wary of Abduh's insistence that, along with jurisprudence, the real hallmark of the ideal Muslim society is *reason*. The only infidel (*kafir*), wrote Abduh, is the man who refuses to examine rational proofs. Being inherently rational, Islam can thus embrace modern science without having to accept the doctrines of secularism or abandoning its own beliefs.[54] This rationalist finding pointed the way forward: the Islamic world could become strong and rich again only by accepting Western science and by modernizing Islam's legal systems, schools, and systems of government along Western lines. He held that

> There is no religion without a state and no state without authority and no authority without strength and no strength without wealth. The state does not possess trade or industry. Its wealth is the wealth of the people and the people's wealth is not possible without the spread of these sciences amongst them so that they may know the ways for acquiring wealth.[55]

In his most important work, *The Unity of Theology* (or *Treatise on the Oneness of God*), Abduh advanced the thesis that Islam is superior to Christianity because it is inherently more receptive to science. To make his case, however, he had to stretch Quranic references so far that his arguments exceed the limits of plausibility. References to the *jinn* (spirits), for example, become references to microbes.[56]

A modern scholar, Norman Calder, has also blamed Abduh for diminishing Islam by rejecting Islamic mysticism. Calder argued that

> [I]f you have a rich, complex and varied tradition, the needs of the 20th century hardly indicate that it should be restricted, rather that it should be accepted in all its richness.... If we ask why there is a tendency for at least some Muslims to make their heritage smaller, we will I think find it goes back to a very great man and a very important thinker, Muhammad Abduh.... He wanted to reform Islam and the method he chose was one of rejection ... one of the things he rejected was the whole mystic tradition. He claimed that much mystic lore was nonsense, *khurafat*; he called upon his followers not to listen to mystics and to get rid of them.... [This] is not a particularly good point of departure for Muslims today trying to find their way forward as Muslims.... Now, perhaps Muhammad Abduh was right; perhaps this was a necessary way forward, a retreat in order to advance. But on the whole, I would be inclined to say that, at that point of transition, Islam started to become a smaller tradition.[57]

Political Activist to Adjust Islam to the Demands of Modern Times: Rashid Rida (1865–1935)

Syrian-born author, editor and political activist Rashid Rida lived and worked in Egypt. He was one of the first Muslim intellectuals to call for the establishment of a modernized but fully Islamic state and for a reformed *sharia*, the body of Islamic sacred laws. He was strongly influenced by the reformist ideas of al-Afghani and especially of Abduh. Indeed, *Al-Manar*, the highly-regarded reformist monthly magazine that Rashid Rida published for 37 years (from 1898 to 1935), was essentially a call for change according to the doctrines of Abduh.[58]

Intellectually, Rashid Rida began precisely where al-Afghani and Abduh had begun. He first raised a fundamental question — "Why are Muslim countries so backward?"— and then answered it by tying religious belief directly to secular power and prosperity. Shakib Arslan, a contemporary Egyptian scholar who wrote about Rashid Rida in Arabic in 1939–1940, described Rashid Rida's position as follows:

> The teachings and moral precepts of Islam are such that if they are properly understood and fully obeyed, they will lead to success in this world as well as the next—and to success in all the forms in which the world understands it, [namely] strength, respect, civilization, happiness. If they are not understood and obeyed, weakness, decay, barbarism are the results.... It is irrelevant to say that modern civilization rests on technical advance, and that Islamic civilization cannot be revived so long as the Muslims are technically backward; *technical skill is potentially universal, and its acquisition depends on certain moral habits and intellectual principles. If Muslims had these, they would easily obtain technical skill; and such habits and principles are in fact contained in Islam.*[59]

Rashid Rida himself favored the traditionalism of the Hanbali (Sunni) school of law and denounced Shiism as full of "fairy tales and illegitimate innovations."[60] He applauded the Wahhabi conquest of the Hijaz (the northern half of the west coast of Saudi Arabia, the cradle of Islam where Mecca and Medina are located) and praised Ibn Saud, the tribal chieftain who shared power with the Wahhabis, for "defending the essential principles of Sunnism better than almost anyone since the first four caliphs."[61] Nevertheless, Rashid Rida's line of thought contained a certain flexibility as well.

He argued, for example, that when holy texts are ambiguous or appear to contradict each other, men should use reason to decide what course of action is most in accord with the spirit of Islam and will further the interests of the Muslim community as a whole. He also tried to break some new ground on the issue of *ijma* (the consensus of Islamic scholars) by asserting that the religious leaders of the Muslim community can exercise not only executive and judicial power but legislative power as well.

That is, there can be a body of "positive law" (man-made law), known as *qanun*, which ultimately derives its authority from the general principles of Islam.[62] This law is independent and is valid so long as it does not conflict with the *sharia*. Rashid Rida concluded that it is the right and the duty of an Islamic state to devise such "a system of just laws appropriate to the situation in which its past history has placed it."[63] Indeed, he contended that this was the original understanding of law-making in early Islam.

The steady, aggressive inroads of the West made it clear to Rashid Rida that new Islamic laws were needed sooner rather than later. He asserted that the duty of *jihad* (by which he meant using force if necessary to defend the practice of or the survival of Islam itself) was binding on all Muslims. The Islamic world, however, could not discharge this duty successfully if it was too weak; therefore, it had to become strong. The only feasible way for it to do so was by adopting the sciences and technology of the West.

One step in this direction—and here Rashid Rida broke sharply with Islamic tradition—was permitting businessmen to charge interest. Charging interest was clearly forbidden by Islamic law, but he argued that the danger of an economic takeover of

Islamic lands by Western capitalism was so acute that such a drastic step was justified and was, indeed, essential.

Of greater importance to us here, however, was his strong belief that Muslims needed a system of law which was not only truly Islamic but which could also be enforced by an Islamic state headed by a true caliph. He felt that

> [Such an exalted leader would have to be] the supreme practitioner of *ijtihad* [independent reasoning], the great *mujtahid* [a man who applies such independent reasoning]: a man capable by intelligence and special training and with the aid of the *ulama* [religious scholars], of applying the principles of Islam to the changing needs of the world, and capable, by the respect in which he is held, of imposing the results of this process on the Muslim governments.... Only if such a caliph existed could a real Islamic society exist.[64]

These qualifications, however, were so demanding that Rashid Rida could think of no candidates for this post. He therefore recommended instead the formation of an Islamic "progressive party." This in turn would set up a seminary designed to train specialists in *ijtihad*. Graduates of the seminary would constitute a new body of religious scholars. Some of them would be descendents of Muhammad's own tribe, the Quraysh. As Hourani succinctly sums up his teaching on this vital point:

> [The purpose of the seminary would be that] in the fullness of time one [of the Qurayshis] might be chosen by electors of all Muslim countries, and be formally invested by "those who bind and loose" as a genuine caliph and restorer of that true Islamic government which was the best of all.[65]

Rashid Rida's ambitious reforms were never put into effect. He died in Syria in 1935.

Political Activist for a Separate Islamic State: Muhammad Iqbal (1878–1938)

Poet, philosopher and political activist, Iqbal is remembered today as the spiritual leader of Indian modernism and as the father of Pakistan.[66] Through Islam, he sought a middle way of avoiding the failings of capitalism and communism: "The soul of both," he wrote, "is impatient and intolerant; both of them know not God, and deceive mankind. One lives by production, the other by taxation and man is a glass caught between these two stones." He was particularly critical of those Westerners who, he declared, "have lost the vision of heaven; they go hunting for the pure spirit in the belly."[67]

Born in the Indian province of Punjab (now in Pakistan) and initially educated in Lahore, Iqbal was a brilliant student. Later, he earned a degree in philosophy from the University of Cambridge in 1905–1908, qualified as a lawyer in London, and received a Ph.D. from the University of Munich. His doctoral dissertation, in English, was entitled *The Development of Metaphysics in Persia* and cast new light on some forms of Islamic mysticism. Iqbal was knighted by the British in 1922.

His poems, written both in Persian and in Urdu, are still quoted by Indian and Pakistani Muslims alike. These works evoke the former achievements of Islam, complain about its contemporary shortcomings and urge the faithful to reform and to become more unified. Specifically, they call for obedience to Islam, for self-discipline, for recognition that everyone is potentially a "vice-regent of God on earth" and for a life of political action rather than a passive withdrawal from the fray.

While studying in London in 1907, Iqbal joined the All India Muslim League and had a mystical experience which reinforced his commitment to Islam. The *ghazal* (lyric poem) he wrote to honor this occasion forecasts triumphs for Islam and failures for the West. Here are some of the verses:

> At last the silent tongue of Hijaz has
> announced to the ardent ear the tiding
> That the covenant which had been given to the
> desert-dwellers is going to be renewed
> vigorously:
> The lion [Islam] who had emerged from the desert and
> had toppled the Roman Empire is,
> As I am told by the angels, about to get up
> Again [from his slumbers].
> You, the dwellers of the West, should know that
> the world of God is not a shop.
> Your imagined pure gold is about to lose its standard value.
> Your civilization will commit suicide with its
> own daggers.
> A nest built on a frail bough cannot be
> durable.
> The caravan of feeble ants will take the rose petal for a boat
> And in spite of all blasts of waves, it shall cross
> the river.[68]

In a famous presidential address delivered at the conference of the All India Muslim League in 1930, Iqbal rejected the idea that Muslims and Hindus could constitute a unified Indian nation. He called instead for the amalgamation of the Muslim provinces of northwestern India:

> I would like to see the Punjab, North-West Frontier Provinces, Sind and Baluchistan [joined together] into a single State. Self-Government within the British Empire or without the British Empire. The formation of the consolidated North-West Indian Muslim State appears to be the final destiny of the Muslims, at least of [those of] North-West India.[69]

In 1934 Iqbal published, in English, *The Reconstruction of Religious Thought*, a book on his philosophy which was based on lectures he had given in India a few years earlier. In it, he called for use of *ijtihad* (independent reasoning) to set up new social and political institutions more appropriate for modern times. However, he took a more cautious position on its use. As the modern scholar Sheila McDonough remarked, "Iqbal tended to be progressive in adumbrating general principles of change but conservative in initiating actual change."[70]

In a letter written in 1937, one year before his death, Iqbal explained the reasons and the geographically larger scope for what would, after partition in 1947, become the state of Pakistan:

> A separate federation of Muslim Provinces ... is the only course by which we can secure a peaceful India and save Muslims for the domination of Non-Muslims [i.e., Hindus]. Why should not the Muslims of North-West India [this area would become West Pakistan] and Bengal [East Pakistan] be considered as nations entitled to self-determination just as other nations in India and outside [the] India area are.[71]

"Father of the Turks": Mustafa Kemal Ataturk (1881–1938)

Founder and first president of Turkey, Ataturk drastically modernized his country's educational and legal systems and forcefully encouraged Turks to adopt a European way of life. He probably did more in a shorter period of time to change his country than any other leader of a state with such a large percentage of Muslims. Unlike virtually all of the Islamic personalities discussed thus far, thanks to his father (an army officer who wanted to help reform the country) Ataturk received his earliest education not at a religious school but at a modern secular school.

In this school, Ataturk, then known as Mustafa, did so well in mathematics that his teacher nicknamed him Kemal, meaning "The Perfect One." Much later in his illustrious career, when he decreed in 1934 that henceforth Turks would have to adopt surnames, the parliament bestowed on him the name of Ataturk ("Father of the Turks"), by which he is now commonly known.

When the Turkish republic came into being in 1923, Ataturk encouraged a breathtaking number of radical reforms in what had been a traditionalist Islamic society. To begin with, he made it clear that he would not let Islam stand in the way of science. He wrote:

> We shall take science and knowledge from wherever they may be, and put them in the mind of every member of the nation. For science and knowledge, there are no restrictions and no conditions. *For a nation that insists on preserving a host of traditions and beliefs that rest on no logical proof, progress is very difficult, perhaps even impossible.*[72]

His reforms included the[73]

disestablishment of Islam. That is, it was stripped of its former status and prestige as the official Turkish religion. For our purposes here, this was the most significant change wrought by Ataturk. Religion became a strictly private affair: Islam was divested of its roles in public life. All the *madrasas* were closed. The Westernized ruling elite in the cities became thoroughly secularized. Only in the countryside did Shiites continue to worship in mosques and at the tombs of saints.[74]

"Six Arrows," i.e., Ataturk's political platform of 1923. These "arrows" were: a republican form of government; nationalism; populism; state-owned enterprises, based on Soviet models, designed to transform Turkey from an agricultural to an industrial state; secularism; and what was known as "a permanent state of revolution," i.e., constant changes in Turkish life.

emancipation of women, symbolized by Ataturk's own marriage to a Western-educated Turkish woman in 1923 and by their divorce in 1925.

prohibition of the fez, the traditional Turkish men's hat, in 1925, as a symbolic move to free citizens from the conservatism of the past. In 1927 Ataturk explained to the parliament:

> Gentlemen, it was necessary to abolish the fez, which sat on the heads of our nation as an emblem of ignorance, negligence, fanaticism, and hatred of progress and civilization, to accept in its place the hat, the headgear used by the whole civilized world, and in this way to demonstrate that the Turkish nation, in its mentality, as in other respects, in no way diverges from civilized social life.[75]

prohibition of the highly conservative Sufi brotherhoods, also in 1925.

jettisoning of the whole structure of Islamic law between February and June 1926. The *sharia* was replaced by Western laws, i.e., the Swiss civil code, the Italian penal code and the German commercial code. This had the effect of ending polygamy; making marriage a civil rather than a religious contract; and allowing divorce as a civil, not religious, action.

replacement of the Arabic script in 1928, used for centuries to write Ottoman Turkish, by the Latin alphabet. This was especially noteworthy because, as the modern scholar Norman Itzkowitz has pointed out,

> Education benefited from this reform, as the young people of Turkey, cut off from the past with its emphasis on religion, were encouraged to take advantage of new educational opportunities that gave access to the Western scientific and humanistic traditions.[76]

passage of voting rights for women. In 1934, women were permitted to vote for members of parliament and to hold parliamentary seats themselves.

Although many Turks welcomed these draconian changes, the Kurds of southwestern Anatolia did not. In 1925 they rebelled in the name of Islam. Within two months, however, the Turkish government quelled their revolt and hanged their leader, Seyh Said. There were other disturbances, too, as Ataturk became less inclined to tolerate any opposition. Decisive leadership was always his strong suit.

Rashid Rida, the author, editor and political activist discussed earlier in this chapter, thought that Ataturk had only one failing. "He was a great man," Rida said, "who unfortunately knew nothing about Islam. If he had known what Islam really was," Rida added, "he would have been the perfect man to bridge the differences between Muslim religious leaders and thereby unify Islam."[77]

Teacher of Islamic Revival in Iran: Ali Shariati (1933–1977)

Iranian teacher and sociologist, Shariati analyzed the problems of contemporary Muslim societies, e.g., Iran under the shah, in the light of Islamic principles.[78] He is remembered today for encouraging Iranian students to participate in what would become, a year after his death, the 1978–1979 nationalist–Islamic revolution in Iran.

Educated in Iran as a teacher, Shariati went to France on a scholarship and received his doctorate in sociology from the Sorbonne in Paris in 1964. When he returned to Iran he was arrested at the border and jailed for about one year because he had been politically active in France. Released in 1965, he began teaching at Iran's Mashhad University. His doctrines offended the government, however, and he was transferred to teaching duties at the Houssein-e-Ershad Religious Institute in Teheran.

Shariati was so popular with the students there that the shah's government again saw him as a threat and sentenced him to eighteen months in prison. Local and international protests prompted his release in 1975. He was then kept under such tight surveillance that he could neither publish nor teach. As a result, he decided to emigrate to the United Kingdom. Three weeks later, he was found dead in his apartment there—possibly murdered, his supporters speculated, by SAVAK, the shah's notorious secret police service.

Most of Shariati's works, which total approximately twenty-six treatises, were not edited by Shariati himself but were transcribed from tapes made of his lectures in Persian. Some of these transcriptions have been translated, but he is not as well-known in the West as in Iran. Nevertheless, his ideas are worth recording. This is how a website summarizes his thought:

> He was neither a reactionary fanatic who opposed anything that was new without any knowledge nor was he [one] of the so-called Westernized intellectuals who imitated the West without independent judgment. Knowledgeable about the conditions and forces of his time, he began his Islamic revival with enlightenment of the masses, particularly the youth. He believed that if these elements of the society had true faith, they would totally dedicate themselves and become active and *mujahid* elements [a *mujahid* is someone who fights actively for Islam] who would give everything, including their lives, for their ideals.... He vigorously tried to introduce the Quran and Islamic history to the youth so that they may find their true selves in all their human dimensions and fight all the decadent societal forces.[79]

Shariati himself consistently stressed the importance of Islam in the modernizing process. Here are three examples from his works:

Islam is what we must return to, not only because it is the religion of our society, the shaper of our history, the spirit of our culture, the powerful conscience and strong binder of our people, and the foundation of our morality and spirituality, but also because it is the human "self" of our people.[80]

Movements of Muslim nations seeking independence will only attain victory when they follow determined, intellectual principles and [an] ideological school of thought in which philosophy, economics, ethics, social and political issues, nationhood etc. have been clearly expressed. The important point to note is that the "place" of this ideological school of thought must be built from the materials and tools Islam has placed at our disposal. Inspiration for its construction must come from the sacred, salvation-giving teachings of the Holy Qur'an.[81]

At this juncture, we see that neither the intellectuals, who do not know Islam, nor the pseudo-religious people, who are unaware of their own time, can fulfill our immediate needs. Only the enlightened Islamic scholar is able ... to extract the refine, with the help of the miraculous revolution that exists in the very nature of the spirit and thought of the true Islam, the vast religious energies which are entrapped there.[82]

Warm tributes to Shariati's work came from Iranian religious leaders. Ayatollah Taleqani said of him: "Shariati created a new *maktab* [doctrine]. It was he who drew the youth of Iran into the revolutionary movement." Ayatollah Beheshti added: "The works of Shariati were essential for the revolution. Those of Imam Khomeini [discussed in the next chapter] were not exactly suitable for winning over the younger generation."[83]

Muslim Anarchist: Sayyid Abul-Ala Mawdudi (1903–1979)

Mawdudi was an Indian Muslim journalist and a conservative reformer whose ideas greatly influenced the course of Muslim nationalism in India. He was not a scholar or a theologian but, rather, a political activist and a passionate believer in Islam.[84] In his reading he had fallen under the spell of the strict fundamentalist teachings of Ibn Taymiyya (d. 1328) and of Muhammad ibn Abd al-Wahhab (d. 1787). Mawdudi himself held that the Muslims of his time were living in abased spiritual conditions which amounted to at least a partial *jahiliyya*, i.e., that "time of ignorance" of the pre–Islamic era. He explained the current weaknesses of Islam in India by pointing to the deplorable fact that Indian Muslims were living side-by-side with Hindus.

In his book, *Jihad in Islam* (1927), Mawdudi called not only for restrictions on non–Muslims living under Islamic rule but also, as a true anarchist, for the overthrow of all existing governments, Muslim and secular alike. He wrote:

> Islam is a revolutionary doctrine and system that overturns governments. It seems to overturn the whole universal social order ... and establish its structure anew.... Islam seeks the world. It is not satisfied with a piece of land but demands the whole universe.... *Jihad* is at the same time offensive and defensive.... The

Islamic party does not hesitate to utilize the means of war to implement its goal.[85]

Mawdudi advocated a return to the Quran and the *sunna* and the creation of a truly Islamic state with Islamic government, banking and economic institutions.[86] His traditionalism knew few bounds. He rejected, for example, a liberal interpretation of the Quran, put forward by a famous translator: the translator felt that a Quranic verse, "Try as you may, you cannot treat all your wives impartially," was a justification for monogamy. Mawdudi denounced this interpretation as suitable only for those Muslims who were "slaves of the West." On a less reactionary note, however, he also favored the use of rational judgments on religious issues so that the principles of Islam could be applied to a modern society.[87]

It was on the basis of all these ideas that he founded, in 1941, the militant Community for Islam (*Jamaat-i Islam*). Although Mawdudi's teachings were denounced by classically trained Islamic scholars as being extremist, his anti–Hindu doctrines and his advocacy of violent revolution struck a responsive chord among Indian Muslims and could not be swept under the carpet. In fact, they helped to fuel tensions between Pakistan and India over the status of Kashmir. Ultimately, they contributed to the creation of the predominately Muslim parts of India as the independent state of Pakistan.

"Proponent of a Moderate Islam": Fazlur Rahman (1911–1988)

A noted Pakistani scholar of Islamic thought, who taught for many years at the University of Chicago, Rahman has been well-described as "a leading proponent of a modernist Islam and amicable relations among peoples of different faiths."[88] If ever adopted, his ideas would go far toward bridging the intellectual gap between the Islamic world and the West.

Rahman had something to say, for example, about ethics. As mentioned earlier, this is a subject which traditionally has not attracted in Islamic thought the same degree of attention it has received in Western philosophy. Rahman himself believed ethics were an integral part of Islam, arguing that in its early years Islam had been motivated by a strong rational and moral concern for correcting the ills of society. This concern, he said, led to a deep commitment to reasoning and rational discourse about ethics. In addressing the fundamental ethical question —"What ought or ought not to be done?"— these early believers (and, by extension, later Muslims as well) could draw upon both reason and revelation to find appropriate answers.[89]

For our purposes here, the most important point Rahman made was this:

> [The first essential step in modernizing Islam is for Muslims to] distinguish clearly between normative Islam and historical Islam.... If the spark for the modernization of old Islamic learning is to arise, then the original thrust of Islam — of the Qur'an and Muhammad — must be clearly resurrected so that the conformities and deformities of historical Islam may be clearly judged by it.[90]

What he called for was simple but at the same time far-reaching — indeed, almost revolutionary. He taught that

> [The initial step of his holistic and contextual approach was] simply studying the Qur'an in its total and specific background (and doing this study systematically in a historical order, not just studying it verse by verse or passage by passage.... A historical critique of theological developments in Islam is the first step toward a reconstruction of Islamic theology. This critique ... should reveal the extent of the dislocation between the world view of the Qur'an and various schools of theological interpretation in Islam and point the way forward toward a new theology.[91]

PART THREE

ISLAMIC FUNDAMENTALISM AND THE FUTURE

Chapter IX

The Challenge of Fundamentalism

Historical Background

"Fundamentalism" is an integral part of most religions and need not be political: it can be a rigorous form of self-discipline and self-renewal. What all fundamentalists have in common is the desire to return to the often-idealized roots of their respective faiths. They want to slough off what they consider to be the accretions and errors built up over past centuries in order to redistill and revivify the essence of their beliefs. Some fundamentalists do in fact advocate violence, including suicide, to achieve their ends, but the culture of violence is not a necessary part of fundamentalism.[1]

Islamic fundamentalism basically calls for a return to the core beliefs articulated in the Quran and the sunna and implemented in the sharia.[2] Today such fundamentalism is fed by two wellsprings.

The first wellspring is intellectual and involves the life of the mind. Its most important single element is the fear that, if left unchecked in Muslim countries, secularism and individualism (including the Western moral code and the rights of women) are cancers that will ultimately destroy Islam. This fear can lead to a strong desire to create a "pure" Islamic society — one which must be carefully shielded from any corrupting foreign influences. This fear also encourages fundamentalists to embrace revelation at the expense of reason.

Other contributing factors are at play here, too. They include a lack of meaning in secular life; the failures in the Islamic world of ideologies borrowed from abroad (capitalism, communism, nationalism, socialism, and liberalism); the shortcomings of orthodox Islam itself; and a hatred of the United States and its allies because of their pervasive secular cultures and their relations with Israel.

The second wellspring of Islamic fundamentalism is pragmatic and involves the life of the body. For the young Muslim men and the very few Muslim women who constitute the foot soldiers and often the cannon fodder of Islamic fundamentalism, this wellspring is frequently (but not always) characterized by relative poverty, limited educational and employment prospects, and living under oppressive and corrupt regimes where advancement is more a matter of family, political or financial connections than of personal ability.

There is no reason to expect, however, that when and if Islamic fundamentalists manage to come to power, they will be able to do a better job than the regimes they replace. Once in power they will face the daunting task of trying to put into practice in the modern world the religious teachings crafted for a much earlier and much simpler time, i.e., the Arabia of the seventh century.³ Zealous fundamentalists are not good at governing a state. Indeed, the early track record of the Shiite clerics in Iran and the whole of the Taliban experience in Afghanistan proves this point very clearly and very painfully.

We have already mentioned four precursors of modern Islamic fundamentalism — the conservative and controversial theologian Ibn Taymiyya (1263–1328); the spiritual founder of revivalism, Muhammad ibn Abd al-Wahhab (1703–1787); the fiery orator and political activist Jamal al-Din al-Afghani (1839–1897); and the most prominent leader of the nineteenth century reformist movement, Muhammad Abduh (1849–1905). In this chapter we will examine important contemporary thinkers and activists, including Sayyid Qutb (1906–1966), Ayatollah Ruhollah Khomeini (1902–1989), and Osama bin Laden (1957–).

Founder of Modern Islamic Fundamentalism: Sayyid Qutb (1906–1966)

Sayyid Qutb was one of the most important Islamic thinkers of the twentieth century but is not as well known to nonspecialists in the West as he should be.⁴ Born in Egypt in 1906, he had a religious upbringing and had memorized the Quran by the age of 10. After receiving a BA in 1933 from a teacher's college in Cairo, he joined the staff of that institution and taught there until 1939, when he was hired by the Egyptian Ministry of Education as a teacher.

A major turning point in his intellectual development came in 1948 when he was sent to the United States to learn about the American educational system. He studied at different universities and received an MA degree in education from Wilson's Teachers' College in the state of Washington. Like many Muslim liberals of his day, Qutb believed that the Islamic world should use the West as its model. His experiences in the United States, however, pointed him in an entirely different direction. As the scholar Lamia Rustum Shehadeh has explained,

> During his stay in the United States between 1948 and 1951, he was shocked by the American bias against Arabs and unstinting support for the newly-established state of Israel, the materialism of the West, and the sexual permissiveness that pervaded the continent. This brought him to the second station in his intellectual life during which he rejected the liberal secularism in which he had believed as a result of what he regarded as the failure of both Marxism and capitalism to provide for the welfare and dignity of humanity. This realization precipitated his inward search for an authentic alternative that would bring the Arab demise to an end. He found his answer in Islamic tradition. He came to believe that Islam had a superior ideology on which the Muslims [could] build to ensure success in this world and the world to come, being the only true path for a moral and political regeneration.⁵

Qutb returned to Egypt in 1951, fired by his new insights: that Islam was a superior creed and ideology; that an Islamic revival was essential for Egypt and, by extension, for the rest of the Islamic world as well; that the West held a deeply rooted, permanent hatred of Islam; and that for Muslims the only correct best path toward strength and moral and political regeneration was not Western ideologies but Islam itself.[6]

Qutb then joined the Muslim Brotherhood (*Ikhwan al-Muslimin*), a reformist-revivalist mass movement which had been founded in Egypt by a young schoolteacher, Hasan al-Banna, in 1928. Qutb soon became one of its main ideologists. When the Muslim Brotherhood was suppressed in 1954 by Nasser's regime, Qutb was arrested that year and was tortured while in prison. Finally released in 1964, a few months later he was charged with plotting against the government and was rearrested. Tried for conspiring to overthrow the government, he was hanged, on Nasser's express orders, in 1966.

Qutb's most incendiary work was entitled *Signposts on the Road*, also known as *Milestones*. It was drawn from his earlier multivolume commentary on the Quran (*In the Shade of the Qur'an*). Both books were written while Qutb was in prison (1954–1964). *Signposts* was published in 1964 when he was released for a short period. Its uncompromisingly revolutionary message was one of the reasons for his subsequent rearrest and execution. *Signposts on the Road* denounced Nasser's government — and, indeed, the whole contemporary world — as languishing in *jahiliyya*, the state of ignorance held to have existed in Arabia before the rise of Islam. Qutb called for an all-out *jihad* against secularism and its "numerous man-made idols," e.g., capitalism and agnosticism.

The modern historian Scott Appleby has described Qutb's views on *jihad* as follows:

> *Jihad* is not restricted to defense of the homeland, Qutb insists. Rather, it is a command to extend the borders of Islam to the ends of the earth.... Here Qutb broke with contemporary interpreters of Islamic law. Like fundamentalists in other religions, he invoked the doctrines of a sage who had legitimated extremism, in this case Ibn Taymiyya [1226–1328], a scholar of Islamic law who had characterized Mongols as "false Muslims" and blessed those who fought them. Qutb also retrieved the practice of *ijtihad*, the use of independent reasoning when no clear text was available from the Koran or the *hadith* (sayings) of the Prophet. Finally, he gave an extreme interpretation of a traditional precept — jihad — by justifying it by recourse to "exceptionalism," the argument that the onset of crisis [here *jahiliyya*] requires extreme countermeasures.[7]

Another important book by Qutb was *Social Justice in Islam*. Initially published in 1948, this work went through six revisions, the last of them in 1964, only two years before his execution. This final edition was the most radical of all and represents his carefully considered views on social justice. As an example, in the last chapter ("At the Crossroads") Qutb concluded that

> The real and profound struggle is [not between communism and capitalism but] between Islam on one hand and both the Eastern and Western blocs on the

other. Islam is the real force that resists the force of the materialistic thought worshipped equally in Europe, America, Russia and China. It is Islam that contains the universal, complete and harmonious conception concerning existence and life, that replaces struggle and conflict with social solidarity in the human sphere and that gives life a spiritual basis that links it to its Creator in heaven and controls its worldly tendencies so that it does not realize purely material goals, even though productive activity is a form of worship in Islam.[8]

Qutb himself is long gone, but his ideas have achieved a certain immortality. His vision of a purely Islamic government helped inspire Ayatollah Khomeini. As noted earlier, his radical ideology was a source of inspiration for the Muslim extremists who assassinated Egyptian president Anwar Sadat in 1981, for the Taliban movement in Afghanistan, and for the terrorist leader Osama bin Laden. (Bin Laden was one of the students of a distinguished Saudi professor of Islamic studies, Muhammad Qutb, who was Qutb's brother.[9]) The French scholar G. Kepel gives us perhaps the most succinct summary of Qutb's importance: Qutb has been "the greatest ideological influence on the contemporary Islamist movement."[10]

Builder of an Islamic State Run by Shiite Clerics: Ayatollah Ruhollah Khomeini (1902–1989)

Ayatollah Ruhollah Khomeini (the honorific *Ayatollah* literally means "sign of God") was the spiritual mentor of the Islamic revolution in Iran. His regime was termed "the rule of the jurisprudential scholar" (*wilayat al-faqih*), and he himself was addressed as *Imam*, a title of honor.[11] His was the first attempt in modern times to create a purely Islamic state, or, more precisely, a Shiite state constructed along socialist lines and run with an iron hand by Shiite clerics. Such a clerical state had no precedent in Islamic history.

It is worthwhile noting here that although Khomeini himself is often labeled, correctly, as a fundamentalist, the roots of the 1978–1979 revolution in Iran were secular as well as religious. The modern scholar Nikki Keddie has pointed out the secular issues:

> The continuing growth of malaise and discontent among most sections of the Iranian population as despotism and repression increased in the 1970s, promised political and economic decentralization failed to materialize, and economic difficulties grew in 1976 and 1977, despite huge oil income, led to an outbreak of opposition beginning in 1977.[12]

Born in Iran in 1902 into a family of Shiite scholars (he was the grandson and son of *mullahs*, i.e., Shiite clerics), Khomeini was known for the depth of his religious learning. He became a Shiite scholar who wrote extensively on Islamic philosophy, law, and ethics. In the 1950s he was acclaimed as an ayatollah (a major religious leader) and later, in the early 1960s, as a grand ayatollah — one of the supreme religious leaders of Iran.

Khomeini was not very active politically until the early 1960s, when he began to speak out both against a land-reform program which forced farmers to borrow money to cultivate the land (the shah was in charge of much of the banking system and made huge profits by lending money to farmers) and against the emancipation of women. His arrest in 1963 sparked antigovernment demonstrations. The next year he was exiled to Turkey for criticizing the shah of Iran, Mohammad Reza Pahlavi, and for instigating riots. He then moved from Turkey to the Shiite holy city of Najaf in Iraq, where he became the acknowledged leader of the anti-shah opposition.

There he published, in 1971 a revolutionary book entitled *Islamic Government*. This puts forward three of his most important beliefs[13]:

1. "Islam knows neither monarchy nor dynastic succession," wrote Khomeini. As examples, he pointed to the facts that the Prophet had asked the Byzantine emperor and the Sassanid shah to give up the power they had obtained illegitimately, and that the martyr Husain ibn Ali (grandson of the Prophet and revered by Shiites as the Third Imam) had met his death trying to keep Islam from degenerating into a monarchy. In Khomeini's judgment, monarchy was an un–Islamic institution.
2. "All the laws and principles needed by man for his happiness and perfection," Khomeini wrote, can be found in Islam, i.e., in the Quran and the *sunna*. Most importantly, "The legislative power in Islam is limited to God alone." The Prophet and the imams were the only ones to know the law perfectly and to possess in full the qualify of justice (*adalat*). Their only legitimate successors are the Islamic jurists, so it follows that "Authority must come officially from the jurists."
3. Islam itself is in grave danger of being corrupted by the perverse doctrines of Christianity and Zionism, which have been encouraged in Iran by the imperialist powers. The *ulama* must purify Islam and proclaim its message. All ties with the "demonic" regime of the shah must be severed.

In 1978 Khomeini was deported from Iraq and moved to a suburb of Paris. Later that year, however, huge street demonstrations erupted in Iran as people from all walks of life demanded an end to the shah's dictatorial secular rule and the abdication of the shah himself. The shah fled to the United States, his main supporter. Khomeini himself returned in triumph to Tehran in 1979, where he was greeted as the religious leader of the revolution.

He soon displaced the first government of Iran after the revolution (a secular government headed by Mehdi Bazargan) and began to lay the groundwork for an Islamic state, building the revolution, in part, on a platform of attacking all things American. He consistently denounced the United States as "the Great Satan," not only because he saw it as evil but also because it was *alluring*—the true test of a diabolical threat.[14] He also exploited the 444-day takeover of the American embassy in Tehran (in which 52 Americans were held captive from 1979 to 1981) to humiliate the United States and to help cement clerical rule in Iran.

Under his leadership, Shiite clerics made government policy, while Khomeini himself made the final decisions on the most important matters. Hundreds of Iranians who had worked for the shah's regime were executed; members of the political opposition were jailed or killed. Khomeini was determined to steer Iran away from the West and make it a theocratically ruled state. The modern scholar Milton Viorst has noted that

> [Khomeini] perceived himself above all as an avenger of the humiliations that the West had for more than a century inflicted on the Muslims of the Middle East.... He was merciless and cunning. His well-advertised piety complemented a prodigious skill in grasping and shaping Iran's complex politics. Most important, he knew how to exploit the feelings of national resentment that characterized his time.[15]

In an infamous *fatwa* (in this context, a binding decree, not just a legal opinion) issued in 1989, Khomeini called for the death of the British writer Salman Rushdie because of the heresies allegedly contained in Rushdie's novel *The Satanic Verses* (1988).[16] This provocative book featured a character modeled on the Prophet Muhammad and depicted him and his transcription of the Quran in a negative light. Rushdie had to go into hiding under the protection of Scotland Yard but continued to write and make public appearances. In 1998 the Iranian government announced it would no longer seek to enforce the *fatwa* issued nine years earlier.

Although Iran's economic development suffered grievously under Khomeini's rule, and Khomeini himself prolonged the bloody Iran-Iraq war in an elusive hope of victory, he always retained his charismatic appeal to the Shiite masses of Iran and remained the supreme political and religious decision maker. He promised the masses an "Islamic state" without defining precisely what that was.

For rank-and-file Iranians, however, any other system probably offered more hope than life under the shah, so they accepted what Khomeini offered (although in fact they had no choice in matter), either in hopes of more social justice or of more Shiite religious observances. When Khomeini died in 1989, his funeral procession was escorted by as many as one million weeping followers, who desperately tried to kiss or touch his corpse, jostling it so much that it nearly fell to the road.

Author of Orientalism, or How the West Misperceives Islam: Edward W. Said (1935–2003)

Born in Jerusalem in 1935 of Palestinian parents, Said was educated in the United States, earning a doctorate from Harvard, and for four decades was a distinguished teacher and author at Columbia University in New York. A Christian and polymath, he wrote more than twenty books on subjects as diverse as the author Joseph Conrad, musicology, comparative literature, and the Middle East; was an excellent pianist and music critic; and was a passionate, eloquent spokesman for the cause of Palestinian nationalism.

For our purposes here, Said is best remembered for his brilliant work, *Orientalism* (1978), a citation from which was used in the introduction to this book.

"Orientalism" implies that the knowledge about Islam that is produced in Western scholarly discourses is not actually knowledge about Islam itself, but knowledge about *Western conceptions of Islam* and about the *Western interests of domination* that underlie these concepts.[17] As Said himself put it,

> Under the general heading of knowledge of the Orient, and within the umbrella of Western hegemony of the Orient during the period from the end of the eighteenth century, there emerged a complex Orient suitable for study in the academy, for display in the museum, for reconstruction in the colonial office, for theoretical illustration in anthropological, biological, linguistic, racial, and historical theses about mankind and the universe, for instances of economic and sociological theories of development, revolution, cultural personality, national or religious character.[18]

Obituaries honoring Said after his death in 2003 did not fail to point out the importance of *Orientalism*. The *Washington Post* said that it was "a seminal examination of the way the West perceives the Islamic world. It was translated into twenty-six languages and helped establish an academic field of post–Colonial studies."[19] The *Financial Times* judged that

> [Said was] one of the late 20th century's most influential thinkers about the relations between culture and politics.... *Orientalism* ... established his reputation by bringing together his two personae — professor of English literature at Columbia and member of the Palestine National Council. It caught the imagination of students all over the world with its thesis that western academic learning about Islam and the Muslim peoples was not detached and scientific, as it liked to present itself, but one of the instruments the west used to impose its domination.[20]

Author of Rethink Islam: Mohammed Arkoun (1928–)

An Algerian scholar, Arkoun was professor of the history of Islamic thought at the Sorbonne in Paris and is best known for his efforts to rethink and reshape the relationship between Europe, Islam, and the Mediterranean world. In 2001, for example, he delivered a series of lectures at the University of Edinburgh which dealt, respectively, with "Islam, Europe, and the 'West': The Need for an Intellectual Shift;" "Inaugurating a Critique of Islamic Reason;" and "The Concept of Prophetic Discourse: From Revelation to the Revelatory Function of Religious Discourse."[21]

Although widely considered a leading contemporary authority on Islam, Arkoun's views have consistently been rejected by traditional Islamist intellectual circles as being too secular and too liberal.[22] The reaction of the conservatives was understandable. In *Rethinking Islam: Common Questions, Uncommon Answers* (1989), for example, Arkoun wrote:

> Nationalist ideology and the demand for a return to a mythical version of Islam today exercise the same sort of pressure on scientific rationality as did the legal-

theological teaching of the Middle Ages. So-called Islamic thought has never engaged in reflections on the ideological function of discourse. As a result, assertions derived from the Qur'an are uniformly taken as truth so long as they are guaranteed by the experts who founded the great schools of interpretation or by the ulema [sic] deemed to be authorities by the consensus of believers. The person trained inside this dogmatic closure cannot think about the problems of ideology. Such a person will, quite to the contrary, absorb [a given text] as totally true.... *I envisage the Qur'an as a linguistic space where several types of discourse (prophetic, legislative, narrative, sapiential) work simultaneously and intersect each other.*[23]

A publisher's synopsis of Arkoun's most recent book, *The Unthought in Contemporary Islamic Thought* (2002), also makes it clear why Islamic conservatives will probably never be counted among Arkoun's supporters:

Arkoun's approach subjects varying belief-systems (including non-belief), traditions of exegesis, theology and jurisprudence to a critique aimed at liberating reason from dogmatic constructs. By treating Islam as a religion as well as a time-honored tradition of thought, Mohammed Arkoun's work aims at overcoming the limitations of a purely descriptive, narrative and chronological treatment of history. He does so by recommending that the entire development of Muslim thought, from the Qur'anic worldview to the range of contemporary discourses, be subjected to critical analysis—*an analysis that will engender a discussion as to how Islamic studies and thought can be brought to the level of the fertile criticisms witnessed in European scholarship and historical development since the 17th century.*[24]

From a secular point of view, the Swedish scholar Ulrika Mårtensson has pointed out that

Arkoun is a good example of thinkers who see cultural interaction as a benign potential, rather than a threat. He also pinpoints the watertight relationship between the classical Islamic sciences and the institution of the *ulama*, that is, the religious leadership. Their refusal to change their thought-patterns is as much a social as an intellectual refusal: opening up to the impact of modern sciences on their classical ones means giving up their social authority as the community's sole spiritual guides—or a least some of them perceive it that way.[25]

Advocate of the Islamization of Science: Seyyed Hossein Nasr (1933–)

Born in Tehran (Iran) in 1933, Nasr received his doctorate from Harvard in 1958, where he specialized in Islamic cosmology and science. After teaching at Tehran University, at Harvard and at the American University of Beirut, he emigrated to the United States in 1979, joining the faculty of George Washington University in

Washington, D.C. in 1984. He is currently that university's Professor of Islamic Studies.

Nasr has already been quoted three times in this book and has been acclaimed by his supporters as one of the most prolific scholars of Islamic and comparative religious studies in the world today. He has published extensively, chiefly on the concept of the "Islamization of science." This should be viewed as an effort to implant conservative Islamic values into the field of Western science, which is otherwise held to lack an ethical foundation.[26]

In one of his early books, *Science and Civilization in Islam* (1968), Nasr discusses the achievements of Islamic scientific thought in medicine, astronomy, mathematics, algebra, chemistry, physics, geography, and natural history. His advocates claim that his work is based on original sources and remains one of the best overviews or brief surveys of the entire scientific corpus of the Islamic world.

In the Introduction to *Science and Civilization in Islam*, Nasr explains what he means by "Islamic science." Because this concept is not self-evident, it is perhaps useful to cite him here at some length. He tells us:

> To the Muslim, history is a series of accidents that in no way affect the non-temporal principles of Islam. He is more interested in knowing and "realizing" these principles than in cultivating originality and change as intrinsic virtues.... The arts and sciences came to possess instead a stability and a "crystallization" based on the immutability of the principles from which they had issued forth; it is this stability that is too often mistaken in the West today for stagnation and sterility....
>
> The arts and sciences in Islam are based on the idea of unity, which is the heart of the Muslim revelation. Just as all genuine Islamic art ... provides the plastic forms through which one can contemplate the Divine Unity [*tawhid*] manifesting itself in multiplicity, so do all the sciences that can properly be called Islamic reveal the unity of Nature....
>
> The Western world has [ever since the fifteenth century] concentrated its intellectual energies upon the study of the quantitative aspects of things, thus developing a science of Nature, whose all too obvious fruits in the physical domain have won for it the greatest esteem among people everywhere, for most of whom "science" is identified with technology and its applications. Islamic science, by contrast, seeks ultimately to attain such knowledge as will contribute toward the spiritual perfection and deliverance of anyone capable of studying it; thus its fruits are inward and hidden, its values more difficult to discern. To understand it requires placing oneself within its perspective and accepting as legitimate a science of Nature which has a different end, and uses different means, from those of modern science.[27]

Although this citation sums up accurately Nasr's own point of view, his opinions remain controversial and are not widely shared by other specialists working in the field. Indeed, many Muslim and non–Muslim scientists today are suspicious of what they see as a conservative religious enterprise to create a new category of "Islamic science"—one which must be treated differently from the familiar Western (and now globally accepted) concept of science.

These critics also point out that in the works of Islamic astronomers, God or the Quran are not mentioned except in well-defined invocations or supplications, even though a work itself may be as long as two hundred or more folios. Other Islamic thinkers also resist making generalizations about Islam and science over a period of hundreds of years, thinking it more fruitful to concentrate instead on specific branches of science and on specific sects of Islam at given times and places.

"The Luther of Islam": Abdolkarim Soroush (1945–)

Soroush was hailed not only as "the foremost Iranian and Islamic political philosopher and theologian" but also, because of his strong desire to reform his religion, as "the Luther of Islam."[28] He was educated both in religious studies, especially Islamic law and exegesis, and in modern science, i.e., analytical chemistry. In London he also studied the history and philosophy of science and became an activist in student politics directed against the shah's regime. He returned to Iran when the revolution began and thereafter became a stern critic of the hegemony of the Shiite clerics.

An academic meeting in Washington, D.C., sponsored by the Middle East Institute (MEI) in 2000 focused on a collection of Soroush's essays in English, which were published in 2002 as *Reason, Freedom, and Democracy in Islam*. At that meeting, Soroush analyzed the link between religion and freedom.[29] In Iran, he indicated, oppressive regimes had based their political power on Islam. But when religion began to play a more active role in the political process, the regimes began to restrict freedom of speech and assembly. As a result, he concluded, Iranians now see religion as being essentially authoritarian.

It is this fact which has driven his own work. Indeed, as the Swedish scholar Ulrika Mårtensson has pointed out, Soroush both wants to save Islam from being an instrument of authoritarian government and to save Muslims from an authoritarian rule legitimized by their own religion. Soroush thus has two interrelated goals: secularization and democratization.[30]

In Soroush's view, the proper role of philosophers is to try to reconcile religion and freedom, that is to say, to give religion a new definition and to link democracy to religion. Soroush hoped to convince his fellow Iranians that it is possible to be a good Muslim and still to enjoy freedom. The task he set for himself was to find a theoretical foundation linking the immutable aspects of Islam to the changeable aspects of peoples' daily lives.

At the MEI meeting, Soroush also stressed that there were two concepts of religion — a maximalist view and a minimalist view. In the former, everything has to be derived from religion. This view, he said, is prevalent in Iran today and is the cause of most of Iran's current problems. Soroush said that this view had to be replaced by a minimalist view, i.e., one which recognizes that some values, e.g., human rights, can usefully be borrowed from outside Islam, though they must be adapted to the needs of Islamic societies.[31]

Soroush spelled out clearly his concerns for the future of Islam in a perceptive interview given in 2002. This question was put to him:

How do you view the future of the Moslems' intellectual and social life — in other words, what major and essential problems do you find in the path of the next two or three generations of Moslems?

He replied:

> This is a huge problem and I am not sure if I can do justice to it.... I have distinguished between two kinds of Islam: Islam of identity and Islam of truth. In the former, Islam is a guise for cultural identity and a response to what is considered the "crisis of identity." The latter refers to Islam as a repository of truths that point toward the path of worldly and otherworldly salvation....
>
> I fear that Moslems, in their confrontation with Western civilization, wish to turn to Islam as an identity.... I think one of the greatest theoretical plagues of the Islamic world, in general, is that people are gradually coming to understand Islam as an identity rather than a truth. So, I believe that the Islam of identity should yield to the Islam of truth. The latter can coexist with other truths; the former, however, is, by its very nature, belligerent and bellicose. It is the Islam of war, not the Islam of peace.[32]

Syrian Modernist and Reformer: Aziz al-Azmeh (c. 1949–)

Born in Damascus, al-Azmeh received his Ph.D. in Oriental Studies at Oxford in 1977. Subsequently, he taught in a number of different countries and published extensively, chiefly in Arabic and English but also in German and French. Known as a modernist and as a reformer of Islam, he had some strong words to say in the 1996 edition of his book, *Islams* [sic] *and Modernities* about what he termed the "Islamization of knowledge." In his view,

> The two strands — skepticism towards science and the scientific validation of the Koranic texts in the name of *i'jaz* [the inimitability of the Quran] — are continuing today, having taken different courses. Ultimately, they led to the formulation of the notion of the "Islamization of Knowledge": not only of natural sciences, but equally of social sciences.
>
> Correlatively, this trend has been inimical to the development of the more historically apposite tendencies in the exegesis of Modernist Reformism, namely, those calling for turning to the Koranic text with the equivalent of modern historical, philological and analytical scholarship. In this vein, some of the best and most innovative attempts to study the Koran scientifically have been marginalized during this century.[33]

In a subsequent interview with the *Iran Bulletin*, al-Azmeh also had criticism of Islamic fundamentalism:

> Fundamentalism is an attitude towards time, which it considers to be of no consequence, and therefore finds no problem with the absurd proposition that the initial conditions, the golden age, can be retrieved: either by going back to the texts without the mediation of traditions considered corrupt (because they

represent Time between the present and its putative beginnings)..., or by the re-formation of society according to primitivist models seen to be copies of practices in the golden age, as with what are recognized as fundamentalist movements.[34]

In that same interview, al-Azmeh made some further observations about fundamentalism. He was so eloquent on this subject that it is worth quoting him at some length:

> We must — again — resist the temptation, again widely held, to see a "return" to Islam: this is unhistorical, it does not take seriously the profound changes undergone by our societies, and does not account for the "absence" of that which is supposed to be "returning," quite apart from it assenting to the political Islamist reading of itself: no, no organic answer can satisfy the critical gaze, and we must move elsewhere for explanations....
>
> We must also be conscious of how untraditional this neo-traditionalism of Islamism [violence-prone fundamentalism] is, and how very much out of keeping with social practice it pretends to represent: otherwise it would not have required — whenever it sought to expand — the deployment of such an extraordinary and contentious amount of violence, in ways small no less than dramatic. It does so because it is out of keeping with social life.[35]

Fugitive Most Wanted by the United States: Osama bin Laden (1957–)

Shortly after the 11 September 2001 terrorist attacks on New York and Washington, D.C., the United States Federal Bureau of Investigation updated and reissued a "most-wanted" poster containing a photograph and a description of Osama bin Laden. The poster read in part:

> FBI TEN MOST
> WANTED FUGITIVE
> MURDER OF U.S. NATIONALS OUTSIDE THE UNITED STATES; CONSPIRACY TO MURDER U.S. NATIONALS OUTSIDE THE UNITED STATES; ATTACK ON A FEDERAL FACILITY RESULTING IN DEATH
> USAMA BIN LADEN
> CAUTION
> USAMA BIN LADEN IS WANTED IN CONNECTION WITH THE AUGUST 7, 1998 BOMBINGS OF THE UNITED STATES EMBASSIES IN DAR ES SALAAM, TANZANIA, AND NAIROBI, KENYA. THESE ATTACKS KILLED OVER 200 PEOPLE. IN ADDITION, BIN LADEN IS A SUSPECT IN OTHER TERRORIST ATTACKS THROUGHOUT THE WORLD.
> CONSIDERED ARMED AND EXTREMELY DANGEROUS

The poster described bin Laden as "the leader of a terrorist organization known as al-Qaeda, 'the Base," and called attention to the $25 million reward being offered

FBI "most wanted" poster: Osama Bin Laden.

by the United States Department of State for "information leading directly to the apprehension or conviction of Osama Bin Laden," and the additional $2 million dollar reward offered by the Airline Pilots Association and the Air Transport Association.[36]

When this book was finished (late in 2004), Osama bin Laden was the world's best-known theorist and practitioner of rage-driven *jihad*. An extremist fundamentalist and fervent Arab nationalist who was the mastermind behind numerous deadly terrorist attacks, he is neither an Islamic scholar nor a deep thinker.[37] Nevertheless, he merits our attention here because he acted out some of the most radical fundamentalist ideas which have been circulating in Islamic learning since the time of the traditional theologian Ibn Taymiyya, who died in 1328. In short, bin Laden led by example, not by writing or teaching.

Born in Saudi Arabia in 1957, bin Laden was the seventeenth son of Muhammad bin Laden, an illiterate but brilliant Yemeni longshoreman who with his brothers founded a construction company (the Ben Laden Group) in Saudi Arabia. The company did extremely well. It profited mightily from Saudi government contracts and built huge mosques in Mecca and Medina, fast highways, and princely palaces. The fortune of the bin Laden family has been estimated at billions of dollars.[38] The family was so rich that it was able to extend financial help to the royal family of Saudi Arabia when the Sauds found themselves temporarily short of cash.

Osama bin Laden, raised to be a strict and devout Muslim, earned a degree in economics and public administration in 1981 from the highly conservative King Abdul-Aziz University in Jeddah, Saudi Arabia. As mentioned earlier, one of his teachers was Muhammad Qutb, a distinguished professor of Islamic studies and the brother of the executed fundamentalist Sayyid Qutb. While bin Laden was still a student, the Soviets invaded Afghanistan. Bin Laden decided to help the *mujahadeen* (literally "holy warrior") resistance. He traveled to Afghanistan and Pakistan to meet with the Islamic scholars and leaders who in earlier years had been guests at the bin Laden family home in Saudi Arabia. He raised large amounts of money for the *mujahadeen* cause.

After graduating from the university, bin Laden fought with the *mujahadeen* in Afghanistan and, beginning in about 1995, produced numerous policy statements declaring war against the United States, calling for the overthrow of the royal family of Saudi Arabia, and issued *fatwas* urging Muslims "to kill Americans and their allies, civilian and military, [as] an individual duty."[39] Because it is important to understand bin Laden's thinking, we shall cite several of these public statements at some length.[40]

"Declaration of War Against the Americans Occupying the Land of the Two Holy Places," i.e., the Mosques of Mecca and Medina in Saudi Arabia. (1996)

Issued by bin Laden in August 1996 from his stronghold in the mountains of Afghanistan, this long, rambling declaration runs to twenty-two pages in the English translation published in 2001 by Yonah Alexander and Michael Swetnam in their book *Osama bin Laden's al-Qaida*. Some of bin Laden's key assertions are summarized below in italics, followed by quotations from the texts involved.[41]

The problems of the Islamic world are due to the Jews and the Americans and their allies. Bin Laden tells his readers,

It should not be hidden from you that the people of Islam had suffered from aggression, iniquity and injustice imposed on them by the Zionist-Crusaders alliance and their collaborators; to the extent that the Muslims' blood became the cheapest and their wealth as loot in the hands of the enemies.... The people of Islam awakened and realized that they are the main target for the aggression of the Zionist-Crusader alliance.

With God's help, Muslims defeated the Soviet Union in Afghanistan and can defeat the United States as well. Bin Laden writes that

[I am living in] a safe base in the high Hindu Kush mountains in Khurasan [an historical region comprising what is now northeastern Iran, southern Turkmenistan, and northern Afghanistan]; where by the Grace of Allah the largest infidel military forces in the world was destroyed. And the myth of the superpower was withered in front of the Mujahideen cries of *Allah u Akbar* [God is great]. Today we work from the same mountains to lift the iniquity that has been imposed on the Ummah [the Islamic community] by the Zionist-Crusader alliance.... We ask Allah to bestow victory on us. He is our Patron and He is the Most Capable. From here, today we begin the work, talking and discussing the ways of correcting what has happened to the Islamic world in general, and the Land of the Two Holy Places in particular.

In Saudi Arabia, conditions are intolerable now and are getting worse. Here are some of the grievances Bin Laden lists:

People are fully concerned about their everyday livings; everybody talks about the deterioration of the economy, inflation, ever-increasing debts and jails full of prisoners. Government employees with limited income talk about debts of tens of thousands and hundreds of thousands of Saudi Riyals [the currency of Saudi Arabia].... Great merchants and contractors speak about the hundreds and thousands of millions of Riyals owed to them by the government.... [In addition to failing to pay its debts, the Saudi government is guilty of] ignoring the divine Shar'iah law; depriving people of their legitimate rights; allowing the Americans to occupy the land of the Holy Places [during the Gulf War]; imprisonment, unjustly, of the sincere [Islamic] scholars.

According to bin Laden, *Ibn Taymiyya would have agreed that using* jihad *to expel the Americans from Saudi Arabia is a primary duty for Muslims today.* Bin Laden tells us:

If there is more than one duty to be carried out, then the most important one should receive priority. Clearly, after Belief there is no more important duty than pushing the American enemy out of the holy land. No other priority, except Belief, could be considered before it. [For] the people of knowledge, Ibn Taymiyyah stated, "to fight [*jihad*] in defense of religion and Belief is a collective duty; there is no other duty after Belief than fighting the enemy who is corrupting the life and the religion. There are no preconditions for this duty and the enemy should be fought with one's best abilities."[42]

Despite its military power, the United States is cowardly and can be defeated:

We say to the Defense Secretary [William Perry].... Where was this false courage of yours when the explosion in Beirut took place in 1983? You were turned into scattered bits and pieces at that time; 241 [Americans], mainly marines, were killed.... But your most disgraceful case was in Somalia ... when tens of your soldiers were killed in minor battles and one American pilot was dragged in the streets of Mogadishu you left the area carrying disappointment, humiliation, defeat and your dead with you.... You have been disgraced by Allah and you withdrew; the extent of your impotence and weaknesses became very clear.

Death is better than dishonor. Bin Laden exhorts his followers:

Death is better than life in humiliation! [Bin Laden is making a key point here: humiliation leads to the irretrievable loss of a man's personal honor, which is the bedrock of Islamic culture.] ...My Muslim brothers of the world: Your brothers in Palestine and in the land of the Two Holy Places are calling upon your help and asking you to take part against the enemy — your enemy — and their enemy, the Americans and the Israelis.... O you horses [soldiers] of Allah: ride and march on. This is the time of hardship, so be tough. And know that your gathering and cooperation in order to liberate the sanctities [sic] of Islam is the right step toward unifying the whole world of the Ummah under the banner of "No God but Allah."

"THE NEW POWDER KEG IN THE MIDDLE EAST" (1996)

Following is an interview with bin Laden which appeared in the October–November 1996 issue of the militant–Islamist magazine *Nida'ul Islam* (*The Call of Islam*), published in Sydney, Australia. In it bin Laden discusses Saudi Arabia and other issues of the day. These are two of the key questions, and the answers.[xliii]

[*Interviewer's question*:] As part of the furious international campaign against the Jihad movement, you were personally the target of a prejudiced attack, which accused you of financing terrorism and being part of an international terrorist organization. What do you have to say about that?

[*Excerpt from bin Laden's answer*:] After the end of the cold war, America escalated its campaign against the Muslim world in its entirety, aiming to get rid of Islam itself. Its main focus in this was to target the scholars and the reformers who were enlightening the people to the dangers of the Judeo-American alliance, and they also targeted the Mujahideen.... However, our gratitude to Allah, their campaign was not successful, as terrorizing the American occupiers is a religious and logical obligation. We are grateful to Allah Most Exalted in that He has facilitated Jihad in His cause for us, against the Americo-Israeli attacks on the Islamic sanctities [sic].

[*Interviewer's question*:] What is the responsibility of the Muslim populations towards the international campaign against Islam?

[*Excerpt from bin Laden's answer*:] What bears no doubt is that their fierce Judeo-Christian campaign against the Muslim world, the likes of which has never been seen before, is that the Muslims must prepare all the possible might to repel the enemy on the military, economic, missionary, and all other areas.

CNN Interview (1997)

In a March 1997 Cable News Network (CNN) interview, bin Laden said, among other things:

> We declared jihad against the U.S. government, because the U.S. government is unjust, criminal and tyrannical. It has committed acts that are extremely unjust, hideous and criminal, whether directly or through its support of the Israeli occupation.
>
> The country of the Two Holy Places has in our religion a peculiarity of its own over the other Muslim countries. In our religion, it is not permissible for any non-Muslim to stay in our country. Therefore, even though American civilians are not targeted in our plan, they must leave. We do not guarantee their safety, because we are in a society of more than a billion Muslims.[44]

"Jihad Against Jews and Crusaders" (1998)

Under the banner of the "World Islamic Front," this statement, issued in February 1998 by bin Laden and four other radical Islamic leaders from Egypt, Pakistan and Bangladesh, contained the following *fatwa*:

> The ruling to kill the Americans and their allies—civilians and military—is an individual duty for every Muslim who can do it in any country in which it is possible to do it, in order to liberate al-Aqsa Mosque [in Jerusalem] and the holy mosque [in Mecca] from their grip, and in order for their armies to move out of all the lands of Islam, defeated and unable to threaten any Muslim.
>
> This is in accordance with the words of Almighty God, "and fight the pagans altogether as they fight you altogether," and "fight them until there is no more tumult or oppression, and there prevail justice and faith in God...."
>
> We—with God's help—call on every Muslim who believes in God and wishes to be rewarded to comply with God's order to kill the Americans and plunder their money wherever and whenever they find it. We also call on Muslim ulema [sic], leaders, youths, and soldiers to launch the raid on Satan's U.S. troops and the devil's supporters allying with them, and to displace those who are behind them so that they may learn a lesson.[45]

Barbara Metcalf, an American scholar, has made an interesting point about bin Laden's *fatwa*:

> A little noted aspect of Osama bin Laden's leadership was his claim to authority, despite his lack of a traditional education, to issue *fatwa*. His call to make *jihad* incumbent on all Muslims deployed a technical distinction of Islamic legal thought, saying that *jihad* was an individual duty, *farz 'ain*, rather than a duty on some subset of the *umma* (e.g., political leaders, soldiers), *farz kifaya*.[46]

ABC Interview with Osama bin Laden (1998)

The first part of this interview, which took place in May 1998, consists of questions put to bin Laden by his followers. The second part consists of questions posed to him by the American Broadcasting Corporation (ABC) reporter John Miller. Here are some points made by bin Laden on the wrongs committed against Muslims and on the certain defeat of the Jews and the Americans:

> The wrongs and crimes committed against the Muslim nation are far greater than can be covered in this interview. America heads the list of aggressors against Muslims. The recurrence of aggression against Muslims everywhere is proof enough. For over half a century, Muslims in Palestine have been slaughtered and assaulted and robbed of their honor and of their property.... They [the Americans] rip us of our wealth, resources and oil. Our religion is under attack. They kill, murder our brothers. They compromise our honor and dignity and dare we utter a single word of protest, we are called terrorists.
>
> We are certain that we shall — with the grace of Allah — prevail over the Americans and the Jews, as the Messenger of Allah promised us in an authentic prophetic tradition when He said the Hour of Resurrection shall not come before Muslims fight Jews and before Jews hide behind trees and behind rocks.... We anticipate a black future for America. Instead of remaining United States, it shall end up separated states and shall have to carry the bodies of its sons back to America.[47]

Time Magazine Interviews (1998)

In two interviews with *Time Magazine* in December 1998, bin Laden reaffirmed his *fatwa* and also spoke about chemical and nuclear weapons:

> The International Front for Jihad against the U.S. and Israel has, by the grace of God, issued a crystal-clear fatwah calling on the Islamic nation to carry on jihad aimed at liberating holy sites. The nation of Muhammad has responded to this appeal.
>
> Acquiring weapons for the defense of Muslims is a religious duty. If I have indeed acquired [chemical and nuclear weapons], then I thank God for enabling me to do so. And if I seek to acquire those weapons, I am carrying out a duty. It would be a sin for Muslims not to try to possess the weapons that would prevent the infidels from inflicting harm on Muslims.[48]

Audiotapes (after 2001)

American forces have been hunting for bin Laden since the 11 September 2001 terrorist attacks on the United States. Believed to be hiding in the tribal border region between Afghanistan and Pakistan, he subsequently issued several audiotapes. Excerpts from an audiotape released in January 2004, for example, convey the flavor of his thought. He said:

> My message is to incite you against the conspiracies, especially those uncovered by the occupation of the crusaders in Baghdad under the pretext of weapons

of mass destruction, and also of the situation [in Jerusalem].... The occupation of Iraq is the beginning of the full occupation of the Gulf states. The Gulf is the key for control of the world in the point of view of the big powers because of the presence of the biggest deposits of oil.[49]

Bin Laden and the Pursuit of Learning

In the next chapter we shall explore the impact that bin Laden's thought may have on the future of Islamic learning. It is worth repeating that bin Laden is neither an Islamic scholar nor a deep thinker. Nevertheless, he has played a crystallizing role in the contemporary pursuit of learning in the Islamic world. As the modern scholar Bernard Lewis reminds us,

> Osama bin Laden and his Al-Qa'ida followers may not represent Islam, and many of their statements and actions directly contradict basic Islamic principles and teachings, but they do arise within [the] Muslim civilization, just as Hitler and the Nazis arose from within Christendom, and they too must be seen in their own cultural, religious, and historical context.[50]

Chapter X

Conclusions: Future Prospects for Islamic Learning

We have now examined, albeit briefly, 92 noteworthy Islamic personalities and cultural achievements. Islamic learning is nearly 1,400 years old and will doubtless continue into the foreseeable future. It is therefore not unreasonable for us to ask at this point: what might Islamic learning look like in the early decades of the twenty-first century?

Challenges

There can be no single, or simple, answer to this question. Much of what will happen will depend not on religious factors per se but on political, economic, military and social developments in the Islamic world. These developments cannot be foreseen with any confidence. All that seems clear is that, taken as a whole, the third world — including the Islamic portion of that world — is not in very good shape right now and is not likely to fare much better in the decades immediately ahead.

The reason that prospects for the third world remain so clouded is that little if any real progress has been made in addressing a familiar litany of intractable problems. These include ethnicity; massive urbanization; rapid population growth and demographic shifts resulting in large numbers of young people, who face poor prospects in life; widespread poverty, exacerbated by a highly unequal distribution of income; a lack of individual responsibility and accountability; a pronounced lack of political, economic and social freedom; low levels of education[1]; corrupt leaders whose main goals are to enrich themselves and to stay in power; AIDS and other grave health problems; and unchecked environmental degradation.

The Islamic world itself faces two additional challenges: secularism and individualism. Secularism focuses not on otherworldly concerns but on life here on earth; individualism puts a high value on being a free, self-contained person who is relatively unrestrained by either church or state. In the liberal democracies of the developed world, these two concepts have walked hand-in-hand and have spread widely.

They are very likely to spread even further throughout the world. The problem here is that, as stated in the chapter on fundamentalism, many Muslim traditionalists fear that if left unchecked in their own countries, secularism and individualism (including the Western moral code and the rights of women) will become cancers that will ultimately destroy Islam, at least as the traditionalists would like to see it practiced.

Their fears appear to be well-founded. Secularism and individualism have already had major impacts on Christianity and other religions: there is no reason why Islam should be immune. This fact helps explain the growing appeal of Islamic fundamentalism, which deals with secularism and individualism, quite effectively, simply by banning them.

Except for some liberal intellectuals (few of whom still live in the Islamic world: most are in the United States or in Europe), Islamic learning has not yet risen to the intellectual challenges posed by the secularism and individualism of the late twentieth and early twenty-first centuries. These liberal intellectuals include Mohammed Arkoun (1928–), Abdolkarim Soroush (1945–) and Aziz al-Azmeh (1949–), all of whom have been discussed earlier. For the most part, however, the response of Muslims today to these challenges has been protective and defensive. This is understandable—no one likes to see their religion come under fire—but some responsibility must fall on individual Muslims themselves for taking the easy route of blaming others for their troubles and for not embarking on the difficult path of reforming the practice of Islam.[2]

Is reform possible? It is a fact of life that autocratic governments in the Islamic world (and elsewhere) do not welcome or, indeed, even tolerate, much freedom of thought. At the same time, the conservative religious leaders (the *ulama*) fear—correctly—that free thought will erode their religious power base and thus, ultimately, their political, economic and social power base as well. When autocratic governments are inseparably linked with the *ulama*, as in Saudi Arabia, prospects for independent thought are slim indeed.

That said, it is also clear that the current problems of the Islamic world cannot be laid entirely at Islam's doorstep. As we have seen, history proves that Islam is not intrinsically hostile to the life of the mind: there have been periods of brilliance when Islamic learning has flourished. The later political and other failings of Islamic states therefore cannot be due to Islam alone: if they were, these periods could never have occurred. Secular failings must be explained in secular terms, not in religious terms. In our own times, for example, autocratic rule and independent thought have never made good bedfellows.

Themes in the Future

A reasonable guess is that in the coming decades Islamic learning will revolve around three main themes, which are not mutually exclusive but can exist simultaneously, even in the same country. These themes are (1) "steaming as before," (2) a further shift toward fundamentalism, and (3) opening wide the gate of *ijtihad*.

First, *steaming as before* was the traditional nautical phrase entered in the deck log when a steamer was making a long ocean passage and was navigating uneventfully on the same course laid down during the previous watch. Here *steaming as before* will be used to suggest that Islamic learning (i.e., the classical religious learning, not modern secular studies, which are, in fact, flourishing in the Islamic world) may well continue on its present traditional course, without acknowledging the need to make any significant alternations.

Second, if large numbers of Muslims should conclude that mainstream Islam is ineffective (if, for example, the Islamic world slips even further behind the Western world), they may become more receptive to what is billed as an earlier, purer and thus — or so the fundamentalists claim — more successful form of Islam.[3] Such a shift toward fundamentalism seems highly likely because, as the modern scholar Ira Lapidus has pointed out,

> In some respects the emergence of extremist political Islam is the outcome of the historical processes of the last century. Islam used to be one element of the multilayered sense of self held by most Muslims.... However, the destruction of historical forms of small communities and the reduction of peoples to an undifferentiated mass mobilized for political struggle, the decline of the "ulama" and Sufi authority and the emergence of a new radical religious intelligentsia, and the global forces of media and migration *have for many people reduced the choice of identity to one between Islam and the secular world of nation-states. This polarization has had devastating worldwide consequences.*[4]

Third, as mentioned earlier, the gate of *ijtihad* was never firmly shut in Sunni jurisprudence but was always open to some extent; it remained fully open (in theory, at least) in Shiite jurisprudence. It is therefore conceivable that, with the help of their coreligionists in the West, who live and work in countries where much greater freedom of expression is possible, reform-minded Muslims may begin using independent thought to hammer out a modern version of Islam. This might be one which shuns the excesses of Western secularism, individualism and materialism, while at the same time upholding the importance of *tawhid* (the divine unity) and of human reason.

Rushing in where angels fear to tread, this book will end with a short but possibly controversial summary of Islamic learning, and an equally brief forecast of its prospects in the decades immediately ahead.

Islamic Learning Weighed in the Balance

Taken as a whole over the past 1,400 years, Islamic learning has not achieved a diversity, depth and breadth surpassing that achieved by other world cultures over the same long period of time. In recent centuries, the focus of world learning has shifted decisively away from the Islamic world and toward Western centers. There have been several periods of Islamic brilliance but, arguably, the only truly outstanding achievement of Islamic learning since the seventeenth century has been in architecture, namely, the Taj Mahal. What is certain is that the Islamic world can never again aspire to be a center of learning until political conditions change so substantially that much greater intellectual freedom is tolerated and, indeed, encouraged.

Prospects for the Future

Islamic fundamentalism, which has long played a modest but visible role in Islamic learning, will grow in the years ahead, largely because the prospects for the third world, including the Islamic portion thereof, are so bleak. Perceived humiliations of Muslims are likely to spur the growth of fundamentalism, too. Saddam Hussein's ignominious surrender to American forces in December 2003 is perhaps the most compelling recent example.

Radical fundamentalism will continue to present itself to potential followers under an benevolent guise. Writing in the *International Herald Tribune* in 2003, the correspondent David Rohde aptly described this approach as that of "a romantic liberation movement ... a militant ideology ... that combines Islam's powerful call for social justice with a critique of Western corporate imperialism and the corrupt Muslim elites who benefit from it."[5]

As a result of its potential for growth and its inherent anti-intellectualism, fundamentalism will pose the greatest challenge to Islamic learning in the years ahead. At the same time, however, such fundamentalism contains the seeds of its own destruction. Fundamentalist doctrines may have great emotional appeal, but since they are based more on faith than on reason, they can never be the basis on which a modern country can be governed successfully.

We may therefore hazard the guess that if fundamentalists do come to power in various parts of the Islamic world, they will have no more success than fundamentalists have had to date in Iran, the Sudan or Afghanistan. The good news, then, is that while mainstream Islamic learning may need to be modernized, it is not likely to be replaced by Islamic fundamentalism in the foreseeable future.

Appendix 1

The Decorative and Other Arts of Islam

This book has already touched on some of the decorative and other arts of Islam but it may be useful to consider them here, if only very briefly. It is a shame that European, Chinese and even Japanese art is more familiar to most Westerners than is Islamic art. As Linda Komaroff, Curator of Islamic Art at the Los Angeles Country Museum of Art, has pointed out,

> Islamic art is perhaps the most accessible manifestation of a complex civilization that often seems enigmatic to outsiders. Through its brilliant use of color and its superb balance between design and form, Islamic art creates an immediate visual impact. Its strong aesthetic appeal transcends distances as time and space, as well as distances in language, culture, and creed.[1]

Because Islamic art is such a vast subject, art historians have worked out numerous ways of dividing it into smaller units which are easier to analyze. Some of these subdivisions are based on chronology; others are based on cultural entities.

Examples of the former include the early Islamic period (seventh through tenth century), the early medieval period (eleventh through mid-thirteenth century), the late medieval period (mid-thirteenth through fifteenth century), the late Islamic period (sixteenth through eighteenth century), and Islamic art under European influences and contemporary trends (eighteenth century to the present). Examples of the cultural entities in which Islamic art flourished include the Ottoman Empire, the Islamic lands in the West (e.g., Spain), Iraq, Iran, Egypt, India, China, Indonesia, and Africa.[2]

Art historians distinguish between Islamic art that was based on religious sources (the Quran and the *hadith*) and that which emerged as a manifestation of Islamic culture itself. In this appendix we shall look quickly at different kinds of Islamic art, often the work of anonymous artists, without drawing such a subtle distinction. We will refer to Islamic architecture; the written word, including calligraphy; arabesques; carpets; woodwork; metalware; ceramics; tiles; stucco and stone; figurative painting; and music.

Calligraphy from the Quran, Topkapi Palace in Istanbul. (Photograph courtesy of André Kahlmeyer.)

Islamic Architecture

As mentioned in Chapter IV, the most important expression of Islamic art has been architecture, especially the architecture of monuments and mosques. Of these, the Taj Mahal stands preeminent. It is one of the very few man-made objects which is difficult to praise too highly, so even though it was discussed earlier it can usefully be revisited now.

The refined elegance of the Taj represents such an apogee of Islamic learning that this building will be used here to represent — and, indeed, to overshadow — any other Islamic monument or mosque. If one of the purposes of architecture is to use physical forms to communicate the experience and ideas of a given culture, then the Taj deserves the highest possible marks. It captures, more perfectly than any other Islamic building, intellectual discipline or work of art, that "lightness of being" which so often can be felt in the best of Islamic culture. The acoustics inside the main dome are such that a single note of a flute will echo five times. Writing in 1903, the French novelist Pierre Lotti was most impressed. He reported that

> The sonority of this white mausoleum is almost eerie with its ceaseless echoes. When the name of Allah is chanted, the exaggerated sound of the voice is prolonged for several seconds and lingers endlessly in the air, like the vibrations of an organ.[3]

Art historian Henri Stierlin asks rhetorically, "Wherein lies the aesthetic value of the Taj Mahal?" and answers himself as follows:

> [It is] chiefly in an extraordinary sense of measure, in an absence of vain ostentation, and in a sort of mystical quality that accords with the Muslim vision of the heavenly cities of the next world that await the faithful. The dematerialized surfaces of the luminous marble, reflected in the waters of the Gardens of Paradise, conjure up the vision of an eternal and radiant universe. The Taj Mahal seems to glow with a radiance expressive of divine perfection, as it were a proof of the existence of God.[4]

The Written Word

To many Muslims, the Arabic language has a divine origin because it was the medium through which the revelations of the Quran were transmitted to Muhammad. The sanctity of Arabic writing gave rise to a wide range of scripts and a calligraphic tradition (see the following section) going back to the earliest days of Islam.[5]

The Arabic alphabet now has 28 letters, each of which may have as many as four different forms. This alphabet originally sprang from a script used for Nabatean, a dialect of Aramaic used in northern Arabia and Jordan about one thousand years before the beginning of the Islamic era. The earliest inscription that has been found which is unmistakably Arabic is in Sinai; it dates from c. 300. Unlike the Roman alphabet used in English and many European languages, Arabic writing runs from right to left.[6]

Manuscripts and books were important to Islamic rulers. The Umayyad caliph al-Hakam II (961–976), for example, assembled a magnificent library in Cordoba, Spain. His chief librarian was named Tailed, a high-ranking eunuch who boasted that there were 400,000 books in the royal library. The catalogue of the library, i.e., a listing of the books which contained only the names of the authors and titles of the other books in the library, ran to forty-four volumes of fifty folios each.[7]

Since the spread of Islam, writers from many lands outside the Arabian peninsula (e.g., Iran, Turkey, Lebanon, Iraq, India, Muslim Spain, Egypt and Syria) have written. Some of their works have been mentioned in this book. During modern times, the coming of independence and the greater spread of literacy has led to a prolific Arabic press. Arabic poetry and literary works are much appreciated by those who know the language but with the exceptions of the Quran itself and *The Thousand and One Nights*, not many ancient and modern works in Arabic are familiar (in translation) to Western readers.

The Egyptian author Naguib Mahfouz (1911–), however, won the Nobel Prize for literature in 1988. Praising his skills (he has written more than thirty novels), the Swedish Academy for Letters noted that "through his works rich in nuance — now clear-sightedly realistic, now evocatively ambiguous—[Mahfouz] has formed an Arabic narrative art that applies to all mankind."[8]

It is also worth noting that on one Friday evening in 1994, Mahfouz — then an old man, diabetic and nearly blind — was stabbed several times in the neck on a Cairo street. He survived the attack and told the Egyptian interior minister: "This incident is an opportunity to ask God to make the police defeat terrorists and to plead for the country to be purified of this evil in defense of people, liberty and Islam."[9] His assailants were Muslim radicals who had pronounced a death sentence on him in 1989 and who tried to assassinate him because of his advocacy of peace with Israel and his unorthodox depictions of Christ and Muhammad in his 1959 novel, *Children of Gebelawi*, a work banned in Egypt.

Arabic poems seem to bridge the linguistic and cultural gap between the Islamic world and the West more readily than Arabic prose. Here is one such poem, entitled "Youth." It is undated but was written by an Egyptian poet at some point between the 1920s and 1967. In a very rough paraphrased translation it reads as follows:

> Its beauty all a-quiver, a new flower proudly glows in the wind on the bank of the river. Rippling its petals, the unbidden breeze reveals the flower's hidden secrets. The flower admires its reflection in the water until the wind erases it; feeling rejected, the flower then turns away. The fate of this flower is to fulfill its destiny by dying in a silent shower of spilled petals. What does this tell us about youth — once so glad, beautiful, glimmering, and touched by madness. Where, indeed, is youth? It is a quickly-decaying blossom admiring its own image in the water.

Aniconism: Its Importance in Islamic Architecture and Calligraphy

Aniconism means "opposition (for example, by Sunni Islam) to the use of visual images on religious monuments to show living beings, deceased religious figures, or intangible creatures such as angels." On the other hand, Shiite Islam has a powerful iconographic tradition.[10]

The most important expression of Islamic art has always been architecture, especially the architecture of monuments and mosques. These buildings have often been embellished not with figures but with calligraphy, literally "beautiful writing." Calligraphy was used because Sunni Islam, like Judaism, has traditionally put a high value on aniconism. The initial purpose of aniconism was to prevent the worship of idols. It was based on the belief that only God is the author of life. A person who creates a likeness of a living being is, in so doing, falling into the sin of pride by setting himself up as a rival to God.

This is a failure known as *shirk*—i.e., accepting as God that which is not God, thereby debasing the concept of divinity.[11] Sunni tradition holds that on the Day of Judgment, God will ask anyone who has dared to make a picture of a living thing to try to bring it to life. The Quran illustrates the impossibility of this task by stating that although Jesus (whom Muslims consider a prophet) was able to breathe life into a clay bird, he could do so only with God's permission.[12]

During the earliest period of Islam, figural representations of any kind were strictly prohibited. The Caliph Umar (r. 634–644) is said to have acquired in Syria a metal censer with figures on it. Umar used this censer to perfume the mosque at

Medina but in 783 a governor of Medina had the figures removed.[13] In the Dome of the Rock, the huge area (nearly 335 square yards) still covered by mosaic decoration, which originally extended much further, does not contain a representation of a single living creature.[14] Later on, under the Abbasid, Shiite and Turkish dynasties, such figures were tolerated in private homes and in palaces, but rarely on public buildings, unless they were woven into designs which were chiefly ornamental rather than representative.

It is thanks to aniconism, then, that in visual matters the artistic energy of Islam focused chiefly on architecture and on calligraphy, not on figurative painting or sculpture, as has been the case in the West and in non–Muslim Asia. The Swedish scholar Ulrika Mårtensson offers a more detailed explanation of this fact. It was the religious leadership of Islam, she says, who were against figural arts for the reasons stated above. Thus it is the *public religious buildings* which are decorated exclusively with calligraphy. Since public calligraphy almost always involves citations from the Quran as the living Word of God, it in effect fulfills the same function as icons did in Byzantine Christianity, namely, making the divinity present in the places of public worship.[15]

There can be little doubt that, as the art historians Abdelhebir Khatibi and Mohammed Sielmassi have noted, "Calligraphy, the art which combines images with the written word, is perhaps at its most brilliant in the Islamic world."[16] Islamic calligraphy reached its zenith in Ottoman Turkey. Its practitioners there were so famous that a popular saying arose: "The Quran was revealed in Mecca, recited in Egypt, and written in Istanbul."[17]

There are at least seven different calligraphic styles of Arabic: kufic, thuluth, naskhi, Andalusian maghribi, riq'a, diwani, and ta'liq (or farisi).[18] The earliest and in some ways the most visually impressive of these is kufic, named after the town of Kufa in Iraq. As noted earlier, kufic was used by the early Muslims to record the Quran. This thick, angular, stately, formal script also appeared on tombstones, coins and buildings. It passed out of general use in about the twelfth century but continued to be employed as a decorative contrast to other accompanying scripts.

Arabesques

Arabesques have been used very frequently in Islamic art since c. 1000 and were also popular in Europe from the Renaissance until the nineteenth century. They are designs based on repetitive and strictly geometrical forms or patterns of leaves and flowers. While useful, lovely and decorative from a practical point of view, they also have a spiritual quality: to Muslims they can evoke the infinite vastness of God. This is due to their potential for being repeated indefinitely in one, two or even three dimensions.

Carpets

Islamic carpets are often works of art. Muslims have traditionally used small but sometimes exquisitely woven prayer carpets, typically measuring about three feet

Top: Calligraphy from the Quran, entrance of the Sultanahmet Camii (Blue Mosque) in Istanbul, which was completed in 1616. *Bottom:* Quranic calligraphy from the Rustem Pasha Mosque in Istanbul. (Both photographs courtesy of André Kahlmeyer.)

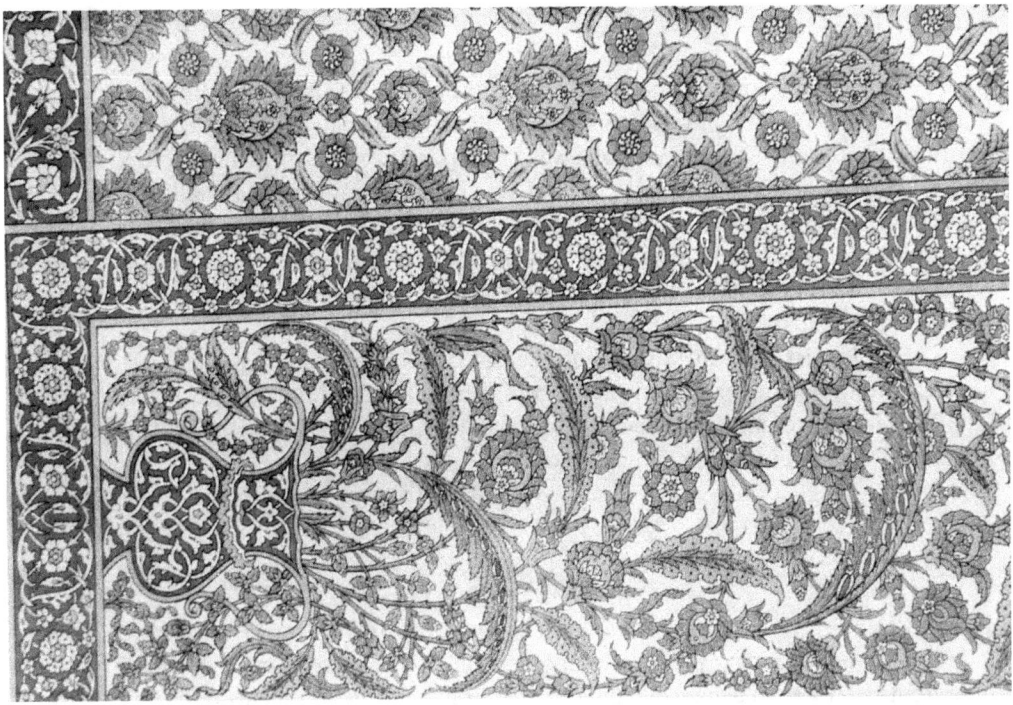

Detail of a faïence (tin-glazed earthenware) panel from the mosque of Ibrahym Agha in North Africa. (Photograph by the author.)

by five feet, for their personal devotions. At the other extreme, carpet makers working for Islamic rulers, especially in Iran during the sixteenth and seventeenth centuries, produced immense floor carpets. Probably the biggest carpet ever woven in Iran was made in 1540 for the mosque of Ismail Shah: it measures 37 feet 9 inches by 17 feet 6 inches.[19] The art historian Henri Stierlin tells us,

> The size is amazing, but the fineness of the weave is even more so. One large wool carpet, measuring 5.5 × 3 meters [more than 18 feet × 9 feet], has no less than 7,400 knots per 10 × 10 centimetre square, while some small prayer carpets ... sometimes count more than 10,000 knots. In India in the 17th century, carpets knotted on silk might have an incredible 20,000 knots.[20]

Woodwork

Wood has been used extensively in mosques and madrasas. Examples of fine woodworking include minbars (pulpits in mosques), boxes to hold Qurans, screen-like partitions known as maqsuras, and doors. Decorative nuances were achieved by making use of the natural grain and structure of the wood, as well as by inlays made of ivory, mother-of-pearl, tortoise shell, and woods of different colors.[21]

Metalware

Bronze and copper were the most popular metals used in workshops during most of the 634 years of Ottoman rule (1290–1924). Because of the frequent warfare of this era, the making of weapons was an important industry which needed skilled craftsmen. Many swords were works of art. Thanks to advanced metallurgical techniques used in hand-forging, a Turkish scimitar would take such a keen edge that it could cut in half a silk handkerchief floating in the air. Indeed, European rulers sometimes sat for their portraits holding a Turkish scimitar or other elegant weapon made in Muslim lands.[22]

The largest and finest piece of Islamic metalware that exists is a vast, elaborately-decorated bronze cauldron weighing about two tons. It has a diameter of seven and one-half feet and was made for the conqueror Tamerlane in Samarkand in the early fifteenth century.[23]

Ceramics

Lusterware was pottery with an iridescent metallic (often golden) sheen in the glaze. It was a luxury product which often depicted courtly scenes. Made by master craftsmen, it was so expensive that only the upper classes could afford it.[24] Even without this costly sheen, however, Islamic ceramics could still be objects of utility and beauty.

This large shallow bowl, painted over glaze with enamel, was made in Iran in the early thirteenth century. It depicts an Iranian leader and his troops seizing a stronghold of the Assassins, an Islamic sect dating from the eleventh to thirteenth centuries. In Arabic, *hashshashin* means "hashish smoker" and refers to their alleged practice of smoking hashish to induce visions of paradise before launching suicidal attacks. There is no historical evidence to support this romantic theory, but the crusaders picked up the term "assassin" in Syria and introduced it to Europe upon their return. (Freer Gallery of Art, Smithsonian Institution, Washington, D.C. Purchase, F1943.3.)

Tiles

Made in a remarkable range of techniques, designs and colors, tiles are one of the most definitive features of Islamic architecture. For example, as mentioned earlier, the octagonal walls of the Dome of the Rock are faced with white, green, black and yellow Turkish tiles bearing stylized floral motifs. Fine tiles were widely used elsewhere, too.

These beautiful tiles grace the entrance to the circumcision room in the private part of the Sultan's Topkapi Palace in Istanbul. (Photograph courtesy of André Kahlmeyer.)

Stucco and Stone

One of the specialties of the Seljuq Turks of Anatolia was the use of carved stone and stucco for architectural decoration. Typical compositions included traditional geometric and vegetal patterns, e.g., arabesques, as well as animal motifs. The strong contrasts of sunlight and shadow in Turkey gave these stone carvings a sense of life: as the light changes over the course of the day, the shaded and illuminated areas of the stones seem to move.[25]

Figurative Painting

We do not have space here to explore Islamic figurative painting in any depth, especially the impressive achievements of Persian miniaturists. To touch only very lightly on what is a complicated subject, we can began by noting that Abbasid palaces were decorated with murals, some of which showed human figures. Restored fragments of wall paintings from the harem of the palace of Caliph al-Mutasim (r. 833–841), for example, depict two women dancers pouring out wine.[26] As mentioned earlier, Firdawsi's poem "Shahnama" (*Book of Kings*), is the national epic of Iran. Completed in 1010, it was illustrated with 250 lifelike figures.

The full development of figurative imagery in the Islamic world, however, dates from the late twelfth century; by the thirteenth and fourteenth centuries different styles of painting had appeared.[27] Chinese influences are evident in the art of the Ilkhan (Mongol) regime in Iran, which lasted until 1336. The modern historian Ira Lapidus says,

> One type of human figure, was aristocratic, elongated, motionless, with facial features precisely drawn, perhaps gesturing slightly with a movement of the head or finger; a second type was a caricature with highly exaggerated expressions of comedy or pain. Thus the Ilkhan regime continued the cosmopolitan aspect of Iranian monarchy, reinforced by Mongol concepts of authority and political destiny.[28]

It is interesting to note that subjects and themes derived from Islam itself appear somewhat infrequently in Persian art.[29] Under the Timurid dynasty, the miniaturist Behzad (c. 1460–1535), the greatest painter of his time and Director of the Royal Library, often produced miniature paintings which contained several scenes, usually on secular subjects, each independent of the other.[30] In some cases, human figures were gracefully portrayed to convey the design of the painting rather than a sense of photographic reality.[31] In others, a familiar event of contemporary urban life is shown in great detail. In 1494, for example, Behzad depicted Caliph Harun al-Rashid in a Turkish bathhouse, assisted by busy attendants dressed in work clothes. The caliph's crown is shown perched on the top of the clothes that he removed before entering the bath itself.[32]

By the sixteenth century, the Ottoman art of illustrating manuscripts moved beyond the confines of classical Islamic literature and began to reflect contemporary

"Caliph Harun al-Rashid in a Bathhouse." (By permission of the British Library, OR. 6810, f 27v.)

events celebrating the power of the Ottoman Empire. New illustrations showed circumcision festivals, athletic performances, guild performances, court events and portraits of the leading men of the time. One of the most famous works of this era is the *Shah-name-i Al-i Osman* (*Book of Kings of the House of Osman*) by the artist Arifi (d. 1561–1562).[33]

In India, artists drew inspiration from Persian, Mughal and Hindu techniques.

A depiction of the marriage of Akbar (1542–1605), for example, reflects a Persian use of color and a Mughal interest in line and form. Classic Indian literary works such as the *Mahabharata* and the *Ramayana* were illustrated as well. On other fronts, the leading artist at the Safavid court in the early seventeenth century, Riza-i Abbasi, drew a number of single-figure studies of his low-life companions—for example, a man playing a bagpipe.

Music

Islam has only a limited tradition of ceremonial religious music. The Sufis have used music (and dance) for their worship; otherwise, religious music has been confined to the verbal but very melodious call to prayer and the chanting of the Quran. Secular folk music has been traditionally popular in Islamic culture, where it has often been the province of women professionals, usually soloists.[34] Secular music contains both composed and improvised portions, using both percussion and melodic instruments. Many musical instruments used in the West—e.g., bagpipes, guitar, lute, oboe, tambourine, viols, and zithers—originally come from the Middle East.[35]

Appendix 2

Expertise in Islamic Thought

Traditional scholars of Islamic thought had to master a number of highly specialized subjects. A list of these subjects was kindly provided by a Muslim scholar, Munir Zilanawala, who read part of the manuscript of this book.[1]

1. Classical Arabic — vocabulary, grammar, style, morphology, rhetoric and poetry
2. Islamic credal belief (*aqida*), spiritual excellence (*ihsan*), and purification of the soul (*tazkiyat al-nafs*)
3. The Quran in Arabic, including:
   a. the circumstances behind the revelation of each verse (*asbab al-nuzul*) and a grasp of what is essential to exegesis (*tafsir*)
   b. the abrogated (*mansukh*) and abrogating (*nasikh*) verses
   c. the general (*amm*) and particularized (*khass*) verses
   d. the plain (*mubayyan*) and ambiguous (*mujmal*) verses
   e. the restricted (*muqayyad*) and unrestricted (*mutlaq*) verses
   f. the apparently clear (*zahir*) and the firmly unequivocal (*nass*) verses
   g. the reports of the Companions of the Prophet, referring to interpretations of particular verses
   h. the several modes of Quranic recitation (*qiraat*)
4. The content, context, reliability, and significance of individual Prophetic narrations (*hadith*). These number several hundred thousand (of many different levels of authenticity and import) and have been compiled into six famous and several dozen lesser known collections. *Hadith* are the theme of a large number of single- and multi-volume commentaries.
5. The biography (*sira*) of the Prophet, including an examination of the polytheistic society of his time, his lineage, his childhood, his married family life and personal behavioral norms, the first revelations, his interaction with the angel Gabriel, his mode of preaching, persecutions by non–Muslims, the migration (*hijra*), var-

ious battles, dealings with non–Muslims, compacts made, the development of the early Muslim community, his final victory and the dispensation of justice

6. Islamic legal and intellectual history, covering the sayings and writings on various branches of Islamic sciences, especially jurisprudence (*fiqh*), of successive generations of scholars, from the time of the Prophet down through the centuries

7. Islamic legal methodology (*usul al-fiqh*) and the extensive array of analytical tools that are used to weave varying and even factually contradictory Quran and *hadith* evidence into a unified whole in order to reach a well-founded rule of law on the question at hand

8. The general objectives (*maqasid*) of the Sacred Law of Islam (*sharia*), which were articulated by al-Shatibi, a fourteenth-century jurist, as the protection from harm of humanity's five "necessities"—religion, life, property, intellect, and progeny

Appendix 3
Ethical Traditions in Islam

This is an annotated and abridged version of a private communication from the Islamic scholar Muhammed Hassanali. It is used here with his kind permission.[1]

There are numerous references in the Quran (and in the *sunna*) to the ethical dimensions of human life. Here are some examples from the Quran:

> Good and evil are not alike, even though the abundance of evil may tempt you. Have fear of God, you men of understanding, so that you may triumph.[2]
>
> Have you thought of him that denies the Last Judgment? It is he who turns away the orphan and has no urge to feed the destitute. Woe betide those who pray but are heedless in their prayers; who make a show of piety and forbid almsgiving.[3]
>
> Do not devour one another's property by unjust means, nor bribe the judges with it in order that you may wrongfully and knowingly usurp the possessions of other men.[4]
>
> Have We not given [man] two eyes, a tongue, and two lips, and shown him the two paths [of right and wrong]?[5]

A Web of Interconnected Concepts

Islamic ethics today consist of a web of interconnected ideals and standards and their applications in daily life. Ethics in Islam cannot be understood without reference to the larger universe of ideas that were part and parcel of pre–Islamic Arabia and the ideas that Muslims encountered when they came into contact with other cultures. To appreciate the diversity of Islam's heritage of ethical thought, one must look at the whole spectrum of Islamic values and at their underlying moral and ethical assumptions.

The Islamic scholar Fazlur Rahman (1911–1988) argued that Islam in its initial phase was moved by a deep rational and moral concern for reforming society. This moral intentionality, he believed, was encouraged by a strong commitment to reasoning and rational discourse. Like other religions, especially Judaism and Christianity, when Islam posed the question "What ought or ought not to be done?" it could answer the question by referring to clearly defined sources of moral authority.

For Islam, the relationship between the Quran and the Prophet's life (as a model of behavior) created a framework within which values and obligations could be determined. The process of determination and elaboration involved the use of reason. Indeed, it is the continuing interaction between reason and revelation (and the potential and limits of the former in relation to the latter) that forms the basis of formal expressions of Islamic ethical thought.

The concept of the ideal ethical value in the Quran is referred to as *taqwa*. In its various forms *taqwa* represents, on the one hand, the moral grounding that underlies human actions; on the other, it signifies the ethical conscience which makes human beings aware of their responsibilities to God and society. Applied to the wider social context, *taqwa* thus becomes the universal, ethical mark of a truly moral community.

For Muslims, the message of the Quran and the example of the Prophet's life remain inseparably related as paradigms for moral and ethical behavior. They gave early Muslim thinkers the basis for forging legal tools embodying moral imperatives. The elaboration of these legal tools lead to the norms and statutes that give substance to the concept of law in Islam (*sharia*): each school of legal thought developed juridical codes to embody its own interpretation of how Muslims should respond to God's commands in conducting their daily lives.

Alongside such legal expressions there also emerged a set of moral assumptions that articulated ethical values. They were rooted in a more speculative and philosophical conception of human conduct, as a response to the Quran and the Prophet's life. Social groups in Islam, as well as the schools of law, were not clearly defined in the first three centuries of Muslim history. Most were still in a formative stage, and their subsequent boundaries and positions were not yet fully elaborated.

A key to understanding the gradual process of definition and distinction was the public discourse of the emerging Islamic society in its first three centuries. Conquests and expansion resulted in contact with cultures whose intellectual heritages (e.g., philosophical, moral, and ethical assumptions) were selectively appropriated by Muslims, who then refined and developed them further. The integration of intellectual and philosophical legacies from Greece, India, and Iran, for example, formed a tradition of intellectual activity that would lead to a cosmopolitan heritage for the emerging Islamic civilization.

These incorporations widened Islam's ability to articulate ethical and moral values outside of its own legal codes. Since clear-cut distinctions in Islam between religion, society, and culture are difficult to sustain, it is a good idea to refer to the whole spectrum of Islamic values (legal, theological, philosophical and mystical) when looking for the moral assumptions and commitments underlying Islamic ethics.

Theological and Traditionalist Approaches

The emergence of an intellectual tradition of enquiry based on using rational tools to understand Quranic injunctions led Muslims to create a formal discipline devoted to the study of the *kalam* (literally "speech," but in this context, the word of Allah, i.e., theology). *Kalam* has no counterpart in the Western tradition. Although its orientation is theological, its approach is rationalist and much of its subject matter is philosophical since it encompasses epistemology, analysis, cosmology, and metaphysics. The goal of this discipline is to make comprehensible and justify God's word. *Kalam* involved Muslims in the elaboration and definition of certain ethical concerns, namely the

precise meanings of Quranic ethical attributes (justice, obligatory, good, evil, etc.)

relationship between human free will and divine will

capacity of human beings to derive, through reason, the knowledge of objective ethical norms and truths.

Two clear positions emerged from this process. The first was associated with the Mutazili movement, which urged Muslims to adopt the rationalistic approaches of the Greek philosophers. The second was based on a traditionalist approach.

The Mutazili movement argued that since God is just, human beings must possess free will since they are going to be held fully accountable for their actions. The Mutazilis also maintained that since ethical notions do have objective meanings, human beings must possess, as well, the intellectual capacity to grasp these meanings. From this perspective, reason is therefore a key attribute and capacity which is *independent of revelation*. The ability to use reason endows humans with the ability to make empirical and rational observations and to draw ethical conclusions.

Historically, the Mutazili movement died out. Its liberal views were not deemed acceptable by the majority of Sunni traditionalists, but some of its thoughts were incorporated into later interpretations of Islam. It must be emphasized that the traditionalists were not opposed to the use of reason *per se*. They parted company with Mutazili rationalists only over the *value* to be placed on reason. For them, reason was an aid and a useful tool for affirming issues of faith, but in defining ethical obligations it played a secondary role vis-à-vis revelation.

Traditionalists today still argue that the final basis for moral obligations must remain Islam's foundational texts, namely, the Quran and the *sunna*. They want these texts to continue to be elaborated and applied as God's commands and prohibitions, to be formulated through the Islamic juridical schools of thought, and to be implemented through the *sharia*.

Philosophical Approaches

The integration of the philosophical legacy of antiquity in the Islamic world was a major enabling factor in the use of philosophical tradition among Muslim intellectuals. It gave rise to such figures as al-Farabi, Ibn Sina, Ibn Rushd and others. These thinkers became well known in medieval Europe as philosophers, commentators, and exponents of the classical tradition going back to Plato and Aristotle.

The term *adab* evokes the moral, ethical, intellectual, and literary discourse that emerged during the eighth to the tenth centuries. In modern Arabic, *adab* means "literature," but it also connotes a wide range of qualities—ethics, education and upbringing, high moral principles and correct behavior, scholarship and knowledge, all at once.[6] The public discourse of *adab* is grounded in philosophical and moral language and concerns and represents a significant part of the cosmopolitan heritage of ethics in Islam. This discourse also reflects efforts to reconcile religiously and scripturally derived values with an intellectually and morally based ethical foundation. The Muslim philosophical tradition of ethics is therefore doubly significant: not only for its value in continuing and embracing classical Greek philosophy but also for its commitment to synthesizing Islam and philosophical thought.

Sufi Perspectives

Sufism, the mystical and esoteric dimension of Islam, emphasizes the personal search for divine love and knowledge. A major goal of Sufi teaching is to enable an individual to find intimacy with God. To do so, it believed that seekers must have an intense inner life of devotion and moral action that will lead to spiritual awakening. For Sufis, the observance of the *sharia* is to be complemented by adherence to a path of moral discipline leading the seeker through several spiritual "stages," each representing inner spiritual growth. The ultimate goal is love and union between the seeker and God. Sufis believe that the inner awareness of morality results in the outward expression of ethical acts.

In their institutional setting, Sufi groups teach conformity to traditional Muslim values, adding the components of discipline and inner purification. Since the practices that instill discipline and moral awareness vary considerably across the range of cultures and traditions encountered by Islam, many local practices were appropriated. Sufi ethical practices thus provide a bridge for incorporating into Muslim moral behavior the ethical values and practices of local traditions.

It has also been held that Sufism is a necessary complement to Islamic jurisprudence (*fiqh*): the personal experience of divine love is said to be a prerequisite for truly understanding the meaning of equality before the law. In this manner, Sufi concepts are closely related to the guiding principles of Islamic justice and ethics.

Islamic Ethics Today

The practice and influence of the diverse ethical heritage in Islam has continued among Muslims in the contemporary world. There is a growing realization among Muslims of the values of their heritage — as well as recognition of the need to adapt that heritage to the changing circumstances ushered in by the globalization of human society. Today, ethical questions faced by Muslims cannot be answered by unified and monolithic responses. Instead, they must (from the point of view of liberal Muslims) take into account the diversity and pluralism that has characterized the Muslims of the past as well as the present, while remaining open to the possibilities and challenges of new ethical and moral discoveries.

Appendix 4
Noteworthy Islamic Personalities and Cultural Achievements

The Prophet Muhammad (c. 570–632)
The Quran (Uthmanic recension, 644–656)
Dome of the Rock (691/692)
Great Mosque of Damascus (715)
Muhammad ibn Ishaq (d. c. 767)
Abu Hanifah (699–767)
Caliph al-Mansur (d. 775)
al-Mufaddal (fl. 762–784)
Great Mosque of Cordoba (784–785)
Caliph al-Rashid (786–806)
Abu Nuwas (c. 747–c. 813)
Caliph al-Ma'mun (r. 813–833)
Jabir ibn Hayyan (c. 721–c. 815)
Muhammad al-Shafii (767–820)
Muhammad ibn Musa al-Khwarizmi (c. 800–c. 850)
The Thousand and One Nights (ninth century)
Ahmad ibn Hanbal (780–855)
al-Bukhari (d. 870)
Yaqub ibn Ishaq al-Kindi (800–873)
Muslim ibn al-Hajjaj (c. 817–875)
Thabit ibn Qurra (836–901)
al-Tabari (839–923)
Muhammad ibn Zakariya al-Razi (c. 865–930)
Abu al-Hasan al-Ashari (873/874–935)
Abu Nasr al-Farabi (c. 878–c. 950)
al-Mutanabbi (915–965)
Brethren of Purity (c. 969)
al-Azhar University (c. 970)
al-Numan (d. 974)
Abu Sulayman Muhammad al-Sijistani (c. 932–c. 1000)
Muhammad ibn Ahmad al-Muqaddasi (c. 946–c. 1000)
The House of Knowledge (1005)
Abu al-Qasim al-Zahravi (936–1013)
Firdawsi (c. 935–c. 1020)
Hamid al-Kirmani (d. c. 1021)
Ibn Sina (980–1037)
Ibn al-Haytham (c. 965–c. 1040)
al-Biruni (973–1048)
al-Ma'arri (d. 1057)
Ibn Hazm (994–1064)
Nasir-i Khusraw (1004–c. 1092)
Abu Hamid al-Ghazali (1058–1111)
al-Hariri (1054–1122)
Omar Khayyam (1048–1131)
Zamakhshari (1075–1144)
al-Idrisi (1100–1165/1166)

Usama ibn Munqidh (1095–1188)
Ibn Rushd (1126–1198)
Mustansiriyya College (1233)
The Alhambra (1258–1358)
Ibn al-Arabi (1165–1240)
Jalal al-Din al-Rumi (1207–1273)
Nasr al-Din al-Tusi (1201–1274)
Ibn al-Nafis (1213–1288)
Sa'di (c. 1213–1291)
Ibn Taymiyya (1263–1328)
Ibn Battuta (1304–1368/1369)
Hafiz (1325/1326–1389/1390)
Ibn Khaldun (1332–1406))
al-Kashi (c. 1380–1429)
al-Maqrizi (1364–1442)
Mehmed II (1432–1481)
Babur (1483–1530)
Sidi Ali Reis (fl. 1552–1557)
Suleyman I the Magnificent (1494/1495–1566)
Sinan (1498–1588)
Akbar (1542–1605)
The Taj Mahal (1632–1654)
Mulla Sadra (1571–1640)

Ahmed Nedim (1681–1730)
Shah Wali Allah (1702/1703–1762)
Muhammad ibn Abd al-Wahhab (1703–1787)
Muhammad ibn Ali al-Sanusi (1787–1859)
Mirza Ghalib (1797–1869)
Deoband movement (1866–)
Jamal al-Din Afghani (1839–1897)
Sayyid Ahmad Khan (1817–1898)
Muhammad Abduh (1849–1905)
Rashid Rida (1865–1935)
Muhammad Iqbal (1877–1938)
Mustafa Kemal Ataturk (1881–1938)
Sayyid Qutb (1906–1966)
Ali Shariati (1933–1977)
Sayyid Abul-Ala Mawdudi (1903–1979)
Fazlur Rahman (1911–1988)
Ayatollah Ruhollah Khomeini (1902–1989)
Edward W. Said (1935–2003)
Mohammed Arkoun (1928–)
Seyyed Hossein Nasr (1933–)
Abdolkarim Soroush (1945–)
Aziz al-Azmeh (c. 1949–)
Osama bin Laden (1957–)

Glossary of Selected Islamic Terms

adab a word connoting a wide range of qualities: ethics, education, upbringing, high moral principles, and correct behavior

alim a man learned in Islamic religious and legal studies

Allah God

aql intellect

asabiyya the esprit de corps inherent in tribalism

bedouin desert-dwelling nomads

bidah religious innovations

bismillah a traditional invocation: "In the Name of God, the Compassionate, the Merciful"

caliph title of early Islamic rulers

Dar al-Harb the non–Muslim world

Dar al-Islam the Muslim world

dawa reformist missionary program

devshirme the Ottoman policy of selecting Christian boys for conversion to Islam and for military or administrative training

falsafa philosophy

fatihah the short prayer which comprises the opening lines of the Quran

fatwa a formal opinion, or some cases a decree, of a religious scholar

fawatih the cryptic letters beginning some chapters of the Quran

fiqh jurisprudence

fitnahs literally "disorders," e.g., the four civil wars (680–692)

fitra an innate human ability to know God

ghazal lyric poem

ghazu a raid

grand mufti senior legal counselor

hadith a record of the life, utterances, teachings or actions of Muhammad

hajj the annual pilgrimage to Mecca

Hijaz the northern half of the west coast of Saudi Arabia — the cradle and heartland of Islam, where Mecca and Medina are located

hijra Muhammad's migration to Medina in 622, which marks the beginning of the Islamic era

hisba the duties of citizens

ijma the consensus of Muslim scholars on religious issues

ijtihad independent reasoning

imam a Shiite religious leader

intifada "uprising," e.g., Palestinian protests against Israeli rule

islam "to surrender," i.e., the religious requirement that believers must surrender themselves totally to God

Ismailis a Shiite branch and doctrine

isnad the chain of oral transmission of a *hadith*

isra Muhammad's miraculous Night Journey

jahiliyya "the time of ignorance": Arabia before the rise of Islam

jihad holy war or holy struggle

jinn spirits

jumud stagnation

Kabah the Kabah sanctuary in Mecca, which houses the Black Stone (probably a meteorite)

kafir a highly pejorative term for "infidel," that is, a non–Muslim

kalam theology

kanun (or qanun) "positive law," i.e., man-made or "Sultanic" law

Khalifa al-Rashidin the four "rightly guided" caliphs who were the companions and immediate successors of Muhammad: revered by the Sunnis

kufic an early Arabic script

kufr unbelief

liwan prayer hall

madhhabs the four Sunni schools of jurisprudence

madrasa college of Islamic studies

mashhad a shrine for pilgrims, e.g., the Dome of the Rock

masoom innocent or pure

matn the subject matter of a *hadith*

mihrab prayer niche in a mosque

miraj Muhammad's ascension into heaven

muezzin crier in a minaret who issues the daily calls to prayer

muhtasib guardian of the public morality

mujtahid a scholar of Islamic law who is permitted to use independent thought on doctrinal issues

mullah a Shiite cleric

Muslim one who surrenders him or herself to Allah and is a follower of Islam

muttafaq *hadith* agreed to be authentic

qadi a judge

qas idahs odes

qasidas formal odes

qibla the direction of prayer, i.e., facing the Kabah in Mecca

qiyas analogical deductions from the Quran, the *sunna* and *ijma*

Quran the holy scripture of Islam

riddah literally "apostasy," i.e., civil wars occurring when some of the Arabian tribes wanted to break away from the Islamic community after the death of Muhammad

salaf "Elders," i.e., the first generations of Islam

salat Sunni Islam's requirement of obligatory prayers five times a day

sarqis songs

sawm the annual fast during the month of Ramadan

shahada the Muslim profession of faith

sharia the body of Islamic sacred laws

shay thing

shaykh a master or leader

Shaytan Satan (the devil), also known as Iblis

Shiites one of the two major branches of the Islamic world (*see also* Sunnis)

shirk elevating someone or something to the point where this person or object encroaches upon the dignity of God

sihar halal "lawful magic": the mesmerizing effect of Arabic poetry

Sufism the mysticism of Islam

sunna the customary social and legal traditions and obligations of the Muslim community, based on the life, teachings and practices of Muhammad

Sunnis one of the two major branches of the Islamic world (*see also* Shiites)

sura a chapter of the Quran

tafsir exegesis, i.e., a learned explanation or critical interpretation of a text, e.g., the Quran

tajdid program of Islamic reform

Glossary of Selected Islamic Terms

tajwid a style of Quranic recitation

talib student

taqiyah Shiite doctrine of dissimulation

taqlid "imitation," i.e., following the established doctrines of the Islamic schools of law

taqwa the concept of ideal ethical values in the Quran

tasawwuf putting aside base attitudes and cultivating virtues instead

tawhid the oneness of God

ulama religious scholars

umma the Islamic community

usul al-fiqh the collective sources of Islamic jurisprudence

Wahhabis followers of the eighteenth century fundamentalist preacher al-Wahhab

zakat annual religious tax

Notes

Preface

1. The name of the Quranic angel is actually "Gibril" but "Gabriel" is used here because Muslims believe he is the same as the angel Gabriel.
2. To clarify one minor point about Arabic, it can be mentioned that in Arabic there is only one article, *al-* ("the"). When the word appearing after *al-* begins with either t, th, d, dh, r, z, s, sh or n, the "l" of the *al-* changes and becomes this letter. Only the "l" of "*al*" would therefore change. For example, the Arabic word for "sun" (*shams*) can be written either as *as-shams* or *al-shams*. Both are correct, but stylistically, it is thought to be better not to mix the two spelling conventions. Therefore, in the interests of constancy and simplicity, only *al-* will be used in this book.

Introduction

1. Said, *Orientalism*, p. 59.
2. After Crone, "Rise of Islam," p. 31.
3. Middle East Institute, "Islamic Civilization," pp. 3–4.
4. Private communication of 3 April 2003 from the Muslim reader Shahab Mushtaq transmitting a summary of Professor King's lecture, which can also be found at the website http://www.uni-frankfurt.de/fb13/ign/astronomy_in_baghdad/lecture.html. Islamic interest in astronomy can clearly be seen in the spread of the astrolabe, an instrument used to solve problems in positional geography. The astrolabe is believed to have been invented by Hipparchus of Biythynia in Alexandria (Egypt) in about 160 BCE and was first described in Alexandria by the Greek philosopher John Philoponus in the sixth century CE. By the ninth century, Islamic scientists were making extensive use of this device for astronomical observations and to reckon time. It remained one of the most important tools of astronomy until as late as the end of the eighteenth century, functioning much like a slide rule or even as a primitive analog computer.
5. Middle East Institute, "Islamic Civilization," p. 7.
6. After "Global Connections," p. 1.
7. Dividing up more than 1,400 years of Islamic history into manageable units is something of a challenge. In this book I have followed many of Waldman's chronological divisions.
8. Cited by Said, *Orientalism*, p. 38. Cromer's account is of course a very biased one. It is not surprising that an Egyptian might have trouble expressing himself clearly, especially in English, when talking to a senior officer of the British colonial elite.
9. Private communication of 20 February 2003.
10. Haqqani, "America needs to listen."
11. U.S. Department of State, "Fact Sheet," p. 1.
12. Counting from west to east on a map of the world, in September 2003 Muslim populations were estimated (by the Muslim Council of Britain and by the United States Central Intelligence Agency) to total 1.5 billion people, distributed as follows: North America (10.4 million), Latin and Central America (2.2 million), European Union (10.0 million), Arab League (284.4 million), sub-Saharan Africa (254.0 million), Turkey (62.4 million), Iran (65.4 million), Azerbaijan and the "stans" [the successor states of the former USSR] (48.5 million), India (133.3 million), Pakistan and Bangladesh (230.0 million), Afghanistan (22.7 million), Russia (26.7 million), China (133.1 million), other Southeast Asia (30.0 million), and Indonesia (196.3 million). See "In the Name of God," p. 4.

13. This book is not a political analysis of radical Islamic fundamentalism but since fundamentalism attracts so much attention in the West these days, a personal comment may be in order here. My own view is that even a vast (and highly unlikely) upsurge of Western interest in and knowledge about the Islamic world in general and about Islam *per se* would have very little impact on the anti-Western, violence-prone strain of fundamentalism. Today, such fundamentalism is largely a response by the Islamic world to the repeated humiliations it has suffered at the hands of the West. As Osama bin Laden told his followers, "Death is better than life in humiliation!" Although it is difficult for outsiders to know what radical fundamentalists really think, a reasonable guess is that, from their point of view, these humiliations are part of their history and cannot easily be erased. Another reasonable guess is that radical fundamentalists feel that even in the unlikely event the West does learn a great deal more about Islam, it will never change its own behavior, which they consider to be anti–Islamic in the extreme.

Chapter I

1. In a private communication of 22 May 2003, Ulrika Mårtensson, a Swedish scholar, volunteered a more detailed explanation of the Islamic tenet that the faithful must surrender to God. Lightly edited, her comments are that this is true concerning logical reasoning. From a philosophic point of view, the reasons for this are as follows: the basic ontology [a theory about the nature of being] of Islamic learning is Neoplatonism [discussed later in this book], which in Islam means a rather Aristotelian interpretation of Plotinus. What we have here is a relation between forms in reality, where God is associated with the highest Forms, and man is "His image," that is, one of the imperfect forms that correspond to the divine Forms. Reason is one of the perfect Forms. Since human reason is by necessity imperfect, it has to surrender to divine guidance, not to human authority — which would be idolatry. But this should not be mistaken for submitting reason to the Quran in a literal sense. It means instead that reason must be "enlightened" through rational study and by aid of the religious quest. Thus submitting reason to God's guidance has a much wider implication than simply following the letter of the Quran.

2. Adapted from Robinson, "Knowledge," p. 208.

3. Robinson, "Knowledge," p. 208.

4. In a private communication of 7 September 2003 the Muslim scholar Muhammed Hassanali mentioned that "Religious or theological philosophy (*kalam*) has no counterpart in the Western tradition. Although its orientation is theological, much of its subject matter is philosophical since it encompasses epistemology, analysis, cosmology, and metaphysics. Furthermore,, its approach is rationalist and, as such, its methods are philosophical. The epistemological foundation and role of religious philosophy in medieval Islamic civilization thus differs from that of medieval Christian theology."

5. Private communication of 29 March 2003 from Rachel Woodlock, an American scholar.

6. Quran, *sura* 35:1–2.

7. Quran, *sura* 22:78.

8. Lapidus, *Islamic Societies* pp. 816–817. Italics added. In a private communication of 22 May 2003, the Swedish scholar Ulrika Mårtensson explained that the caliphate worked much like traditional Christian monarchies. State power was legitimized by the *ulama* as a vice regency of God, but there was a clear distinction between the state as political leadership and the *ulama* as religious leadership. Hence the Islamic caliphate is no different from the Roman Empire or later European premodern monarchies.

9. Today this lack of a central authority in Islam has importance consequences for the growth of radical fundamentalism. As the Oxford scholar James Piscatori has noted, the established religious authorities now find themselves in competition with unofficial religious leaders and preachers, Sufi movements, radical groups and lay intellectuals. See "In the Name of God," p. 5. Thus even if the religious authorities could agree on a party line eschewing violence, their followers would still be heavily influenced by these self-appointed spokesmen for Islam.

10. Private communication of 28 April 2003 from the American scholar Vika Gardner.

11. Quran, *sura* 2:225. In this citation, one line of Dawood's translation has been replaced by a better version.

12. In a private communication of 11 April 2003, Fazi Rahman, a Muslim reader of the manuscript of this book, added that "A *hadith* of the Prophet states that if you see something wrong, you should change it with your hands if you can; if you can't, then with your tongue; and, if not, you should at least dislike it in your heart. Plus, anyone who shares in a good deed gets the full reward of that deed. So helping a charity is a very good idea." Rahman's e-mail has been lightly edited.

13. Quran, *sura* 2:184.

14. Quran, *sura* 85:22.

15. In a private communication of 7 September 2003, which has been lightly edited, the Muslim scholar Mohammed Hassanali explained this

dispute as follows: "The Mutazils [followers of a sect that urged Muslims to adopt the rationalistic approaches of the Greek philosophers] believed that the Koran is created. This was considered an affront to the traditional view that held that the Koran is the uncreated (and eternal) word of God. The traditionalists believe that as the Koran is uncreated and divine, its interpretation must be literal, and is valid for all time. The Mutazils argue that only God is uncreated, hence the Koran must have been God's creation. They buttress their argument by pointing out that the Koran contains Moses's words, which are temporal; hence the Koran cannot be eternal. They believe that one needs to interpret the Koran through the use of reason to make it relevant to one's particular time and circumstances. Although the Mutazils have long disappeared, their rational legacy endures. Some Muslims espouse the view that there is a one Divine Scripture and that the Koran, the Bible, and other holy books are only the physical manifestations of this divine scripture."

16. The six *hadith* collections that are accepted by Sunni Muslims are the compilations, with approximate dates, by: al-Bukhari (middle 800s), Muslim ibn al-Hajjaj (middle 800s), Ibn Maja (late 800s), Abu Dawud (late 800s), al-Tirmidhi (late 800s), and al-Nisai (around 900). One other compilation—Ibn Hanbal's *Musnad* (first half of ninth century)—is sometimes added to this list. After "Hadith," p. 1.

17. Some Muslims in modern times have argued that the *hadith* also contain many scientific facts about organogenesis (the origin and development of the organs of the human body) and other aspects of human biology. Here is one example, cited in a private communication of 9 April 2003 from a Muslim reader, Shahab Mushtaq: "Imam Muslim narrated from Hudhayfa ibn Asad that the Prophet Muhammad said—upon him and his House blessings and peace: 'After the sperm-and-ovum drop has been [in the uterus] forty-two days, Allah sends it an angel that gives it form and fashions its hearing, sight, skin, flesh, and skeleton.' The time frame given above is in conformity with embryological observation. The embryo reaches the sixth week without showing the semblance of human form but by the seventh week of its life—about three centimeters in size and beginning to move—that semblance becomes visible in the formation of the essential organs, including the sensory organs and grown bone tissue. The arms and legs have lengthened. The foot and hand areas are distinguishable and they have digits. The first recordable brain wave activity occurs. This organogenesis peaks precisely at 42 days." Mushtaq himself does not share this view. He says that while some Muslims may believe that *hadith* have a basis in scientific fact, the main intent of such believers is to provide evidence that the Prophet was divinely guided, since there is no possible way he could have known these things during his lifetime.

18. Adapted from Bukhari, "Revelation," p. 1.

19. In a private communication of 19 May 2003, a Muslim reader, Munir Zilanawala, summarized five formal requirements for a "sound" *hadith*. These are: (1) the *hadith* must go back to the Prophet, (2) the narrators must be morally upright, (3) the narrators must be known to have had accurate memories, (4) the text and transmission of the *hadith* must not be at variance from established standard narrations, and (5) both the text and the chain of transmission must be without any "hidden flaw" that alerts experts to suspect inauthenticity.

20. Cited in a private communication of 30 June 2003 from the Muslim reader Shahab Mushtaq. In a private communication of 8 July 2003 the Swedish scholar Ulrika Mårtensson added: "Actually, this is precisely how footnotes function in modern scholarship: you have to support your statements with a genealogy of scholarly opinions."

21. Private communication of 28 April 2003 from the American scholar Vika Gardner.

22. *Encyclopaedia of Islam*, p. 1026.

23. Adapted from a private communication of 19 May 2003 from Munir Zilanawala. It should be added that in a private communication of 22 May 2003 the Swedish scholar Ulrika Mårtensson explained that in classical Sunni Islamic jurisprudence, it is *nowhere* sanctioned to take up arms against a Muslim ruler. *Jihad* was carried out in organized campaigns, exactly like the Roman war campaigns. The modern interpretation—that any Muslim can call for *jihad* against any government, Muslim or non-Muslim—is a result of non-jurists taking interpretatory license.

24. Quran *Sura* 2:190.

25. Some of these points on *jihad* are drawn from Asani, "On Pluralism," p. 58.

26. Metcalf, "'Traditionalist' Islamic Activism," p. 3.

27. "In the Name of God," p. 11.

28. From a private communication of 7 September 2003 from the Muslim scholar Mohammad Hassanali.

29. In a private communication of 8 July 2003 the Swedish scholar Ulrika Mårtensson added that the *sharia* is classically divided into two categories: (1) services to God (*ibadat*) and (2) communal relations (*muamalat*). Muslims agree that the first category, which contains the major tenets of the faith, is eternally unchangeable. Islamic reformers, however, have argued that the second category, which deals with interpersonal matters (e.g., ritual prescriptions about impurity in food and

human relations, and law) could and should change in accordance with changing circumstances.

30. Private communication of 28 April 2003 from the American scholar Vika Gardner.

31. Ansari, "Islamic Ethics," p. 1.

32. In a private communication of 11 April 2003, Fazi Rahman, a Muslim reader of the manuscript of this book, cited the views of one reader of Canada's *Maclean's* magazine. That reader wrote in the 26 October 1998 edition of *Maclean's*: "The real reasons why after 1492, Western Europe began a trajectory dramatically outpacing China and the world of Islam in wealth creation and political liberty [were] superior weapons, disease, slavery, and two new, recently depopulated continents to plunder."

33. In a personal communication of 1 December 2003, the German scholar André Kahlmeyer said that the Shiite point of view arose the following incident. When Muhammad came back from his last pilgrimage, at the small lake of Khumm (between Mecca and Medina), he took Ali's hand and said to him: "Everyone, whose patron I am, shall also have Ali as his patron." Shiites regard this as Muhammad's designation of Ali as his successor. Sunnis know this story, too, but they interpret it differently. They believe that because of his severity, Ali was not very popular and that Muhammad said this to him to increase his authority.

34. For Sunnis, an Imam is a religious leader only in the limited sense that he conducts the Friday prayer, etc. For Shiites, however, an Imam is God's deputy on earth, i.e., an absolute ruler. Thus while there have been many thousands of Sunni Imams, the Shiites recognize only eleven or twelve Imams.

35. After Rahman, "Islamic thought," p. 2.

36. After Lapidus, *Islamic Societies*, pp. 94–95.

Chapter II

1. Quran, *sura* 81.
2. Doughty, *Arabia Deserta*, pp. 96–97.
3. Lings, *Muhammad*, p. 7.
4. After Dawood, *Koran*, p. 1.
5. Some elements in this assertion are drawn from Crone, "Meccan Trade," p. 5.
6. Two of the best biographies of Muhammad are W. Montgomery Watt's *Muhammad: Prophet and Statesman* and *Muhammad at Medina*. Ling's *Muhammad* (see bibliography) is also worth consulting because of its heavy reliance on primary Arabic sources. This gives the full flavor of local traditions.
7. Some of this discussion follows Crone, "The Rise of Islam," p. 10.
8. Cited by Lings, *Muhammad*, p. 21.
9. Cited by Lings, *Muhammad*, p. 25.
10. Quran, *sura* 96:1–2.
11. I have lightly edited Dawood's translation of this *sura*.
12. This listing is adapted from Dawood, *Koran*, pp. 7–8.
13. In a private communication of 3 July 2003 the Muslim reader Shahab Mushtaq says that this killing "was the result of the Jews violating a treaty that they had signed with the Muslims. The punishment carried out what had been specified in the treaty, which had been approved by the Jews."

Chapter III

1. In a lecture given in the United Kingdom, probably in 2003, the Muslim scholar Aftab Malik discussed the importance to Islam of the spoken word and the personal influence of a teacher. He said: "Although Islamic culture valued writing as a memory aid it also recognised the dangers of the way books allowed for the decontextualisation of knowledge from the authoritative control of a given teacher or school, and could thus be used for claiming religious authority independent of proper certification. Classical Islamic culture — take thirteenth-century Baghdad, for example — emphasised the importance of internalising knowledge: until knowledge is internalised and recognized by an authoritative teacher to have been integrated properly into the general understanding and conduct of the student, it was not viewed as knowledge at all." The source of this quote is a private communication of 30 June 2003 from the Muslim reader Shahab Mushtaq.

2. In a private communication of 8 July 2003 the Swedish scholar Ulrika Mårtensson pointed out an exception to this rule. The Mutazilite school of theology holds that the Quran is *inspired* by God's word. Since God is eternal, argue the adherents of this school, His word can never be embodied in the material world, that is, in the piece of writing which is the Quran as a physical book. To equate God with His creation, they assert, is *shirk*.

3. After Dawood, *Koran*, p. 1.
4. Private communication of 22 March 2003 from Munir Zilanawala, Harvard University.
5. Cited by Dawood, *Koran*, p. 4.
6. Quran, *sura* 1:1–7.
7. Lings, *Muhammad*, p. 69.
8. Quran, *sura* 81.
9. Quran, *sura* 24:35.
10. In a private communication of 6 April 2003, Muhammed Hassanali, a Muslim scholar, provided some interesting historical footnotes. He

said that this part of history may have been added to provide legitimacy to Uthman's compilation of the "canonical" Quran. Hassanali noted that this event also raises an important question: is the Quran public property or private property? If it was passed on to Umar's daughter, it would seem that the collected Koran was private, and thus not canonical. If it was public property, i.e., if it belonged to the *umma* (the Muslim community as a whole), it should never have been passed to Umar's daughter. Hassanali noted that there is evidence that this problem was understood by the Muslim community at that time. In any case, the Uthmanic recension has long been considered by Muslims to be canonical and the Quran considered to be public property.

11. In this book, space does not permit discussion of all the Islamic reform movements of the eighteenth to the twentieth centuries. Only a handful of them can be noted here. For a more complete listing, totaling roughly forty reform movements in Arabia, Caucasus/Inner Asia, India, Southeast Asia, Egypt and North Africa, East Africa, and West Africa, see Lapidus, *Islamic Societies*, pp. 464–465. It should be noted, too, that Lapidus draws a technical distinction between reformism and modernism. Islamic reformism was, he says, the doctrine of the *ulama* (religious scholars); Islamic modernism, on the other hand, was the doctrine of the Muslim political elites and the intelligentsia. These latter groups held that the defeat of Muslims by Western powers had revealed the vulnerabilities of the Islamic world. These weaknesses could be corrected, they believed, by repudiating the medieval forms of Islamic civilization — but not Islam itself. Islam's own principles of rationality, ethical activism and patriotism would be used to strengthen the Islamic world. (See Lapidus, *Islamic Societies*, pp. 459–460.) In practice, however, there was a good deal of overlap between reformism and modernism. As Lapidus himself indicates (on p. 628), Sir Sayyid Ahmad Khan (1817–1898) was both a reformer and a modernizer. In the interest of simplicity, then, these two terms will be used interchangeably in this book.

12. Ringgren, "Qur'an," p. 7. This is an excellent introduction to the Quran and has been used extensively here.

13. Lightly edited private communication of 13 June 2003 from the Swedish scholar Ulrika Mårtensson.

14. Private communication of 3 July 2003 from the German scholar André Kahlmeyer.

Chapter IV

1. The political history of the Islamic world, i.e., its dynasties and their rulers, cannot be discussed in any depth in this book because it is far too complicated. For example, focusing on Jerusalem alone, the modern archeologist Kay Prag listed a total of 182 caliphs or other rulers between 632 and 1918. See Prag, *Jerusalem*, pp. 50–54.

2. In discussing the Dome of the Rock I have drawn heavily on my earlier book, *Four Paths to Jerusalem* (2002), which describes Jewish, Christian, Muslim, and secular pilgrimages to Jerusalem over the last 3,000 years.

3. For details on the Jerusalem's importance as a center of Muslim pilgrimage, see Janin, *Four Paths*.

4. After Elad, "Pilgrims and Pilgrimage," p. 301.

5. After Vernoit, "Artistic Expressions," p. 258.

6. Cited by Janin, *Four Paths*, p. 174.

7. This account is drawn from Elad, "Pilgrims and Pilgrimage," p. 301.

8. "Dome of the Rock," p. 2.

9. "Dome of the Rock," p. 5.

10. This description follows Prag, *Jerusalem*, pp. 121–129.

11. Rosen-Ayalon, "Art and Architecture," p. 388.

12. Quran, *Ya Sin*, p. 308.

13. Prag, *Jerusalem*, p. 117.

14. Jarrar, "Two Islamic Construction Plans," p. 382.

15. Prag, *Jerusalem*, pp. 124–125.

16. "Great Mosque of Damascus," p.1.

17. Cited in Medieval Sourcebook, "Ibn Battuta," p. 32.

18. Watt, "Muhammad," p. 1.

19. Ibn Ishaq, "Muhammad," p. 2.

20. Cited by Malik, "Life of *Imman* Abu Hanifah," pp. 1–2.

21. Cited by Malik, "Life of *Imman* Abu Hanifah," p. 2.

22. After "Euclid," pp. 1–5.

23. Middle East Institute, "Islamic Civilization," p. 7.

24. Cited in "Arabic Numeral System," p. 2.

25. Cited in "Arabic Numeral System," pp. 1–2.

26. "Arabic Numerals," p. 2.

27. "Arab Contributions to Mathematics," p. 1.

28. Cited in Arab Gateway, "Arabic Poetry," p. 1.

29. Bloom and Blair, *Islam*, p. 89.

30. Casey, "Visits to Mosques," p. 3.

31. Watt, "Harun al-Rashid," p. 2.

32. Cited by Bloom and Blair, *Islam*, p. 143.

33. Cited by Vernoit, "Artistic Expressions," p. 256.

34. Cited by Bloom and Blair, *Islam*, pp. 129–130.

35. The Ismailis came into existence in 765,

when Ismail, son of the sixth imam Jafar ibn Muhammad, was accepted by a minority of Shiites as their new imam.

36. Cited by the Muslim scholar Hassanali, "Jabir ibn Haiyan [sic]," p. 2.
37. Ead, "Alchemy," p. 9.
38. Cited in a private communication of 30 June 2003 from the Muslim reader Shahab Mushtaq.
39. Hassanali, "al-Khawarizimi [sic]," p. 1.
40. After Bloom and Blair, *Islam*, p. 128.
41. Adapted from a private communication of 13 June 2003 from the Swedish scholar Ulrika Mårtensson.
42. See Haddawy, *Arabian Nights*.
43. Adapted from Haddawy, *Arabian Nights*, pp. xiv–xv.
44. Haddawy, *Arabian Nights*, pp. 16–17, 18.
45. Ahmad, Hassan. "Imam Ahmad ibn Hanbal," p. 2.
46. Adapted from a personal communication of 13 June 2003 from the Swedish scholar Ulrika Mårtensson.
47. Cited in a private communication of 30 June 2003 from the Muslim reader Shahab Mushtaq.
48. O'Conner and Robertson, "al-Kindi," pp. 2–3.
49. Cited in a personal communication of 3 June 2003 from the Islamic scholar Muhammad Hassanali.
50. This section is drawn from Kennedy-Day, "al-Kindi," p. 1.
51. Kennedy-Day, "al Kindi," p. 2.
52. Kennedy-Day, "al-Kindi," p. 3.

Chapter V

1. Waldman, "Islamic World: Fragmentation and Florescence," p. 1.
2. Middle East Institute, "Islamic Civilization," p. 9.
3. After "Thabit ibn Qurra," p. 1.
4. Some of the comments in this section are drawn from private communications of 20 May 2003 and 13 October 2003 from the Swedish scholar Ulrika Mårtensson.
5. Cited by al-Nur, "Al-Tabari," p. 1.
6. Cited by al-Nur, "Al-Tabari," p. 2.
7. These comments on al-Razi are drawn from the U.S. National Library of Medicine's Internet article, "Islamic Culture and the Medical Arts, pp. 1–3, and from Hassanali, "al-Razi," pp. 1–2.
8. Robinson, "Knowledge," p. 215.
9. al-Nur, "al-Ash'ari," p. 1.
10. In a private communication of 13 June 2003, the Swedish scholar Ulrika Mårtensson advanced the thesis that what al-Ashari really did was to distinguish between two levels of reality: the absolute and the relative. On the absolute level, he considered God as the Almighty, the First Cause, and Truth: the Quran is God's Word. On the relative level, human beings have a free will to choose their actions, the Quran is subject to human reason (in the process of interpretation), and truth itself can be grasped only by rational human thought.
11. al-Nur, "al-Ash'ari," pp. 5, 7.
12. After Lapidus, *Islamic Societies*, pp. 91–92.
13. Netton, "al-Farabi," p. 1.
14. After Lapidus, *Islamic Societies*, p. 79.
15. Lapidus, *Islamic Societies*, p. 152.
16. After Netton, "al-Farabi," p. 4.
17. Cited in "Islamic Political Philosophy," p. 3.
18. Poetry Portal, "Al-Mutanabbi," p. 1.
19. Cited by Bloom and Blair, *Islam*, p. 144.
20. Both citations are from a private communication of 20 July 2003 from the Islamic scholar Muhammad Hassanali.
21. This account is drawn from a private communication of 17 September 2003 from the Islamic scholar Muhammad Hassanali.
22. Islam for Today, "Al-Azhar University," p. 1.
23. A variety of terms have been coined by Western scholars to describe the political aspects of Islam today. Among these terms are "Islamist" and "Islamism." Their precise meanings seem to vary from one author to another, but in general they refer to political programs which focus on Islam, not just as a religion but as the basis of a political ideology as well. The scope of what this implies also varies. Some Islamists use these terms to mean that Islam should be the basis of an Islamic country's constitution; others use them to indicate that Islam should be one of several competing ideologies. Although in casual usage "Islamism" and "fundamentalism" are often treated as being identical, this is not quite correct. "Islamism" deals with political programs. "Fundamentalism" is a literalist approach to the Quran and the *sunna*; it may — or may not — have a political ideology attached to it.
24. Fuller, *Political Islam*, p. 184.
25. "Conversation with Aziz al-Azmeh," p. 3.
26. After Halm, *Fatimids*, p. 1.
27. Private communication of 3 June 2003 from the Islamic scholar Muhammad Hassanali.
28. Cited by Hassanali, "Qadi An Numan" [sic], p. 29.
29. Atiyeh, "al-Sijistani," p. 1.
30. After Atiyeh, "al-Sijistani," p. 2.
31. Atiyeh, "al-Sijistani, " p. 2.
32. Cited by Janin, *Four Paths*, pp. 76–77.
33. Foundation for Science Technology, "Al-Muqaddasi," p. 1. This section draws extensively on this article.

34. Adapted from Foundation for Science Technology, "Al-Muqaddasi," pp. 4–5.
35. Cited by Halm, *Fatimids*, pp. 73–74.
36. Cited by Halm, *Fatimids*, pp. 77–78.
37. These comments are drawn from Malaspina Great Books, "Zahrawi," pp. 1–2, and Hassanali, "Abu al-Qasim al-Zahravi," pp. 1–2.
38. Vernoit, "Artistic Expressions," p. 270.
39. Grabar, *Miniatures*, p. 100.
40. After Assaad, "al-Kirmani," p. 1.
41. After Halm, *Fatimids*, pp. 53–54.
42. Assaad, "Kirmani," p. 2.
43. Medieval Sourcebook, "Ibn Sina," p. 1.
44. Medieval Sourcebook, "Ibn Sina," pp. 1–2.
45. Cited by O'Conner and Robertson, "Ibn Sina," p. 4.
46. Nasr, "Avicenna," p. 3.
47. After Hassanali, "Ibn al-Haytham," pp. 5–6.
48. Cited by O'Conner and Robertson, "al-Haytham," p. 3.
49. O'Conner and Robertson, "al-Haytham," p. 1.
50. Oxford University Gazette, "Oxford Don 'Solves,'" p. 1.

Chapter VI

1. Cited by Janin in *Four Paths*, pp. 94–95.
2. After Bloom and Blair, *Islam*, p. 105.
3. Cited by Hermi, "Al-Biruni," p. 1.
4. In a private communication of 7 September 2003, which has been abridged and lightly edited, the Muslim scholar Muhammed Hassanali had this to say about the pursuit of knowledge in Islam: "The pursuit of knowledge is central to the Islamic message. The goal of knowledge is not mere contemplation but the discovery of action that leads to ultimate felicity. In the intellectually fertile environment of medieval Islamic civilization, an intense debate existed among competing intellectual disciplines. This debate, which endured across continents and centuries even as these disciplines evolved, focused on the issues of the identify and foundations of the "real" knowledge that one ought to acquire and make the basis for action. For many, such knowledge was to be found in Islamic law. For others, "real" knowledge was esoteric and mystical; hence the path to salvation lay in seeking the right teacher. Still others thought "real" knowledge consisted of a rational understanding of God's nature and attributes. Still others regarded "real" knowledge to be the philosophical wisdom of the ancients as found in the Neoplatonized Aristotelian view of the world."
5. Cited by Hermi, "Al-Biruni," p. 4.
6. Hermi, "Al-Biruni," p. 2.
7. After O'Conner and Robertson, "al-Biruni," p. 3.
8. After Bloom and Blair, *Islam*, p. 130.
9. Cited by Robinson, "Knowledge," p. 228.
10. Cited by Robinson, "Knowledge," p. 228.
11. After Bloom and Blair, *Islam*, p. 145.
12. "Al-Ma'arri," p. 1.
13. Both poems are cited in "Al-Ma'arri," pp. 3, 6.
14. After Haddad, "Ibn Hazm," p. 1.
15. Cited by Janin, *Four Paths*, p. 81.
16. Cited by Janin, *Four Paths*, p. 82.
17. "Sayyidna Nasir Khusraw," p. 1.
18. "Ismaili Poetry," p. 4.
19. Cited by Bloom and Blair, *Islam*, pp. 119–120.
20. Cited by Ghose, "Mysticism," p. 5.
21. Rabia was the only woman I found mentioned, and then only in passing, during the year I spent researching this book. This confirms that "Islamic learning" was traditionally an activity for men only.
22. Islamic tradition holds that each century a "renewer" (*mujaddid*) appears to restore the true knowledge and correct practice of the faith.
23. The *ulama* were not a homogeneous group. In a private communication of 16 May 2003, Omid Safi of Colgate University's Department of Philosophy and Religion mentioned that in medieval Islam "the category of the *ulama* is in fact a heterogeneous group comprised of a whole host of people with various levels of learning, professional income, and involvement in the transmission of knowledge." Popular preachers and storytellers formed the lower ranks of the *ulama*. Perhaps it was such men al-Ghazali had in mind when he denounced those who pursued religious learning only as a way to advance their own careers.
24. al-Ghazali, "Remembrance," p. 3. In a private communication of 22 May 2003, Leor Halevi, Assistant Professor of History at Texas A&M University, noted that this *hadith* does not necessarily represent al-Ghazali in an original way: *hadith* of that sort, regarding the angels of death and the punishment in the grave, etc., had received wide circulation before al-Ghazali's time.
25. After Musallam, "Ordering of Muslim Societies," p. 175.
26. After Musallam, "Ordering of Muslim Societies," p. 174.
27. After Musallam, "Ordering of Muslim Societies," p. 182.
28. Cited by Musallam, "Ordering of Muslim Societies," p. 182.
29. After Musallam, "Ordering of Muslim Societies," p. 185.
30. After Musallam, "Ordering of Muslim Societies," p. 185.

31. Private communication of 5 July 2003 from McGill professor Wael Hallaq.
32. Private communication of 8 August 2003 from Dr. James Piscatori of Wadham College, Oxford.
33. Adapted from Mutahhari, "The Role of *Ijtihad* in Legislation," p. 2. The Iranian scholar and theologian Murtada Mutahhari (1919/1920–1979) was one of the few high-ranking *ulama* to be in continuous contact with Ayatollah Khomeini during the long prerevolutionary period. Mutahhari was assassinated in 1979.
34. Al Hariri, "Al Hariri of Basrah," p. 4.
35. Al Hariri, "Al Hariri of Basrah," pp. 5–6.
36. Al Hariri, "Al Hariri of Basrah," p. 2.
37. O'Conner and Robertson, "Omar Khayyam," p. 1.
38. Cited by Bloom and Blair, *Islam*, p. 152.
39. After Bloom and Blair, *Islam*, p. 152.
40. Cited in Medieval Sourcebook, "Zamakhshari," pp. 2–3.
41. Cited in Medieval Sourcebook, "Zamakhshari," p. 3.
42. "World Maps of al-Idrisi," p. 2.
43. Jwaideh, "Idrisi," p. 2.
44. Much of the information in this section is drawn from Jwaideh, "Idrisi," pp. 2–6.
45. After Maalouf, *Les croisades*, p. 288, and Janin, *Four Paths*, p. 101.
46. Cited by Janin, *Four Paths*, p. 101.
47. Cited by Janin, *Four Paths*, pp. 101–102, and Medieval Sourcebook, "Usamah ibn Munqidh," p. 2.
48. "Ibn Rushd," p. 1.
49. Cited in Medieval Sourcebook, "Ibn Rushd," p. 1.
50. Quran, *sura* 7:184.
51. Quran, *sura* 88:17.
52. After Hassanali, "Ibn Rushd," p. 10.
53. A key reason why the vizier Nizam al-Mulk established *nazamiyyas* in all the major cities of the Seljuq realm was to defend Sunni orthodoxy against efforts by the Shia Fatimids and their Ismaili supporters to overthrow the Sunni caliphate. This was a deadly serious business. Indeed, al-Mulk himself was murdered by an Ismaili assassin in 1092.
54. Nakosteen and Szyliowicz, "Islamic Era," p. 5.
55. After Bloom and Blair, *Islam*, pp. 120–121.
56. Nasr, *Science and Civilization in Islam*, cited in a private communication of 3 June 2003 from the Islamic scholar Muhammad Hassanali.
57. Cited by Bloom and Blair, *Islam*, pp. 121–122.
58. Bloom and Blair, *Islam*, p. 180.
59. Cited by Bloom and Blair, *Islam*, p. 179.
60. "Symmetric Patterns," pp. 1–3, and Addington, "Four Types of Symmetry," pp. 1–4.
61. "Ibn al-Arabi," p. 1.
62. Robinson, "Ibn al-Arabi," p. 1.
63. Robinson, "Knowledge," p. 235.
64. Adapted from a private communication of 15 June 2003 from the Swedish scholar Ulrika Mårtensson.
65. "Life of Rumi," p. 4.
66. "Life of Rumi," p. 2.
67. Cited by Bloom and Blair, *Islam*, p. 63.
68. After Hassanali, "al-Tusi," p. 1.
69. "Twelver" Shiites are so-named because of their belief that the twelfth of their Imams mysteriously withdrew from the world and will reappear only at the end of time. In his absence, the Shiite community is guided by highly trained scholars formally known as *mujtahids* and popularly called *mullahs*. In modern times, *mullahs* have played a major political role in Iran and elsewhere, trying to cast national policies into a purely Islamic mold.
70. After Cooper, "al-Tusi," p. 1.
71. After O'Conner and Robertson, "al-Tusi," p. 4.
72. "Ibn al-Nafis," p. 1.
73. "Ibn al-Nafis," p. 1.
74. Cited by Bishiri, "Brief Note," p. 10.
75. "Masterpieces of Sa'di," p. 2.
76. Bishiri, "Brief Note," p. 3.
77. From a private communication of 17 September 2003 from the Muslim reader Shahab Mushtaq.
78. Cited by Bishiri, "Brief Note," p. 8.
79. Adapted from a private communication of 15 June 2003 from the Swedish scholar Ulrika Mårtensson.
80. Cited in Medieval Sourcebook, "Ibn Battuta," p. 40.
81. After Pavlin, "Ibn Taymiyya," p. 1.
82. In a private communication of 15 June 2003 the Swedish scholar Ulrika Mårtensson noted the political context of Ibn Taymiyya's preaching. This took place after the Mongol onslaught and the fall of the Abbasid empire, which left the Islamic community without a caliph of the Prophet's family as its leader. Ibn Taymiyya called for unity and a return to the pristine virtues of the first Muslim community in Medina as a way to strengthen the Muslim community of his own time. It is possible that some modern Islamic thinkers may find the political situation today to be similar, but even graver, than it was in Ibn Taymiyya's time. For this reason, they attach considerable importance to his writings.
83. Cited by Thornton, "Ibn Taymiyya," p. 1.
84. Cited by Thornton, "Ibn Taymiyya," p. 1.
85. Cited by Haddad, "Ibn Taymiyya," p. 1. Italics added.
86. Cited by Haddad, "Ibn Taymiyya," p. 2.
87. After Haddad, "Ibn Taymiyya," pp. 3, 7.

88. Cited in Medieval Sourcebook, "Ibn Battuta," p. 1.
89. Cited in Medieval Sourcebook, "Ibn Battuta," p. 27.
90. Cited in Medieval Sourcebook, "Ibn Battuta," p. 50.
91. "Biography of Hafiz," p. 2.
92. Cited by Bloom and Blair, *Islam*, p. 166.
93. Cited by Vernoit, "Artistic Expressions," p. 264.
94. Cited in "Biography of Hafiz," pp. 4–5.
95. *Encyclopedia of Islam*, "Ibn Khaldun."
96. Issawi, "Ibn Khaldun," p. 7.
97. Cited by Issawi, "Ibn Khaldun," p. 3.
98. Cited by Issawi, "Ibn Khaldun," p. 3.
99. Waldman, "Islamic World: Migration and Renewal," p. 16.
100. After Bloom and Blair, *Islam*, p. 141.
101. *Encyclopedia of Islam*, "Ibn Khaldun."
102. The first two quotes are cited in the *Encyclopedia of Islam*, "Ibn Khaldun." The third quote is from Bloom and Blair, *Islam*, p. 139.
103. Cited in the *Encyclopedia of Islam*, "Ibn Khaldun."
104. Cited by O'Conner and Robertson, "al-Kashi," p. 2.
105. Cited by Bloom and Blair, *Islam*, p. 170.
106. Cited by Bloom and Blair, *Islam*, p. 170.
107. After Bloom and Blair, *Islam*, p. 170.
108. After Dold-Samplonius, "Kashi, al-," p. 2.
109. Cited by O'Conner and Robertson, "al-Kashi," p. 3.
110. Cited by O'Conner and Robertson, "al-Kashi," p. 4.
111. After Halm, *Fatimids*, p. xiii.
112. Modern estimates are that the Black Death killed about one-third of the populations it infected. This suggests that al-Maqrizi's figure of 900,000 people was too high.
113. Cited by Bloom and Blair, *Islam*, pp. 175–176.
114. Unless otherwise attributed, this account comes from Janin, *Four Paths*, pp. 117–118.
115. Cited in Medieval Sourcebook, "Al-Makrisi," p. 13.
116. Cited in Medieval Sourcebook, "Al-Makrisi," p. 9.

Chapter VII

1. Hodgson, Rethinking World History, p. 97.
2. After Lapidus, *Islamic Societies*, pp. 253, 255, 260.
3. For text and illustrations, see Waugh, "Memoirs of Babur."
4. Cited by Waugh, "Memoirs of Babur," p. 3.
5. Cited by Waugh, "Memoirs of Babur," p. 10.
6. Cited by Waugh, "Memoirs of Babur," p. 17.
7. Cited in Medieval Sourcebook, "Sidi Ali Reis," p. 1.
8. Cited in Medieval Sourcebook, "Sidi Ali Reis," pp. 1–2.
9. Cited in Medieval Sourcebook, "Sidi Ali Reis," pp. 2–3.
10. Cited in Medieval Sourcebook, "Sidi Ali Reis," p. 33.
11. After Dale, "Islamic World," p. 62.
12. Hooker, "Suleyman," p. 1.
13. After Hooker, "Suleyman," p. 65.
14. Both citations are cited by Hooker, "Suleyman," p. 2.
15. Cited by Bloom and Blair, *Islam*, p. 189.
16. Cited by Bloom and Blair, *Islam*, p. 189.
17. After Bloom and Blair, *Islam*, p. 191.
18. After "Sinan," p. 1.
19. Vernoit, "Artistic Expressions," p. 277.
20. Grabar, "Arts, Islamic," p. 2.
21. After Vernoit, "Artistic Expressions," p. 281.
22. Gross, "Magnificent Exhibit," p. 1.
23. Cited in Bloom and Blair, *Islam*, p. 218.
24. After Armstrong, *Islam*, p. 107.
25. After Ballhatchet, "Akbar," p. 4.
26. After Armstrong, *Islam*, p. 107.
27. Cited by Robinson, "Knowledge," p. 239.
28. Cited by Dale, "The Islamic World," p. 80.
29. Stierlin, *Islamic Art*, pp. 180–181.
30. Cited by Nou, Okada, and Joshi, *Taj Mahal*, p. 12.
31. Cited by Nou, Okada, and Joshi, *Taj Mahal*, pp. 19–20.
32. These quotes, from *Les Six Voyages de Jean-Baptiste Tavernier en Turquie, en Perse et aux Indes*, are cited in Nou, Okada, and Joshi, Taj Mahal, pp. 123, 191.
33. Vernoit, "Artistic Expressions," p. 280.
34. After Nou, Okada, and Joshi, p. 22.
35. See Nou, Okada, and Joshi, *Taj Mahal*, p. 23.
36. Nou, Okada, and Joshi, *Taj Mahal*, p. 24.
37. This quote, from Rousselet's *L'Inde des Rajas* (Paris: Hachette, 1875), is cited in Nou, Okada, and Joshi, *Taj Mahal*, pp. 139–148.
38. Cited in Nou, Okada, and Joshi, *Taj Mahal*, pp. 218, 223. Italics added.
39. Cooper, "Mulla Sadra," p. 1.
40. After Armstrong, *Islam*, p. 103.
41. The following discussion is taken from a private communication of 30 May 2003 from Dr. Sajjad Rizvi.

Chapter VIII

1. Hodgson, *Rethinking World History*, p. 97.
2. In *The Future of Political Islam* (p. 5), Gra-

ham Fuller, a former Vice-Chairman of the National Intelligence Council at the Central Intelligence Agency, gives a more detailed account of this process: "The death of Islamic intellectual vigor and curiosity ... led to the decline of creative thinking in Islamic theology, philosophy, science, and technology.... This atrophy of Muslim intellectual vigor was well demonstrated in the collapse of Muslim sciences and even a general passivity toward later scientific and technological development in the West — until that same technology overwhelmed the Muslim world. Even in the face of the West's challenge, *most reformers looked at the West primarily as a warehouse of technological hardware, without grasping the need for the all-important civilizational software or values that made it all function.*" Italics added.

3. After Lapidus, *Islamic Societies*, p. 570.
4. Cited by Vernoit, "Artistic Expression," p. 275.
5. Adapted from Bhat, "Political Thought of Shah Wali-u Allah," p. 2.
6. After "Shah Wali Allah," p. 1.
7. Dale, "Islamic World," p. 89.
8. "Shah Wali Allah," p. 1.
9. After "Shah Wali Allah," p. 5.
10. Lapidus, *Islamic Societies*, p. 378.
11. Upadhyay, "Shah Wali Ullah," p. 6.
12. After Schwartz, *Two Faces*, p. 67.
13. Cited by Hourani, *Arabic Thought*, p. 37.
14. After Robinson, "Knowledge," p. 239.
15. Robinson, "Knowledge," p. 239. Italics added.
16. Vikør, *Sufi and Scholar*, p. 1.
17. Vikør, *Sufi and Scholar*, p. 189.
18. "Mirza Ghalib," p. 1.
19. "Ghalib," p. 1.
20. Ghalib, "Flower," p. 1.
21. "Paper Cartridges," p. 2.
22. Lapidus, *Islamic Societies*, p. 624.
23. The following comments are drawn from "Ghalib — Introduction," pp. 3–4.
24. Cited in "Paper Cartridges," p. 3.
25. Cited in "Paper Cartridges," p. 3.
26. After Lapidus, *Islamic Societies*, p. 465.
27. Robinson, "Knowledge," p. 244.
28. Cited by Metcalf, "'Traditionalist' Islamic Activism," p. 1.
29. After Lapidus, *Islamic Societies*, pp. 626–627.
30. "Deoband Movement," p. 2.
31. After Hourani, *Arabic Thought*, p. 108.
32. Kalin, "al-Afghani," p. 2.
33. Hourani, *Arabic Thought*, p. 112.
34. Cited by Hourani, *Arabic Thought*, p. 112.
35. The following section is drawn from Hourani, *Arabic Thought*, pp. 112–129.
36. Cited by Kalin, "al-Afghani," p. 4. It should be noted that Kalin concludes (on p. 5) that al-Afghani's exact position on a number of issues — for example, the relation between religion, philosophy, and science — remains somewhat obscure.
37. Hourani, *Arabic Thought*, p. 127.
38. After Lapidus, *Islamic Societies*, p. 517.
39. Armstrong, *Islam*, p. 130.
40. Ansari, "The Islamic World," p. 100.
41. Ansari, "The Islamic World," p. 100.
42. After Lapidus, *Islamic Societies*, p. 459.
43. After Lapidus, *Islamic Societies*, pp. 628–629.
44. "Sayyid Ahmad Khan," p. 1.
45. Iqbal, "Sayyid Ahmad Khan," p. 3.
46. Lapidus, *Islamic Societies*, pp. 464, 466
47. Harder, "Muhammad Abduh," p. 5.
48. This account of Abduh's life and career is drawn from Hourani, *Arabic Thought*, pp. 130–160.
49. Hourani, *Arabic Thought*, p. 136.
50. Cited by Hourani, *Arabic Thought*, pp. 140–141.
51. Hourani, *Arabic Thought*, pp. 144–145.
52. Private communication of 4 July 2003 from the Swedish scholar Ulrika Mårtensson.
53. Cited by Hourani, *Arabic Thought*, p. 150.
54. After Hourani, *Arabic Thought*, pp. 148–149.
55. Cited by Harder, "Muhammad Abduh," p. 1.
56. After Harder, "Muhammad Abduh," p. 2.
57. Calder is quoted in private communication of the Islamic scholar Muhammad Hassanali.
58. After Hourani, *Arabic Thought*, p. 226. Many of my comments on Rashid Rida are drawn from pp. 222–244 of this source.
59. Arslan is quoted by Hourani in *Arabic Thought*, p. 228. Italics added.
60. Rashid Rida, cited by Hourani, *Arabic Thought*, p. 231.
61. Rashid Rida, cited by Hourani, *Arabic Thought*, p. 231.
62. After Hourani, *Arabic Thought*, p. 234.
63. Rashid Rida, quoted by Hourani in *Arabic Thought*, p. 235.
64. Hourani, *Arabic Thought*, p. 240.
65. Hourani, *Arabic Thought*, p. 244.
66. After Lapidus, *Islamic Societies*, p. 626.
67. Both citations are from Robinson, *Islamic World*, p. xix.
68. Cited in "Allama Iqbal," pp. 3–4.
69. Cited in "Allama Iqbal," p. 6.
70. McDonough, "Iqbal," p. 3.
71. Cited in "Allama Iqbal," p. 6.
72. Cited by Kalin, "Three View of Science," p. 1. Italics added.
73. After Itzkowitz, "Ataturk," pp. 9–10.
74. After Lapidus, *Islamic Societies*, pp. 503, 508.
75. Cited by Robinson, *Islamic World*, p. xix.

76. Itzkowitz, "Ataturk," p. 10.

77. After Hourani, *Arabic Thought*, p. 242.

78. For a useful account of Ali Shariati's life and work, see Keddie, *Roots of Revolution*, pp. 215–225.

79. "Dr. Ali Shariati," p. 2.

80. From "What is to be done?", cited in "Dr. Ali Shariati," p. 4.

81. From "School of thought and action," cited in "Dr. Ali Shariati," p. 4.

82. From "What is to be done?", cited in "Dr. Ali Shariati," p. 5.

83. Both quotes are from "Dr. Ali Shariati," p. 1.

84. Some of this discussion is drawn from Schwartz, *Two Faces of Islam*, pp. 131–132.

85. Cited by Schwartz, *Two Faces of Islam*, p. 132.

86. In a private communication of 12 September 2003, the Muslim reader Shahab Mushtaq remarked that if one examines these claims for a "return to the Quran and the *sunna*," they turn out to be nonsensical. He noted that in fact Muslims never left the Quran and the *sunna*. Indeed, after Ibn Taymiyya's era they seem to have abandoned both philosophy and the readiness to adopt knowledge no matter what its origins, replacing them instead with a determination to stick to literal interpretations of the Quran and the *sunna*.

87. After Lapidus, *Islamic Societies*, p. 645.

88. Lapidus, *Islamic Societies*, p. 810.

89. Adapted from an undated article in the *Muslim Almanac* ("The Ethical Tradition in Islam," by Azim Nanji) which was forwarded to me as an attachment to a private communication from a Muslim reader.

90. Rahman, *Islam & Modernity*, p. 141.

91. Rahman, *Islam & Modernity*, pp. 145, 151–152.

Chapter IX

1. It is worth noting that Robert Pape, a professor of political science at the University of Chicago, compiled a database of 188 suicide bombings and attacks that took place around the world between 1980 and 2001. His conclusion was that "The data show that there is little connection between suicide terrorism and Islamic fundamentalism, or any religion for that matter.... Rather, what nearly all suicide terrorist campaigns have in common is a specific secular and strategic goal: to compel liberal democracies to withdraw military forces from territory that the terrorists consider to be their homeland. Religion is rarely the root cause, although it is often used by terrorist organizations in recruiting and other efforts in service of the broader strategic objective." See Pape, "The Strategic Logic of Suicide Bombers."

2. The modern Islamic scholar Youssef Choueiri points out that although some scholars object to the use of "fundamentalism" (*usuli*) as a generic term, it is "an eminently endogenous Arabic designation.... Thus, *fundamentalism* in historical Islam was in its early development associated with a scholarly and religious activity, undertaken for the purpose of elucidating the principles and sources of a particular discipline.... Modern and contemporary Islamic fundamentalism combines political action with an ardent desire to discover the original blueprint of a pious community and its ideological principles.... It is then quite legitimate to use "fundamentalism," in spite of its Anglo-Saxon and evangelist connotations, in order to designate intellectual, theological and political movements in the Muslim world." See Choueiri, *Islamic Fundamentalism*, pp. xvi–xvii. For another point of view (i.e., that the expression "Islamic fundamentalism" is both useful *and problematic*), see Denoeux, "The Forgotten Swamp," p. 57 ff.

3. Ironically, modern fundamentalists overlook the fact that early Islam was quite open to learning and to new ideas. It embraced peoples of all races and cultures, willingly accepting their intellectual contributions. This stands in sharp contrast to the cultural hostility, anti-intellectualism, and exclusivism of fundamentalism today.

4. The following account draws on the German scholar André Kahlmeyer's unpublished paper, "Sayyid Qutb: Islamic Fundamentalist."

5. From Shehadeh, "Women in the discourse of Sayyid Qutb," *Arab Studies Quarterly*, Summer 2000, pp. 45–55, cited by Kahlmeyer, "Sayyid Qutb," p. 4.

6. After Kahlmeyer, "Sayyid Qutb," pp. 4–5.

7. From Appleby, "History in the Fundamentalist Imagination" in *The Journal of American History*, September 2002, pp. 498–511, cited by Kahlmeyer, "Sayyid Qutb," pp. 12–13.

8. Cited by Shepard, *Sayyid Qutb*, p. 350.

9. See Rothstein, "Review of *Terror and Liberalism*; Berman, "Philosopher of Islamic Terror," p. 2; and Bergen, *Holy War, Inc.*, pp. 50–51. On these pages, Bergen adds the following details about Muhammad Qutb: "After Sayyid's execution in Egypt in 1966, Muhammad would become the keeper of his brother's flame and the chief interpreter of his written works. Those writings would have a profound effect on bin Laden and the Islamists allied with him.... Qutb makes the case that the only way to establish [a new, truly Islamic order] is through an offensive *jihad* against the enemies of Islam, whether they be non–Islamic societies or Muslim societies that are not following the precepts of the Koran. This is the ideological

underpinning of bin Laden's followers, who target not only the West but also Muslim regimes such as Saudi Arabia, which they regard as apostates from Islam."

10. Kepel, *Jihad: The political trail of Islam*," p. 314, cited by Kahlmeyer, "Sayyid Qutb," p. 12.

11. After Lapidus, *Islamic Societies*, p. 485.

12. Keddie, *Roots of Revolution*, p. 231.

13. The following discussion is drawn from Keddie, *Roots of Revolution*, pp. 207–208.

14. After Fuller, *Political Islam*, p. 182.

15. Viorst, "Ayatullah [*sic*] Ruhollah Khomeini," pp. 1, 2.

16. Shortly after it was issued, this *fatwa* was declared un-Islamic by the religious scholars of al-Azhar University in Cairo and of Saudi Arabia. See Armstrong, *Islam*, pp. 148–149.

17. Adapted from a private communication of 26 September 2003 from the Swedish scholar Ulrika Mårtensson.

18. Said, *Orientalism*, pp. 7–8.

19. "Professor Edward W. Said," p. 1.

20. "Obituary: Edward W. Said," p. 1.

21. "Mohammed Arkoun," p. 1.

22. "Mohammed Arkoun," p. 1.

23. Arkoun, *Rethinking Islam*, p. 94. Italics added.

24. This synopsis, provided by the publisher of Arkoun's book, is cited in "Mohammed Arkoun," p. 3. Italics added.

25. This comes from a private communication of 29 August 2003 from the Swedish scholar Ulrika Mårtensson.

26. This and some other points in this section have been adapted from a private communication of 1 October 2003 from the Swedish scholar Ulrika Mårtensson.

27. "Seyyed Hossein Nasr," pp. 1, 12.

28. Sadri and Sadri, *Reason*, pp. ix, xv.

29. The following comments are drawn from Middle East Institute, "Policy Brief," pp. 1–3.

30. Adapted from a private communication of 2 September 2003 from the Swedish scholar Ulrika Mårtensson. She added that Soroush is an active participant in the ongoing international and philosophical debate about religious truth. Some of the participants in this debate claim that in order to tolerate other faiths, religions must reduce their own claims to possess absolute truth: the very existence of more than one truth leads to conflict and means that one of them must yield. Hence religions must admit that they possess only relative truth. She noted that Soroush argues that several truths can indeed coexist. For example, if I hold that the "truth" you believe in is false, there is no reason why I cannot tolerate your holding it, especially if it does not prevent me from holding my own "truth." (See Chapter 9 in Sadri and Sadri, *Reason, Freedom, and Democracy*.")

31. Middle East Institute, "Policy Briefs," p. 3.

32. Sadri Freedom, and Democracy, Reason, pp. 23–24.

33. Al-Azmeh, *Islams*, p. 122. Italics added.

34. "Conversation with Aziz al-Azmeh," p. 1.

35. "Conversation with Aziz al-Azmeh," p. 7.

36. "FBI Ten Most Wanted Fugitive," pp. 1–2.

37. The Egyptian physician and terrorist leader Ayman al-Zawahiri, who is now Osama bin Laden's deputy, appears to be al-Qaeda's resident intellectual. His father and uncle were both prominent Islamic scholars and clerics; Zawahiri himself has justified the recourse to violence (*jihad*) in two works—*Bitter Harvest* (1991), and *Knights Under the Prophet's Banner* (2001). The latter appears to exist only in manuscript form.

38. Alexander and Swetman, *Usama bin Laden*, p. 3.

39. Cited by Alexander and Swetman, *Usama bin Laden*, p. 6.

40. For a partial listing of bin Laden's public statements, see the Public Broadcast System's "Osama bin Laden v. the U.S.," pp. 1–6.

41. These citations are all from appendix 1A of Alexander's and Swetnam's *Usama bin Laden*.

42. As mentioned earlier in the section on Ibn Taymiyya, he believed that "*Jihad* implies all kinds of worship, both in its inner and outer forms.... Since lawful warfare is essentially *jihad* and since its aim is that the religion is God's entirely and God's word is uppermost, therefore according to all Muslims, those who stand in the way [shall] be fought." Cited by Thornton, "Ibn Taymiyya," p. 1.

43. These citations come from appendix 2 of Alexander's and Swetnam's *Usama bin Laden*.

44. Cited in "Osama bin Laden v. the U.S.," p. 3.

45. Cited by Alexander and Swetman, *Usama bin Laden*, appendix 1B.

46. Metcalf, "'Traditionalist' Islamic Activism," p. 12, endnote 19.

47. From "Interview: Osama bin Laden," pp. 3, 9.

48. Cited in "Osama bin Laden v. the U.S.," p. 5.

49. "Bin Laden Tape Assails U.S. Occupation."

50. Lewis, *Crisis of Islam*, p. 107.

Chapter X

1. According to World Bank president James Wolfensohn, poor countries spend more on military items ($200 billion) than they invest in education. See "World Bank Faults the Rich Countries."

2. Some of these comments have been adapted from a 4 July 2003 private communication from the Muslim reader Shahab Mushtaq.

3. To repeat what was said in the section on the nineteenth century reformer al-Afghani, the claim that returning to the "essence" of Islam will enable Muslims to become strong enough to fend off the encroachments of foreigners is based more on faith than on reason.

4. Lapidus, *Islamic Societies*, p. 835. Italics added.

5. Rohde, "Radicals' Seductive Voice," p. 1.

Appendix 1

1. Komaroff, "Islamic Art," p. 1.
2. After Komaroff, "Islamic Art," p. 3, and Grabar, "Arts, Islamic" pp. 7, 10, 11.
3. This quote from Lotti's *L'Inde (sans les Anglais)*, is cited by Nou, Okada, and Joshi, *Taj Mahal*, p. 96.
4. Stierlin, *Islamic Art*, p. 180.
5. After Khatibi and Sielmassi, *Islamic Calligraphy*, description inside front cover.
6. This paragraph is drawn from "Islam and Islamic History," pp. 1–2.
7. After Imamuddin, *Hispano-Arab Libraries*, pp. 3–4.
8. Cited in "Naguib Mahfouz," p. 13.
9. Boston Globe, p. 2.
10. Ansari, "Islamic World," p. 119.
11. According to the strictest interpretations of *shirk*, the pursuit of wealth to the neglect of one's religious and social obligations is considered to be *shirk*.
12. Quran, *suras* 3:49 and 5:112.
13. Vernoit, "Artistic Expressions," p. 253.
14. An excellent technical description of the Dome of the Rock can be found on pp. 28–34 of Richard Ettinghausen and Oleg Grabar's *The Art and Architecture of Islam, 650–1250* (New Haven and London: Yale University Press, 1994).
15. Adapted from a private communication of 13 June 2003 from Ulrika Mårtensson.
16. Khatibi and Sielmassi, *Islamic Calligraphy*, description inside front cover.
17. Cited in "Islam and Islamic History," p. 3.
18. Khatibi and Sielmassi, *Islamic Calligraphy*, p. 78.
19. After Rice, *Islamic Art*, pp. 254-280.
20. Stierlin, *Islamic Art*, pp. 124-125.
21. After Ertug, *Pursuit of Excellence*, p. 77.
22. After Ertug, *Pursuit of Excellence*, p. 95.
23. After Rice, *Islamic Art*, pp. 212, 278.
24. After Ertug, *Pursuit of Excellence*, p. 146.
25. After Ertug, *Pursuit of Excellence*, p. 185.
26. After Vernoit, "Artistic Expressions," p. 260.
27. This and the following comments are drawn from Vernoit, "Artistic Expressions."
28. Lapidus, *Islamic Societies*, p. 229.
29. After Grabar, *Miniatures*, p. 91.
30. For an excellent introduction to Persian miniature painting, see Grabar, *Mostly Miniatures*. He discusses this unique art form under seven thematic categories: history, religion, animals, the epic, lyric romanticism, realism, and ornament. See pp. 84–121.
31. After Lapidus, *Islamic Societies*, p. 231.
32. After Grabar, *Miniatures*, p. 115.
33. After Lapidus, *Islamic Societies*, p. 263.
34. The most famous woman singer of modern times was the Egyptian Um Kulthum (d. 1975). Her repertoire was based on classical religious singing but also included some secular songs. She also appeared in popular films. See Vernoit, "Artistic Expression," p. 284.
35. After "Middle Eastern Music," p. 1.

Appendix 2

1. Private communication of 19 May 2003 from Munir Zilanawala of Harvard University. His list has been lightly edited.

Appendix 3

1 Appendix 3 is taken from private communications of 7 and 14 September 2003 from the Muslim scholar Muhammed Hassanali. He said that much of this material was adapted from Azim Nanji's article, "The Ethical Tradition in Islam," which appeared in Nanji's *The Muslim Almanac: The Reference Work on History, Faith and Culture, and Peoples of Islam* (Detroit: Gale Research, 1995, pp. 205–211.) Hassanali added that Hugh Kennedy in "Intellectual Life in the First Four Centuries of Islam" in *Intellectual Traditions in Islam* (F. Daftary ed.) provides a more thorough discussion of Muslim thought during the early years of Islam.

2. Quran 5:100.
3. Quran: 107.
4. Quran 2:188.
5. Quran 90:8.
6. "The Concept of Adab," p. 1.

Selected Bibliography

Abu-Rabi, Ibrahim. "The Arab World." In Nasr, Seyyed Hossein and Oliver Leaman, *History of Islamic Philosophy*. London and New York: Routledge, 2001, pp. 1082–1114.

"Abu Raihan al-Biruni, (973–1048 A.D.)." http://members.tripod.com/~wzzz/BIRUNI.html. Accessed 4 April 2003.

Addington, Susan. "The Four Types of Symmetry in the Plane." http://mathforum.org/sum95/suzanne/symsusan.html. Accessed 2 May 2003.

Ahmad, Hassan. "Imam Ahmad ibn Hanbal." http://www.sunnahonline.com'ilm/seerah/0040.htm. Accessed 28 March 2003.

al-Azmeh, Aziz. *Islams and Modernities*. 2nd ed. London and New York: Verso, 1996.

Alexander, Yonah and Michael S. Swetnam. *Usama bin Laden's al-Qaida: Profile of a Terrorist Network*. Ardsley, N.Y.: Transnational, 2001.

al-Ghazalli [sic]. "The Remembrance of Death and the Afterlife." http://www.fordham.edu/halsall/source/alghazali.html. Accessed 11 April 2003.

al Hariri. "Al Hariri of Basrah." Cited in http://www.fordham.edu.halsall/basis/1100Hariri.html. Accessed 28 April 2003.

"Allama Iqbal — Biography." http://www.allamaiqbal.com/person/biography/biotxtread.html. Accessed 27 June 2003.

"al Ma'arri." http://www.humanistictexts.org/al_ma'arri.htm. Accessed 9 April 2003.

al-Nur. "Al-Tabari." http://www.dartmouth.edu/~alnur/ISLAM/GRMUSLIMS/Al_Tabari.htm. Accessed 1 April 2003.

———. "Imam Abu al-Hasan al-Ash'ari." http://www.dartmouth.edu/~alnur/ISLAM/GRMUSLIMS/Al-ashari.htm. Accessed 2 April 2003.

Ansari, Abdul Haq. "Islamic Ethics: Concept and Prospect." http://students.washington.edu/rameez/islam/articles/islamic_ethics.htm. Accessed 9 September 2003.

Ansari, Sarah. "The Islamic World in the Era of Western Domination: 1800 to the Present." In Robinson, Francis (ed.), *The Cambridge Illustrated History of the Islamic World*. Cambridge: Cambridge University Press, 1998, pp. 90–121.

"Arab Contributions to Mathematics and the Introduction of the Zero." http://www.arabicnews.com/ansub/Daily/Day/9804221/1998042208.html. Accessed 7 July 2003.

Arab Gateway. "Arabic Poetry." http://www.al-bab.com/arab/literature/poetry.htm. Accessed 3 April 2003.

"The Arabic Numeral System." http://www-gap.dcs.st-and.ac.uk~history/HistTopics/Arabic_numerals.html. Accessed 20 January 2003.

"Arabic Numerals." http://islamicity.com/mosque/ihame/Ref6.htm. Accessed 20 January 2003.

Arberry, Arthur J. *Modern Arabic Poetry: An Anthology with English Verse Translations*. Cambridge: Cambridge University Press, 1967.

Arkoun, Muhammed. *Rethinking Islam: Common Questions, Uncommon Answers*. Boulder: Westview, 1994.

Armstrong, Karen. *A History of God*. London: Mandarin, 1994.

———. *A History of Jerusalem: One City, Three Faiths*. Hammersmith, Eng.: HarperCollins, 1997.

———. *Islam: A Short History*. London: Phoenix, 2002.

———. *Muhammad: A Biography of the Prophet*. London: Phoenix, 2001.

Asani, Ali S. "On Pluralism, Intolerance, and the Quran." *The American Scholar*, vol. 71., no. 1 (winter 2002), pp. 52–60.

Assaad, S. "Sayyidna Hamid al-Din al-Kirmani." http://ismaili.net/~heritage/hero/hero11.html. Accessed 4 April 2003.

Atiyeh, George N. "al-Sijistani, Abu Sulayman Muhammad (c. 932–c.1000)." http://www.muslimphilosophy.com/rep/H040.htm. Accessed 31 March 2003.

Ballhatchet, Kenneth. "Akbar." http://www.britannica.com/eb/print?eu=5318. Accessed 27 March 2003.

Bashiri, Iraj. "A Brief Note on the Life of Shaykh Muslih a-Din Sa'di Shiraz." http://angelfire.com/rnb/bashiri/Poets/Sadi.html. Accessed 13 September 2003.

Bergen, Peter L. *Holy War, Inc.: Inside the Secret World of Osama bin Laden*. London: Phoenix, 2001.

Berman, Paul. "The Philosopher of Islamic Terror." 23 March 2003 *New York Times* article carried by http://ww2.moriel.org:8004/israel/philosopher_of_islamic_terror.htm. Accessed 4 July 2003.

Bhat, Abdur-Rashid. "Political Thought of Shah Wali-u Allah — An Analytical Study." http://www.alinaam.org.za/library/shahw.htm. Accessed 4 June 2003.

"Bin Laden Tape Assails U.S. Occupation." *International Herald Tribune*, 6 January 2004.

"Biography" [of Seyyed Hossein Nasr]. http://www.seriousseekers.com/Teachers%20and%20Contrib.../teachers_contributors_Nasr.ht. Accessed 29 September 2003.

"Biography of Hafiz." http://www.hafizonlove.com/bio/index.htm. Accessed 9 May 2003.

Bloom, Jonathan and Sheila Blair. *Islam: Empire of Faith*. London: BBC Worldwide, 2001.

Boston Globe, "Recovering Egypt Writer Asks Extremism's Defeat." http://www.boston.com/globe/search/stories/nobel/1994/1994e.html. Accessed 11 August 2003.

Bukhari, Salih. *Hadith*. http://www.usc.edu/dept/MSA/fundamentals/hadithunnah/bukari/001.sbt.html. Accessed 21 February 2003.

Casey, John. "Visits to Mosques Give a Good Insight Into Islam Aesthetics." http://www.telegraph.co.uk/news/main.jhtml?xml=news/campaigns/islam/nislam27.xml. Accessed 22 March 2003.

Choueiri, Youssef M. *Islamic Fundamentalism*. London and New York: Continuum, 2002.

"The Concept of *Adab*." http://www.hf.unib.no/smi/pao/rooke.html. Accessed 10 September 2003.

"Conversation with Aziz Al-Azmeh on Islamism and Modernism Part I." http://www.iran-bulletin.org.Azmeh_1.html. Accessed 4 August 2003.

Cooper, John. "al-Tusi, Khwajah Nasir (1201–74)." http://www.muslimphilosophy.com/rep/H036.htm. Accessed 4 May 2003.

———. "Mulla Sadra (Sadr al-Din Muhammad al-Shirazi) (1571/2–1640). http://www.muslimphilosophy.com/rep/H027.htm. Accessed 20 May 2003.

Coulson, Noel James. "Shar'iah." http://www.britannnica.com/eb/print?eu=108146. Accessed 25 December 2002.

Crone, Patricia. "Meccan Trade and the Rise of Islam." http://www.fordham.edu/halsall/med/crone.html. Accessed 24 February 2003.

———. "The Rise of Islam in the World." In Robinson, Francis (ed.), *The Cambridge Illustrated History of the Islamic World*. Cambridge: Cambridge University Press, 1998, pp. 2–31.

Dale, Stephen E. "The Islamic World in the Age of European Expansion, 1500–1800." In Robinson, Francis (ed.), *The Cambridge Illustrated History of the Islamic World*. Cambridge: Cambridge University Press, 1998, pp. 62–89.

Dawood, N.J. (trans. and ed.) *The Koran*. London: Penguin, 1999.

Denoeux, Guilain. "The Forgotten Swamp: Navigating Political Islam." *Middle East Policy*. Vol. IX, No. 2, June 2002, pp. 56–81.

"Deoband Movement [1866–1947]." http://www.storyofpakistan.com/articletex.asp?artid=A025. Accessed 16 June 2003.

Dold-Samplonius, Yvonne. "Kashi, al-." http://www.britannica.com/eb/print?eu=139045. Accessed 16 December 2002.

"The Dome of the Rock." http://members.tripod.com/~TheHOPE/domerock.htm. Accessed 19 March 2003.

Doughty, C.M. (Edward Garnett, ed.) *Passages from Arabia Deserta*. Harmondsworth: Penguin, 1983.

"Dr. Ali Shariati." http://www.math.nyu.edu/phd_students/amirishs/Html/Shariati.html. Accessed 6 July 2003.

Ead, Hamed Abdel-reheem. "Alchemy in Islamic Times." http:www.levity.com/alchemy/islam01.html. Accessed 20 August 2003.

Elad, Amikam. "Pilgrims and Pilgrimage to

Jerusalem during the Early Muslim Period." In Levine, Lee L. (ed.), *Jerusalem: Its Sanctity and Centrality to Judaism, Christianity, and Islam*. New York: Continuum, 1999, pp. 300–314.

———. "Why Did Abd al-Malik Build the Dome of the Rock? A Re-examination of the Muslim Sources." In Raby, J. and J. Johns (eds.), *Bayt al-Maqdis. Abd al-Malik's Jerusalem*. Oxford: Oxford University Press, 1992, pp. 42–52.

Encyclopaedia of Islam. "Ibn Khaldun." http://www.muslimphilosophy.com/ei/KHALDUN.htm. Accessed 9 May 2003.

———. "Idjtihad." Vol. 3. Leiden, Neth.: Brill, 1971.

Ertug, Ahmet. *In Pursuit of Excellence: Works of Art from the Museum of Turkish and Islamic Arts, Istanbul*. Istanbul: Ahmet Ertug, 1993.

Ettinghausen, Richard, and Oleg Graber. *The Art and Architecture of Islam, 650–1250*. New Haven and London: Yale University Press, 1994.

Euben, Roxanne L. *Enemy in the Mirror: Islamic Fundamentalism and the Limits of Modern Rationalism*. Princeton: Princeton University Press, 1999.

"Euclid." In *Encyclopædia Britannica*. http:www.britannica.com/eb/article?eu=33758. Accessed 22 March 2003.

"FBI Ten Most Wanted Fugitive." [sic] http://www.fbi.gov/mostwant/topten/fugitives/laden.htm. Accessed 20 August 2003.

Foundation for Science Technology and Civilization, "Al-Muqaddasi: An Encyclopaedic Scholar." http://www.muslimheritage.com/day_life/default.cfm?ArticleID=245&Oldpage=1. Accessed 4 April 2003.

Fuller, Graham E. *The Future of Political Islam*. New York: Palgrave Macmillan, 2003.

Garonne, Max. "Fundamental Problems: Religious Writer Karen Armstrong Explains Why Muslim Nations Have Difficulty with Democracy and the Qualities That All Forms of Fundamentalism Share." *Salon News*, 22 October 2001. http://www.salon.com.books/int/2001/10/22/armstrong/index.html. Accessed 26 April 2003.

"Ghalib — Introduction." http://www.cs.wisc.edu/~navin/india/songs/ghalib/intro.g. Accessed 26 April 2003.

Ghalib, Mirza. "Flower." http://www.lib.virginia.edu/area-studies/SouthAsia/Ideas/flower.html. Accessed 12 June 2003.

———. "Ghalib." http://www.lib.virginia.edu/area-studies/SouthAsia/Ideas/preface.html. Accessed 12 June 2003.

Ghose, Sisirkumar. "Mysticism." http://www.britannica.com/eb/print?eu=117397. Accessed 12 April 2003.

"Global Connections: Science & Technology: Historic Innovation, Modern Solutions." http:www.pbs.org/wgbh/globalconnections/mideast/themes/science/index.html. Accessed 21 March 2003.

Grabar, Oleg. "Arts, Islamic." http://www.britannica.com/eb/print?eu=109490. Accessed 16 May 2003.

———. *Mostly Miniatures: An Introduction to Persian Painting*. Princeton and Oxford: Princeton University Press, 2000.

———. *Penser l'art Islamique*. Paris: Éditions Albin Michel, 1996.

"Great Mosque of Córdoba." http://archnet.org/library/sites/one-site.tcl?site_id=31. Accessed 22 March 2003.

"The Great Mosque of Damascus." http://users.telerama.com/~jdehullu/islam/umay_04.htm. Accessed 17 March 2003.

Gross, Benjamin. "Magnificent Exhibit of South Asian Paintings Draws Crowds in Washington." http://uninfo.state.gov/usa/ismal/a072402.htm. Accessed 14 November 2003.

Haddad, G.F. "Ibn Hazm." http://www.sunnah.org/history/Innovators/ibn_hazm.htm. Accessed 10 April 2003.

———. "Ibn Taymiyya." http://www.sunnah.org/history/Innovators/ibn_taymiyya.htm. Accessed 6 May 2003.

Haddawy, Husain (trans. and ed.). *The Arabian Nights*. New York: Norton, 1992.

"Hadith." http://mb-soft.com/believe/txw/hadith.htm. Accessed 28 March 2003.

Halm, Heinz. *The Fatimids and Their Traditions of Learning*. London: Tauris, 1997.

Hanafi, Hassan. "Method of Thematic Interpretation of the Qur'an." In Wild, Stefan (ed.), *The Qur'an as Text*. Leiden, Neth.: Brill, 1996, pp. 195–211.

Harder, Elma. "Muhammad Abduh." http://www.cis-ca.org/voices/a/abduh-mn.htm. Accessed 23 June 2003.

Hassanali, Mohammed. "Muslim Contribution to the Sciences." (A private communication of 21 March 2003, this document gives biographic information on numerous Muslim luminaries. It is cited in the endnotes as "Hassanali," followed by the name of the Muslim thinker being discussed.)

Haqqani, Husain. "America Needs to Listen to Muslims." *International Herald Tribune*, p. 6.

Hermi, Lotfi. "Abu Raihan Al-Biruni." http://www.araf.net/dergi/sayi07/lofti962.shtml. Accessed 7 May 2003.

Hillenbrand, Robert. "Images of Authority on Kashan Lustreware." In Allan, James (ed.), *Islamic Art in the Ashmolean Museum*. Oxford: Oxford University Press, 1995, pp. 167–192.

"History of the Planispheric Astrolabe." http://www.saundersandcooke.com/history.html. Accessed 1 April 2003.

Hodgson, Marshall G.S. *Rethinking World History: Essays on Europe, Islam, and World History*. Cambridge: Cambridge University Press, 1993.

———. *The Venture of Islam*. 3 vols. Chicago and London: University of Chicago Press, 1974.

Hooker, Richard. "Suleyman." http://www.wsu.edu:8080/~dee/OTTOMAN/SULEYMAN.HTM. Accessed 13 May 2003.

Hourani, Albert. *Arabic Thought in the Liberal Age, 1789–1939*. Cambridge: Cambridge University Press, 1986.

"Ibn al-Arabi or Ibn Arabi, Muhyi al-Din Muhammad bin ali al-Hatimi al-Tai." http://www.infoplease.com/ce6/people/A0824825.Html. Accessed 2 May 2003.

"Ibn al-Nafis." http://www.timelinescience.org/resource/students/blood/ianafis.htm. Accessed 5 May 2003.

"Ibn Rushd." http://www.bysiness.co.uk/ulamah/biobnrushd.htm. Accessed 30 April 2003.

"Ijtihad." http://www.wikipedia.org/w/wiki.phtml?title=Ijtihad&printable=yes. Accessed 1 April 2003.

Imamuddin, S.M. *Hispano-Arab Libraries*. Karachi: Pakistan Historical Society, 1961.

"In the Name of God: A Survey of Islam and the West." *The Economist*, 13 September 2003, pp. 3–16.

"Interview: Osama bin Laden." http://www.pbs.org/wgbh/pages/frontlilne/shows/binladen/who/interview.html. Accessed 23 August 2003.

Iqbal, Muzaffar. "Sayyid Ahmad Khan (1817–1898/1232–1316)." http://www.cis-ca.org/voices/k/syydkhn-mn.htm. Accessed 21 June 2003.

Ishaq, Ibn. "Life of Muhammad." http://www.fordham.edu/halsall/source/muhammadi-sira.html. Accessed 24 February 2003.

"Islam and Islamic History in Arabia and the Middle East: Arabic Writing." http://islam.org/Mosque.ihame/Ref3.htm. Accessed 4 February 2003.

Islam for Today. "Al-Azhar University, Cairo." http://www.islamfortoday.com/alazhar.htm. Accessed 3 April 2003.

"Islamic Political Philosophy: Al-Farabi, Avicenna, Averroes." http://www.fordham.edu/halsall/source/arab-yy67s11.html. Accessed 2 April 2003.

"Ismaili Poetry: Nasir-I Khusraw Poetry." http://www.amaana.org/ISWEB/ismpoet2.htm. Accessed 11 April 2003.

Issawi, Charles. "Ibn Khaldun." http://www.britannica.com/eb/print?eu=42867. Accessed 16 December 2002.

Itzkowitz, Norman. "Ataturk, Kemal." http://www.britannica.com/eb/print?eu=117163. Accessed 7 July 2003.

Janin, Hunt. *Four Paths to Jerusalem: Jewish, Christian, Muslim, and Secular Pilgrimages, 1000 BCE to 2001 CE*. Jefferson and London: McFarland, 2002.

Jarrar, Sabri. "Two Islamic Construction Plans for al-Haram al-Sharif." In Rosovsky, Nitza (ed.), *City of the Great King: Jerusalem from David to the Present*. Cambridge: Harvard University Press, 1996, pp. 380–416.

Jwaideh, Wadie. "Idrisi, al-Sharif al-." http://www.britannica.com/eb/print?eu=42986. Accessed 10 April 2003.

Kahlmeyer, André. "Sayyid Qutb: Islamic Fundamentalist." Unpublished paper of 1 June 2003 for a graduate seminar on Modern Arab Political Thought, taught at the Lebanese American University in Beirut by Dr. Fawwaz Traboulsi.

Kalin, Ibrahim. "Sayyid Jamal al-Din Muhammad b. Safdar al-Afghani (1838–1897)." http://www.cis-ca.org/voices/a/afghani-mn.htm. Accessed 17 June 2003.

———. "Three Views of Science in the Islamic World." http://www.kalam.org/papers/kalin.htm. Accessed 18 June 2003.

Keddie, Nikki R. *Roots of Revolution: An Interpretative History of Modern Iran*. New Haven and London: Yale University Press, 1981.

Kennedy-Day, Kiki. "al-Kindi, Abu Yusuf Ya'qub ibn Ishaq (d. c. 866–73)." http://www.muslimphilosophy.com/ip/kin.htm. Accessed 29 March 2003.

Khatibi, Abdelkebir, and Mohammad Sielmassi. *The Splendours of Islamic Calligraphy*. London: Thames & Hudson, 2001.

Komaroff, Linda. "Islamic Art." http://www.lacma.org/islamic_art/intro.htm. Accessed 15 December 2002.

Lapidus, Ira M. *A History of Islamic Societies*.

2nd ed. Cambridge: Cambridge University Press, 2002.

Lewis, Bernard. *The Crisis of Islam: Holy War and Unholy Terror.* London: Weidenfeld & Nicolson, 2003.

———. *What Went Wrong? Western Impact and Middle Eastern Response.* London: Phoenix, 2002.

"Life of Rumi." http://www.khamush.com/life.html. Accessed 3 May 2003.

Lings, Martin. *Muhammad: His Life Based on the Earliest Sources.* Cambridge: Islamic Texts Society, 2002.

Maalouf, Amin. *Les Croisades vues par les Arabes.* Paris: Lattès, 1992.

Malaspina Great Books. "Abul Qaisim Zahrawi (-al) (936–1013)." http://www.malaspina.com/site/person_1210.asp. Accessed 5 April 2003.

Malik, Maida. "The Life of *Imam* Abu Hanifah Nu'man ibn Thabit, 80–150 A.H." http:www.sunnah.org/publication/khulafa_rashideen/life_of_imman_abu_hanifah.htm. Accessed 20 March 2003.

"The Masterpieces of Sa'di." http://itsa.ucsf.edu~ico/poetry/sadi/titlepage.html. Accessed 13 September 2003.

McDonough, Sheila D. "Iqbal, Sir Muhammad." http://www.britannica.com/eb/print?eu=43692. Accessed 27 June 2003.

Medieval Sourcebook. "Al-Makrisi: Account of the Crusade of St. Louis." http://www.fordham.edu/halsall/source/makrisi.html. Accessed 22 June 2003.

———. "Ibn Battuta: Travels in Asia and Africa, 1325–1354." http://www.fordham.edu/halsall/source/1354-ibnbattuta.html. Accessed 7 May 2003.

———. "Ibn Rushd (Averroës), 1126–1198 CE: Religion and Philosophy, c. 1190 CE." http://www.fordham.edu/halsall/source/1190averroes.html. Accessed 30 April 2003.

———. "Ibn Sina (Avicenna) (973–1037): On Medicine, c. 1020." http://www.fordham.edu/halsall/source/1020Avicenna-Medicine.html. Accessed 6 April 2003.

———. "Sidi Ali Reis (16th Century CE): Mirat ul Memalik (*The Mirror of Countries*), 1557 CE." http://www.fordham.edu/halsall/source/16CSidi1.html. Accessed 14 May 2003.

———. "Usamah ibn Munqidh (1095–1188): *Autobiography*, Excerpts on the Franks." http://faculty.juniata.edu/tuten/islamic/usama.html. Accessed 8 July 2003.

———. "Zamakhshari (1070–1143 CE): The Discoverer of Truth, c. 1130 CE." http://www.fordham.edu/halsall/source/1130Zamakhshari.html. Accessed 28 April 2003.

Metcalf, Barbara D. "'Traditionalist' Islamic Activism: Deoband, Tablighis, and Talibs." http://www.ssrc.org/sept11/essays/metcalf.htm. Accessed 16 June 2003.

Middle East Institute. "Islamic Civilization: An Overview." http://www.mideasti.org/library/islam/civilization.htm. Accessed 23 February 2002.

———. "Policy Briefs: Islamic Democracy and Islamic Governance." http://www.mideasti.org/html/b-sourush.html. Accessed 5 July 2003.

"Middle Eastern Music." http://www.britannica.com/ebc/print?eu=397399. Accessed 12 December 2002.

"Mirza Ghalib." http://www.boloji.com/ghalib/index.htm. Accessed 26 April 2003.

"Mohammed Arkoun, (1928–)." http://www.cis.ca.org/voices/a/arkoun-mn.htm. Accessed 4 August 2003.

Musallam, Basim. "The Ordering of Muslim Societies." In Robinson, Francis (ed.), *Cambridge Illustrated History of the Islamic World.* Cambridge: Cambridge University Press, 1998, pp. 164–207.

Mutahhari, Murtada. "The Role of *Ijtihad* in Legislation." http://www.al-islam.org/al-tawhid-legislation.htm. Accessed 14 February 2003.

———. *Understanding Islamic Sciences: Philosophy, Theology, Mysticism, Morality, Jurisprudence.* London: Islamic College for Advanced Studies, 2002.

"Naguib Mahfouz: Biased to Grassroots (People & Facts)." http://www.sis.gov.eg/egyptinf/culture/hml/nmahfouz.htm. Accessed 11 August 2003.

Nakosteen, Mehdi K., and Joseph S. Szyliowicz. "The Islamic Era: Influences on Muslim Education and Culture." http://www.britannica.com/eb/print?eu+108330. Accessed 6 September 2003.

Nasr, Seyyed Hossein. "Avicenna." http://www.britannica.com/eb/print?eu=11566. Accessed 6 April 2003.

Netton, Ian Richard. "al-Farabi, Abu Nasr (c. 870–950)." http://www.muslimphilosophy.com/rep/H021.htm. Accessed 2 April 2003.

Nou, Jean-Louis, Amina Okada, and M.C. Joshi. *Taj Mahal.* New York: Abbeville, 1993.

"Obituary: Edward W. Said." http://news.ft.com/servlet/ContentServer?pagena.../FullStory&c=StoryFT&cid=105948012643. Accessed 26 September 2003.

O'Conner, J.J., and E.F. Robertson. "Abu Ali al-Hasan ibn al-Haytham." http://www.gap-dcs.st-and.ac.uk/history/Mathematicians/Al-Haytham.html. Accessed 7 May 2003.

———. "Abu Ali al-Husain ibn Abdallah ibn Sina (Avicenna)." http://www-gap.dcs.st-and.ac.uk/~history/Mathematicians/Avicenna.html. Accessed 7 May 2003.

———. "Abu Arrayhan Muhammad ibn Ahmad al-Biruni." http://www-gap.dcs.st-and.ac.uk/~history/Mathematicians/Al-Biruni.html. Accessed 4 April 2003.

———. "Abu Yusuf Yaqub ibn Ishaq al-Sabbal al-Kindi." http://www-groups.dcs.st-and.ac.uk/~history/Mathematicians/Al-Kindi.html. Accessed 29 March 2003.

———. "Ghiyath al-Din Jamshid Mas'ud al-Kashi." http://www-gap.dcs.st-and.ac.uk/~history/Mathematicians/Al-Kashi.html. Accessed 11 May 2003.

———. "Nasir al-Din al-Tusi." http//www-gap.dcs.st-and.ac.uk/~history/Mathematicians/Al-Tusi_Nasir.html. Accessed 4 May 2003.

———. "Omar Khayyam." http://www-gap.dcs.st-and.ac.uk/~history/Mathematicians/Khayyam.html. Accessed 28 April 2003.

"Osama bin Laden v. the U.S.: Edicts and Statements." http://www.pbs.org/wgbh/pages/frontline/shows/binladen/who/edicts.html. Accessed 23 August 2003.

Oxford University Gazette. "Oxford Don 'Solves' 2,000-Year-Oold Maths Problem," 20 March 1997. http:www.ox.ac.uk/gazette/1996-7/weekly/200397/news/story_5.htm. Accessed 24 March 2003.

Papadropoulo, A. *L'Islam et l'art musulman*. Paris: Éditions d'art Lucien Mazenod, 1976.

Pape, Robert A. "The Strategic Logic of Suicide Bombers." *International Herald Tribune*, 23 September 2003.

"Paper Cartridges and the Sepoy Rebellion." http://www.royao.arsenal.com/cartridge.html. Accessed 12 June 2003.

Pavlin, James. "Ibn Taymiyya, Taqi al-Din (1263–1328). http://www.muslimphilosophy.com/rep/H039.htm. Accessed 6 May 2003.

Poetry Portal. "Al-Mutanabbi." http://www.poetry-portal.com/poets13.html. Accessed 3 April 2003.

Prag, Kay. *Jerusalem*. London: Black, 1989.

"Professor Edward W. Said, 67, Dies; Leading Advocate for Palestinians." http://www.washingtonpost.com/wp-dyn/articles/A2728-2003Sep25.html. Accessed 26 September 2003.

Rahman, Fazlur. *Islam & Modernity: Transformation of an Intellectual Tradition*. Chicago and London: University of Chicago Press, 1982.

———. "Islamic Thought." http://www.britannica.com/eb/print?eu=108140. Accessed 4 February 2003.

Rice, David Talbot. *Islamic Art*. Norwich: Thames and Hudson, 1979.

Ringgren, Helmer. "Qur'an." http://www.britannica.com/eb/article?eu=108143. Accessed 10 December 2002.

Robinson, Francis. "Knowledge, Its Transmission, and the Making of Muslim Societies" In Robinson, Francis (ed.), *The Cambridge Illustrated History of the Islamic World*. Cambridge: Cambridge University Press, 1998, pp. 208–249.

Robinson, Neal. "Ibn al-Arabi, Muhyi al-Din (1164–1240)." http://www.muslimphilosophy.com/rep/H022.htm. Accessed 2 May 2003.

Rohde, David. "Radicals' Seductive Voice: Islam as a Liberating Force." *International Herald Tribune*, 28 October 2003.

Rosen-Ayalon, Myriam. "Art and Architecture in Jerusalem in the Early Islamic Period." In Prawer, Joshua, and Haggai Ben-Shammai (eds.), *A History of Jerusalem: The Early Muslim Period, 638–1099*. Jerusalem and New York: Yad Izhak Ben-Bvi and New York University Press, 1996, pp. 386–412.

Rothstein, Richard. "Review of *Terror and Liberalism*, by Paul Berman." *International Herald Tribune*, 25 April 2003.

Roy, Olivier. *L'Islam Mondialisé*. Paris: Éditions du Seuil, 2002.

Sadri, Mahmoud, and Ahmad Sadri (trans. and eds.). *Reason, Freedom & Democracy in Islam: Essential Writings of 'Abdolkarim Soroush*. Oxford: Oxford University Press, 2002.

Said, Edward W. *Orientalism*. New York: Vintage, 1979.

"Sanusiyyah." http://philtar.ucsm.ac.uk/encyclopedia/islam/sufi/sanusi.html. Accessed 9 June 2003.

"Sayyed Hossein Nasr. Science and Civilization in Islam." http://www.fordham.edu/halsall/med/nasr.html. Accessed 29 September 2003.

"Sayyed Hossein Nasr (b. 1933–)." http://www.cis-ca.org/voices/n/nasr-mn.htm. Accessed 29 September 2003.

"Sayyid Ahmad Khan (1817–1898)." http://www.nmhschool.org/tthornton/sayyid_ahmed_khan.htm. Accessed 28 March 2003.

"Sayyidna Nasir Khusraw." http://www.amaana.org/ISWEB/khusraw.htm. Accessed 11 April 2003.

Schimmel, Annemarie. "Islamic Myth and Legend." http://www.britannica.com/eb/print?eu=108140. Accessed 4 February 2003.

———. "Sufism." http://www.britannica.com/eb/print?eu=108145. Accessed 8 January 2003.

Schwartz, Stephen. *The Two Faces of Islam: The House of Sa'ud from Tradition to Terror*. New York: Doubleday, 2002.

"Shah Wali Allah, 1114–1176/1703–1762." http://www.cis-ca.org/voices/shahwaliallah_mn.htm. Accessed 4 June 2003.

Shepard, William E. *Sayyid Qutb and Islamic Activism: A Translation and Critical Analysis of* Social Justice in Islam. Leiden, Neth.; New York, and Köln, Ger.: Brill, 1996.

"Sinan." http://www.britannica.com/eb/print?eu=69653. Accessed 25 April 2003.

Stierlin, Henri. *Islamic Art and Architecture*. London: Thames & Hudson, 2002.

"Symmetric Patterns at the Alhambra." http://weasel.cnrs.humboldt.edu/~spain/alh/index.html. Accessed 2 May 2003.

Taylor, Andrew. *God's Fugitive: The Life of Charles Montagu Doughty*. London: Flamingo, 2000.

"Thabit ibn Qurra." http://www.umma.org.history/scholars/QURRA.html. Accessed 25 March 2003.

Thornton, Ted. "History of the Middle East Database: Taqi al-Din Ibn Taymiyya." http://www.nmhschool.org/tthornton/taqi_al.htm. Accessed 6 May 2003.

Upadhyay, R. "Muslim Attitude Towards BJP." http://www.saag.org/papers3/paper278.htm. Accessed 20 June 2003.

———. "Shah Wali Ullah's Political Thought — Still a Major Obstacle Against Modernisation of Indian Muslims." http://www.saag.org/papers7/paper629.html. Accessed 4 June 2003.

U.S. Department of State. "Fact Sheet: Islam in the United States." http://usinfo.state.gov/usa/islam/fact2.htm. Accessed 23 March 2003.

U.S. National Library of Medicine. "Islamic Culture and the Medical Arts." http://www.nlm.nih.gov/exhibition/islamic_medical/islamic_06.html. Accessed 2 April 2003.

Vernoit, Stephen. "Artistic Expressions of Muslim Societies." In Robinson, Francis (ed.), *Cambridge Illustrated History of the Islamic World*. Cambridge: Cambridge University Press, 1998, pp. 250–290.

Vikør, Knut S. "The Development of *Ijtihad* and Islamic Reform, 1750–1850." http://www.hf.uib.no/i/smi/paj/vikor.html. Accessed 14 January 2003.

———. *Sufi and Scholar on the Desert Edge: Muhammad b. Ali al-Sansi and His Brotherhood*. London: Hurst, 1995.

Viorst, Milton. "Ayatullah [sic] Ruhollah Khomeini." http://www/time.com/time/time100/leaders/profile/khomeini.html. Accessed 18 August 2003.

Waldman, Marilyn R. "Islamic World." http://www.britannica.com/eb/print?eu=109492. Accessed 27 December 2002.

Watt, William Montgomery. "Harun al-Rashid." http://www.britannica.com/eb/print?eu=40234. Accessed 23 March 2003.

Watt, H. Montgomery. "Muhammad: Prophet and Statesman." http://www.fordham.edu/halsall/med/watt.html. Accessed 20 March 2003.

Waugh, Daniel C. "The Memoirs of Babur." http://faculty.washington.edu/dwaugh/CA/texts/babur1.html. Accessed 13 May 2003.

"World Bank Faults the Rich Countries." *International Herald Tribune*, 24 September 2003.

"World Maps of al-Idrisi." http://www.henrydavis.com/MAPSS/EMwebpages/219mono.html. Accessed 10 April 2003.

Index

Abd al-Rahman 50
Abd al-Wahhab 57, 133–134, 151, 158; see also Wahhabism
Abdolkarim Soroush 166–167, 177
Abu al-Hasan al-Ashari 64–65
Abu Hamid al-Ghazali 4, 60, 65, 82–83, 85, 92
Abu Hanifah 47–48
Abu Nasr al-Farabi 65–66, 197
Abu Nuwas 51
Ahmad ibn Hanbal 53, 56–57
Ahmed Nedim 129–130
Akbar 114, 121–122, 192
al-Aqsa Mosque 40–41, 91, 173
al-Azhar University 67–68, 137, 142, 143
al-Biruni 4, 78–79
al-Bukhari 18, 58, 61
al-Hakim 71, 76, 183
Alhambra 95–96
al-Hariri 87–88
al-Idrisi 90–91
Ali Shariati 150–151
al-Kashi 108–109
al-Khwarizmi 52, 54–55
al-Kindi 39, 58, 60
al-Ma'arri 79–80
al-Ma'mun 52–53, 57
al-Mansur 48–49
al-Maqrizi 109–110
al-Mubarak 18
al-Mufaddal 49
al-Muqaddasi 70–71
al-Mutanabbi 66–67
al-Numan 68–69
Al Qaeda 13, 168, 170
al-Razi 64
al-Sanusi 134–135
al-Shafi 57
al-Sijistani 69

al-Tabari 34, 62–64
al-Zahravi 73
aniconism 184–185
Ayatollah Ruhollah Khomeini 126, 151, 158, 160–162
Aziz al-Azmeh 68, 167–168, 177

Babur 108, 114–115
Book of the Thousand and One Nights (The Arabian Nights) 55–56, 183
Brethren of Purity 67

Cromer, Lord 5, 6

Dar al-Harb (Arabic: the Islamic world) 20
Dar al-Islam (Arabic: the non-Islamic world) 20
Deoband movement 132, 137–138
Dome of the Rock 40–45, 81, 105, 117, 185, 189
Doughty, Charles Montague 26

ethics, traditions of in Islam 21, 152, 160, 195–198

fatwa (Arabic: a legal opinion) 6, 162, 170, 173–174
Fazlur Rahman 152–153, 195–196
Firdawsi 73–74, 190
fitra (Arabic: humans' innate ability to know God) 13
fundamentalism (Islamic) 1, 35, 102, 133–134, 157–162, 167–175, 177–179

Gabriel 1, 17–18, 28, 31, 33, 193
Great Mosque of Cordoba 50
Great Mosque of Damascus 44–46

hadith (Arabic: records of the life of Muhammad) 7, 17–18, 51, 53, 57–58, 61, 63, 80–81,

83, 87, 92, 132–133, 137, 141, 159, 181, 193–194
Hafiz 105–106
Hamid al-Kirmani 74
Haroun al-Rashid 39, 50–51, 190–191
hijra (Arabic: Muhammad's migration to Medina) 29, 193
hisba (Arabic: duty of citizens) 85–86
House of Knowledge 71–73
House of Wisdom 52, 54, 58, 62, 71

Ibn al-Arabi 96–97
Ibn al-Haytham 4, 76
Ibn al-Nafis 99–100
Ibn Battuta 45–46, 102, 104–105
Ibn Hazm 80–81
Ibn Khaldun 65, 106–108, 109
Ibn Rushd 92–94, 96, 197
Ibn Sina 4, 74–76, 197
Ibn Taymiyya 57, 101–104, 133, 151, 158–159, 170–171
ijma (Arabic: consensus of scholars) 18–19, 20, 81, 145
ijtihad (Arabic: independent reasoning) 19–20, 48, 82, 86–87, 103, 132, 134, 138, 140–142, 146–147, 159, 177–178
islam (Arabic: to surrender to God) 12
Islamic doctrines 11–17; sources of 17–21
Islamic thought, complexity of 11
Ismailis 68–69, 73–74, 98–99, 109
isnad (Arabic: footnotes) 18, 57–58, 63
isra (Arabic: Muhammad's night journey) 28–29, 41

Jabir ibn Hayyan 53–54
jahiliyya (the time of ignorance, i.e., Arabia before the rise of Islam) 25, 49, 151, 159
Jamal al-Din al-Afghani 138–140, 142, 144, 158
Jalal al-Din al-Rumi 97–98
jihad (Arabic: struggle or holy war) 19–20, 93, 102–103, 145, 151, 159, 170–171, 173

kufic (Arabic: a formal script) 34–35
kufr (Arabic: unbelief) 13

madhhabs (Arabic: schools of Islamic thought) 48
Mehmed II 112
Mirza Ghalib 135–137
Mohammad Arkoun 163–164, 177
Muhammad 1, 3, 7, 11–12, 14, 17–19, 23, 25–31, 39–40, 42, 46–47, 57–58, 63, 69, 82, 87, 131, 138, 152, 162, 183, 193
Muhammad Abduh 138, 142–144, 158
Muhammad al-Shafti 54
Muhammad ibn Ishaq 27, 46–47

Muhammad Iqbal 146–147
mujahid (singular) or *mujahadeen* (plural) (Arabic: those who fight actively for Islam) 150, 171–172
mujtahid (Arabic: scholar of Islamic law with the right to use independent reasoning) 20, 62, 103–104, 146; see also ijtihad
Mulla Sadra 126–127
Muslim ibn al-Hajjaj 61–62
Mustafa Kemal Ataturk 148–150
Mustansiriyya (Islamic college) 94–95
Mutazili movement 52–53, 57, 65, 197

Nasir-I Khusraw 81–82
Nasr al-Din al-Tusi 98–99

Omar Khayyam 88–89
Osama bin Laden 102, 134, 158, 160, 168–175

Pillars, i.e., the Five Pillars of Islam 14, 16–17

qadi (Arabic: judge) 20, 53, 68, 92
qiyas (Arabic: legal reasoning) 20
Quran (or Koran) 1, 2, 11–13, 16–17, 20, 25, 27, 31–36, 45, 51, 53–54, 57–58, 60, 62–63, 65, 71, 74, 80, 83, 85, 87, 89–90, 93, 97, 102–103, 105, 118, 123–124, 130–133, 138, 140–141, 143–144, 150, 152–153, 157–159, 161–162, 164, 166–167, 181–187, 192–197

Rashid Rida 142, 144–146, 149–150

Sa'di 100–101
Said, Edward W. 3, 162–163
Saud dynasty 134, 145
Sayyid Abul-Ala Mawdudi 151–152
Sayyid Ahmad Khan 140–141
Sayyid Qutb 158–160, 170
Seyyed Hossein Nasr 75, 79, 94, 164–166
Shah Wali Allah 130–133, 137
sharia (Arabic: the body of Islamic sacred law) 20–21, 117, 144–145, 149, 157, 171, 194, 196–198
Shiites (Arabic: adherents of one of the two major branches of Islam) 22–24, 39, 52–53, 67–68, 78, 86–87, 98, 101, 103, 126, 138, 145, 149, 158, 160–162, 166, 184–185; see also Sunnis
shirk (Arabic: idolatry) 13, 63, 133, 184
Sidi Ali Reis 114, 116–117
Sinan 117–121
Sufism 11, 82–83, 96–97, 101–102, 106, 126, 131, 133, 137, 149, 192, 198
Suleyman (the Magnificent) 22, 43, 117–119
Suleymaniye Mosque 117–120
sunna (Arabic: the body of Muslim traditions) 17–20, 23, 54, 57, 102–103, 133, 152, 157, 161, 195, 197

Sunnis (Arabic: adherents of one of the two major branches of Islam) 22–24, 39, 48, 52, 61–62, 64, 67, 82–83, 86–87, 101–102, 133, 138, 145, 184, 197; *see also* Shiites

tafsir (Arabic: exegesis, i.e., a learned explanation) 34, 193
Taj Mahal 40, 122–126, 178, 182–183
taqlid (Arabic: unquestioning acceptance of precedent) 19, 87, 140–141, 143
tawhid (Arabic: the oneness of God) 13–14, 133, 165, 178
Thabit ibn Qurra 62

ulama (Arabic: religious scholars) 47, 57, 83, 101, 138, 141, 143, 146, 161, 164, 173, 177
umma (Arabic: community) 19, 39, 140, 143, 171
Usama ibn Munquidh 91–92
usul al-fiqh (Arabic: sources of Islamic jurisprudence) 20, 47, 194

Wahhbabism 13, 102, 133–134, 145; *see also* Abd al-Wahhab

Zamakhshari 89–90

www.ingramcontent.com/pod-product-compliance
Lightning Source LLC
Chambersburg PA
CBHW080935020526
44116CB00034B/2867